HISTORY OF WORLD ARCHITECTURE

Pier Luigi Nervi, General Editor

LATE BAROQUE AND ROCOCO ARCHITECTURE

Christian Norberg-Schulz

Harry N. Abrams, Inc., Publishers, New York

Editor: Carlo Pirovano

Design: Diego Birelli

Photographs: Bruno Balestrini and Christian Norberg-Schulz

Drawings: Enzo Di Grazia

Library of Congress Cataloging in Publication Data

Norberg-Schulz, Christian.
    Late Baroque and Rococo architecture.
    (History of world architecture)
    1. Architecture, Baroque.   2. Architecture,
Rococo.   I.   Title.
NA590.N63   724'.19   73–980
ISBN 0-8109-1012-8

Library of Congress Catalogue Card Number: 73–980
Copyright 1971 in Italy by Electa Editrice, Milan
© Copyright 1974 in the United States by Harry N. Abrams, Inc., New York
All rights reserved. No part of the contents of this book may be reproduced
without the written permission of the publishers
Harry N. Abrams, Incorporated, New York

Printed and bound in U.S.A.

Architectural criticism has nearly always been concerned with the visible aspect of individual buildings, taking this to be the decisive factor in the formulation of value judgments and in the classification of those "styles" which appear in textbooks, and which have thus become common knowledge. But once it is recognized that every building is, by definition, a work subject to the limitations imposed by the materials and building techniques at hand, and that every building must prove its stability, as well as its capacity to endure and serve the needs it was built for, it becomes clear that the aesthetic aspect alone is inadequate when we come to appraise a creative activity, difficult enough to judge in the past, rapidly becoming more complex in our own day, and destined to become more so in the foreseeable future.

Nevertheless, what has struck me most, on studying the architecture of the past and present, is the fact that the works which are generally regarded by the critics and the general public as examples of pure beauty are also the fruit of exemplary building techniques, once one has taken into account the quality of the materials and the technical knowledge available. And it is natural to suspect that such a coincidence is not entirely casual.

Building in the past was wholly a matter of following static intuitions, which were, in turn, the result of meditation, experience, and above all of an understanding of the capacity of certain structures and materials to resist external forces. Meditation upon structural patterns and the characteristics of various materials, together with the appraisal of one's own experiences and those of others is an act of love toward the process of construction for its own sake, both on the part of the architect and his collaborators and assistants. Indeed, we may wonder whether this is not the hidden bond which unites the appearance and substance of the finest buildings of the past, distant though that past may be, into a single "thing of beauty."

One might even think that the quality of the materials available not only determined architectural patterns but also the decorative detail with which the first simple construction was gradually enriched.

One might find a justification for the difference in refinement and elegance between Greek architecture, with its basic use of marble —a highly resistant material, upon which the most delicate carvings can be carried out—and the majestic concrete structures of Roman architecture, built out of a mixture of lime and pozzolana, and supported by massive walls, to compensate for their intrinsic weaknesses.

Would it be too rash to connect these objective architectural characteristics with the different artistic sensibilities of the two peoples?

One must recognize, therefore, the importance of completing the description of the examples illustrated with an interpretation of their constructional and aesthetic characteristics, so that the connection between the twin aspects of building emerges as a natural, logical consequence.

This consequence, if understood and accepted in good faith by certain avant-garde circles, could put an end to the disastrous haste with which our architecture is rushing toward an empty, costly, and at times impractical formalism. It might also recall architects and men of culture to a more serene appraisal of the objective elements of building and to the respect that is due to a morality of architecture. For this is just as important for the future of our cities as is morality, understood as a rule of life, for an orderly civil existence.

Pier Luigi Nervi

TABLE OF CONTENTS

Introduction

The eighteenth century is generally known as the Enlightenment or the Age of Reason. This does not imply, of course, that man for the first time started to think, but rather that he invented a new way of using his power of reasoning. The significance of the new approach was clearly understood by contemporaries. Thus D'Alembert wrote that the *esprit de système* of the seventeenth century ought to be replaced by a new *esprit systématique*.[1] He thereby pointed out the very essence of the problem: in spite of its unrest and variety, the seventeenth century had been characterized by a general attitude—the belief that the world might be understood as a system deduced from a few immutable *a priori* axioms or dogmas. The Baroque Age offered a multitude of such models: the philosophical systems of Descartes and Spinoza, the absolute monarchy by divine right, the dogmatic structures of Lutheranism, Calvinism, and the Counter-Reformatory Roman Church. A possibility of choice, thus, was introduced, and critical minds were soon led to the conclusion that systems have a relative rather than an absolute value. In the long run, therefore, the *esprit de système* could not satisfy man's need for a secure existential basis. But the lost certainty had to be replaced by something, and the solution was found in the liberation of reason from the fetters of preconceived ideas. Thus Voltaire wrote: "We must never say: let us begin by inventing principles according to which we attempt to explain everything. We should rather say: let us make an exact analysis of things. . . ."[2] Reason, thus, should be applied to the phenomena themselves, rather than to the deduction of "facts" from *a priori* axioms. Man suddenly realized that the conclusions ought to come at the end of the investigation, instead of being stated at its beginning. Reason thereby became the tool of a new empiricism, which already was conceived toward the end of the seventeenth century by John Locke, who said: "Whence has it [*i.e.*, the mind] all the materials of reason and knowledge? To this I answer in one word, from *experience*."[3] The classical British empiricism which was initiated by Locke derived all the contents of the mind from experience, and thus "replaced the metaphysics of the soul with the history of the soul."[4] At the same time natural science was led away from the arbitrary and fantastic assumptions of the past to a new method of observation and analysis. The great protagonist of the new approach was Newton, who replaced metaphysical explanations with systematic description and correlation of phenomena. His importance was immediately recognized, as demonstrated in these lines by Alexander Pope:

Nature and Nature's laws lay hid in night;
God said, "Let Newton be!" and all was light.

The empiricism of Newton, however, did not imply that he rejected philosophy and religion. But he regarded these subjects as the end of human knowledge, rather than as the foundation on which it must be built. Thus he wrote:

The main business of Natural Philosophy is to argue from Phaenomena without feigning Hypotheses, and to deduce causes from Effects, till we come to the very first cause, which certainly is not mechanical. Does it not appear from Phaenomena that there is a being incorporeal, living, intelligent, omnipresent, who in infinite space as in his Sensory, sees the things themselves intimately, and thoroughly perceives them, and comprehends them wholly by their immediate presence to himself?[5]

It would therefore be wrong to interpret the new scientific attitude as directed against religion. Even Voltaire's battle cry of *Écrasez l'infame* was directed against superstition rather than faith, and against the Church (that is, the system) rather than religion.[6] The basic innovation was the rejection of *a priori* ideas and "knowledge," introducing instead a systematic study of nature as it is. The aim was the discovery of regularity in the phenomena themselves, that is, natural laws. Baroque persuasion, thus, was replaced by the free exercise of reason, emancipated from the fetters of dogmas and authority.

The new scientific outlook was closely related to a new idea of freedom. Voltaire defended the doctrine of the freedom of the human will, and said: "In fact, what does it mean to be free? It means to know the rights of man, for to know them is to defend them."[7] And the basic right is the right to influence others by words and teachings. The philosophy of the Enlightenment, thus, opposed the power of convention, tradition, and authority. But rather than consider this opposition as an act of destruction, the enlightened mind wanted to rediscover the "natural" foundation of knowledge. Rousseau considered the state of nature as a standard and norm according to which one can show what is truth and law and what is mere illusion and convention. No wonder, hence, that the old dogmatic systems tended to disintegrate during the eighteenth century. Already during the French Régence royal power was undermined and the court lost its role as the very center of the system. New patrons and new centers of culture replaced the absolute ruler and his palace. In general, the middle class took over from the impoverished and decayed nobility, and the city regained some of its cultural life. Even the Roman Church was secularized, and the great advocates of the Counter-Reformation, the Jesuits, were expelled from most countries.[8] In 1781 Joseph II of Austria closed all convents because their members "were de-

1. *Vienna, Schönbrunn Palace, first project by Fischer von Erlach.*
2. *Project for the hunting lodge of Clemenswerth.*
3. *Hunting lodge of Clemenswerth.*

11

voted to an exclusively contemplative way of life and did not contribute to the good of their neighbor or civil society."[9] What, then, should replace the traditional organizations? Rousseau offered an answer in the concept of a society where the individual is protected by the united power of the political organization, and where the individual will exist only within the framework of the *volonté générale.* "In short, each giving himself to all, gives himself to nobody; and as there is not one associate over whom we do not acquire the same rights which we concede to him over ourselves, we gain the equivalent of all that we lose, and more power to preserve what we have."[10] The centralized and hierarchic system of the seventeenth century, thus, gave place to a multitude of interacting, equal elements.

A profound psychological change resulted. While the Baroque attitude may be characterized by the word *persuasion,* the enlightened mind centered on *sensation.* Accordingly, the illusive, allegorical image was replaced by the natural, true image. Truth and beauty, reason and nature, are but different expressions for the same thing, for one and the same order of being, different aspects of which are revealed in natural science and art. The attitude is well expressed in Newton's maxim: "Nature is always in harmony with itself." Since experience was taken as the point of departure, sensation gained a new fundamental importance, and the eighteenth century offers many valuable studies on the nature of perception, the most famous being Berkeley's *New Theory of Vision* (1709). The attitude of the epoch is well expressed in Berkeley's statement, "Without experience we should no more have taken blushing for a sign of shame, than of gladness."[11] In art the empirical approach led to genres, which correspond to the species of natural objects. Neither the scientist nor the artist creates order; he only ascertains things as they are. This search for the true phenomena led to a study not only of nature, but also of history. In this context we must understand the characteristic dream of the century: the golden age when man lived in close contact with nature and was guided by his natural instincts only. It was the dream of Rousseau and also of the architectural writer Laugier, who went back to the primitive hut to rediscover the true, natural elements of architecture: column, entablature, and pediment.[12] The Greek temple inherited the simple logic of the primitive hut, and thus we understand why Neoclassicism formed the natural goal of eighteenth-century architecture.[13]

But the old systems did not fade away at once. The creation of a new philosophy and science was not accomplished overnight, and the old political systems survived most of the century. Up until about 1760, thus, Late Baroque and Rococo architecture dominated the scene. The Rococo is an interesting transitional phenomenon.[14] It abolished Baroque rhetoric and reflects many characteristic intentions of the Age of Reason, but at the same time its forms express a certain nostalgia for

the *Grand Siècle*. We may liken it to Voltaire, who said: "I do not like heroes, they make too much noise in the world"; but thereupon he wrote his great book, *Le Siècle de Louis XIV*. The Rococo, thus, shows the empirical interest in sensation, but transforms scientific observation into the enjoyment of sensuous stimuli—visual, auditory, gustatory, olfactory, and, last but not least, erotic—which became a main justification of life. At the same time, however, Rococo dwellings are based on a true empirical study of comfortable living, and show a functional differentiation unknown before. Rococo spaces also have an intimacy which contrasts strongly with the infinite extension of Baroque architecture, and reflect the desire for a return to a more natural state of affairs. The form that gave Rococo its name, the *rocaille*, may in fact be characterized as a caprice of nature. Rather than illustrating nature's grand design, however, it expresses its transitory and perishable aspects, thereby defining the Rococo as the end of a development rather than a new beginning.

The Rococo must be distinguished from the Late Baroque architecture which flourished in Central Europe during the first half of the eighteenth century. It represents the natural expression of a belated Counter-Reformation, and reflects as well the ambition of many small monarchies to imitate the Versailles of Louis XIV. But the German Baroque also assimilated ideas from the current Enlightenment and Rococo, and thereby arrived at a singular synthesis which fused monumentality and intimacy, rhetoric and charm, abundance and clarity. Later, we will discuss the different shades of this versatile movement, but we ought merely to point out here that it marks the culmination of the great European tradition. It may be compared to the philosophical system of Leibniz, which also represents a singular synthesis of the *esprit de système* and the *esprit systématique*. Leibniz still accepted the existence of general principles, and considered pure reason greater than sensory perception. But his system had a character different from those of Descartes and Spinoza. While these still operated with simple, static identities, Leibniz introduced a new "dynamic pluralism." His monads are living centers of energy, and the world is constituted by an infinity of such monads.[15] They are all different, but interact and undergo a continuous process of transition from one state to another. Every monad therefore contains its own past and is pregnant with its future. We understand, thus, that Leibniz goes far beyond the Baroque concept of a basically stable, hierarchical system, at the same time that he supersedes the idea of a universe in harmony with itself. His monadology, in fact, points toward the modern idea of a whole which is "more than the sum of its parts," and which consists of an interaction of "self-changing forces."[16] The philosophy of Leibniz, thus, links the Baroque Age with our present world, just as Late Baroque architecture forms one of the "constituent facts" of modern architecture.[17] Both aspects were already brought together in the works of Guarino

Guarini. His *Placita Philosophica* (1665) describes the world as an *ars combinatoria* expressing itself as an incessant, undulating rhythm, and his buildings concretize this concept in pulsating organisms, which are open and indeterminate, but also characterized by a particular formative principle, inherent in the single spatial cell: "Architecture, therefore, is like the encyclopedia, the construction of the new scientific world: a building, precarious in so far as its single parts are concerned, but pregnant in future developments on account of its deliberately systematic nature."[18]

The eighteenth century represents a decisive step toward an open, truly pluralistic world. The centralized models of the Baroque underwent a process of disintegration, and a new world of interacting individual elements was being formed. The most obvious contribution was offered by the new empirical science. Today, however, we begin to understand that the Enlightenment and the scientific development that followed it did not account for the whole relationship between man and his environment, and that the dynamic philosophy of Leibniz was more modern. Still, the Age of Reason pointed out the dangers of *a priori* thinking, a lesson that should never be forgotten. The world, in fact, is still dominated by those who put the conclusion at the beginning.

The Landscape

The landscape ideal of the Baroque epoch found its most characteristic expression in the French garden, as exemplified in the creations of André Le Nôtre. The French garden is conceived as a geometrically ordered, infinite landscape, centered on a palace, which represents the meaningful focus of the system. The real aim, however, is the experience of infinite space, as concretized in a dominant longitudinal axis. All the other elements are related to this axis, chief among them the palace, which divides the world into two halves—the urban world of man and that of openly extended nature. To make this extension effective, the existing topography was transformed into a series of flat terraces, and large surfaces of reflecting water were introduced. The ideas of Le Nôtre were tried out in the gardens of the Tuileries (after 1637), perfected in Vaux-le-Vicomte (1656–61), and culminated with the grand scheme for Versailles (after 1661). Here the entire surrounding landscape is taken into possession by the seemingly limitless system. Versailles represents the very essence of a seventeenth-century environment: domination and strict definition, but also dynamism and openness. Toward the end of the century the whole landscape around Paris was transformed into a network of such centralized and infinitely extended systems.[19] In a still larger context, Paris formed the center of an analogous system, comprising the whole of France.

The absolutist Baroque landscape was inherited by the eighteenth century. Other European powers, great and small, wanted to imitate the

5. *Göllersdorf, chapel of St. John Nepomuk.*
6. *Würzburg, Käppele.*

symbolic solution of Louis XIV, and many centralized and extended environments were created, especially in Austria, Germany, and Russia. Even in democratic England, the French approach dominated early eighteenth-century projects. Among the many examples, we may single out the magnificent first project by Johann Bernhard Fischer von Erlach for Schönbrunn Palace in Vienna, planned shortly after Joseph I was made King of the Romans in 1690 (he became Emperor in 1705). After the defeat of the Turks near Vienna in 1683, Austria consolidated its role as one of the great European powers, and naturally aimed at the creation of a state art analogous to that of France. Schönbrunn obviously was intended as an Austrian Versailles, and the young Joseph I was regarded as a new *Roi Soleil*. In Fischer's project the central part of the façade is crowned by the sun-quadriga of Apollo, "in which our invincible King and Emperor drives the horses."[20] As a whole the design is one of the great visions of architectural history. Over a series of large terraces, an outstretched palace hovers between heaven and earth, surrounded by an extended space that seems to continue infinitely beyond the frame of Fischer's splendid bird's-eye view.[21] A central longitudinal axis is defined by the monumental gate flanked by two Roman triumphal columns, a series of recesses in the terraces, and finally by a large oval *cour d'honneur*. The extended French layout, thus, is combined with ideas taken from ancient Roman architecture, such as the hillside terraces and the terminating *exedra* that resemble the disposition of the Temple of Fortuna in Praeneste (Palestrina). The volumetric relationships, however, as well as the monumental scale created by the main colossal order, are clearly influenced by Bernini's projects for the Louvre. Fischer also explicitly refers to the palace in Persepolis and the Maidan-i-Shah in Isfahan, which he knew from contemporary descriptions.[22] Schönbrunn's situation on the top of a hill departs from the usual Baroque preference for extended, flat sites. At the same time that it echoes medieval solutions, it is related to the elevated position of the great imperial convents of the Late Baroque period. It has a pronounced sacred character, and must be understood as an original expression of monarchy by divine right, unifying the symbolic forms of extension and verticality. In the text to his project, Fischer points out that its position enabled the sovereign to see as far as the borders of Hungary. To create a symbolic spatial totality Fischer thus employed diverse experiences of the architectural past, thereby concretizing his idea of an historical architecture, that is, an architecture that appears as the culmination of a meaningful historical development. In fact, the German emperors wanted to unify "the epochs of Solomon and Augustus,"[23] and Fischer's project manifests all the virtues embraced by this great scheme. Unfortunately, the project remained only on paper. The explanation usually given is that it would have been too expensive. More probably, its architectural scope was too

comprehensive. Schönbrunn did not simply compete with the symbolic centralized extension of Versailles, but added new sophisticated meanings to the current concept of space. Its persuasive rhetoric is Baroque, but its contents are more complex than those of the basically simple dogmatic systems of that period. Its failure, thus, reveals that the Germanic empire was not able to live up to its ideals, or that the latter were in too obvious conflict with a world of imminent enlightenment. In his second project, which was executed, Fischer returned to the conventional type of *Garten-paläste*, remarking with a certain irony: "But everything is changed now, because Schönbrunn has been built in the valley, not on the mountain."[24] If built as originally planned, Schönbrunn would have been the culminating synthesis of the basic experiences of Western architecture, comparable in scope only to the great visions of Leibniz. Whereas the philosophy of Leibniz was directed toward the future, the state architecture of Fischer belonged to a world concept which was approaching its end.

Still, for several decades the European landscape was dominated by the Baroque image of a strictly formalized space, although the solutions hardly reached the richness and originality of the Schönbrunn project. A certain simplification characterizes the layouts of the eighteenth century, reducing Baroque rhetoric and dynamism to elementary geometrical relationships. The centralized system, thus, loses its persuasive momentum and becomes a nostalgic representation of something past. As a characteristic example we may cite the enchanting hunting lodge of Clemenswerth (1736–50), built by Johann Conrad von Schlaun for Clemens August, Elector of Westphalia. The circular disposition has a two-story building (which represents the palace proper) at its very center. Around it we find a regular ring of eight one-story pavilions which served the attendants of the Elector. One of them was built as a small convent with chapel. The solution resembles a permanent encampment,[25] but by means of eight roads radiating out toward infinity between the buildings, it is transformed into a typical manifestation of the Baroque system. Rather than domination and persuasion, however, Clemenswerth expresses a happy gathering together for hunting, solitude, and piety in a world which, in spite of its infinite extension, does not represent a conquest of the real environment but appears as its negation. Clemenswerth, thus, reflects a Rococo attitude, and the simple volumes of the pavilions have the light transparency of the epoch.

The rhetorical greatness of the Baroque landscape, however, lived on in the sacred architecture of the eighteenth century. From the very beginning, the Counter-Reformatory movement had supported the architectural definition of sacred places, and during the following two centuries the landscape of Catholic Europe became saturated with religious monuments: roadside crucifixes, statues of St. John Nepomuk on the bridges,

9. *London, Chiswick House, plan of the garden.*
10. *Karlsruhe, diagrammatic drawing of the city.*

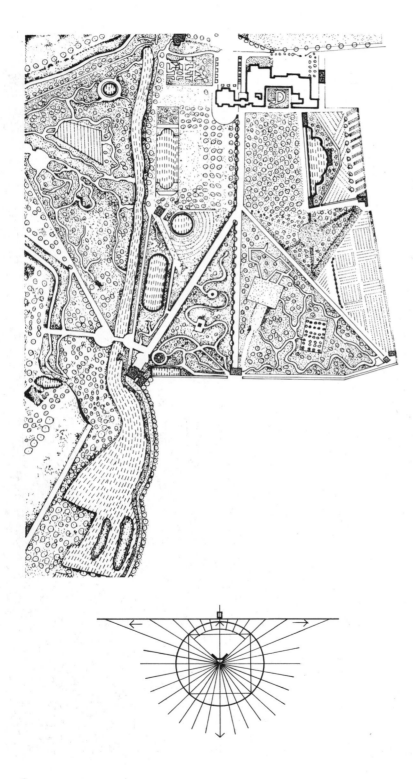

holy graves (mostly in combination with a *via crucis*), pilgrimage churches, and—in Central Europe—a multitude of new and large convents. According to their scale, these monuments functioned as foci of a smaller or larger space. The roadside crucifixes marked the crossroads, whereas statues of St. John Nepomuk bore witness to the true meaning of the bridge, as expressed in Heidegger's words: "A bridge 'gathers' the countryside around it as a landscape around a river."[26] The *via crucis* provided one of the most popular forms of worship of the century. Representing Calvary, it usually consisted of a path leading past the traditional fourteen Stations of the Cross up to the top of a hill, whereby the landscape became part of the meaningful experience.[27] During the seventeenth century the layout was usually irregular, but later the Baroque idea of a longitudinal axis was introduced, leading to such splendid solutions as Balthasar Neumann's Käppele in Würzburg (1748–1824). Here the steep, symmetrical *via crucis* has as its goal a pilgrimage church which, like so many others of the period, gives structure to and dominates the surrounding landscape.[28]

The worship of the Baroque epoch, thus, was actively related to the environment, and the architectural layout symbolized the conquest of an open, extended world. This is particularly evident in the large pilgrimage churches and abbeys of the eighteenth century. The belated Counter Reformatory movement in Central Europe led to the reconstruction of most of the old convents which had been destroyed during the religious wars, as well as the foundation of new ones. As heavenly cities, these convents were situated on the top of hills, serving as foci of the surrounding world. Their symmetrical layout was an expression of perfection, and symbolized the *Civitas Dei* on earth. In fact, the Baroque convents of Central Europe were small, complete worlds, economically successful and spiritually fertile.[29] A pronounced longitudinal axis, however, defines an active relationship to the environment, and the vertical elements, such as domes and steeples, give a meaning to its extension.

As a typical example we may mention the Benedictine monastery of Melk on the Danube in Lower Austria. Its unique position on a rock overhanging the river and its extraordinary dimensions (the building is 1050 feet in length) make Melk an extremely impressive solution to one of the leading building types of Late Baroque architecture. The monastery dates back to 1089, and in general the layout follows an older disposition. The architect Jacob Prandtauer, however, unified the once separate elements into a single continuously extended building (1702–27) and introduced a longitudinal axis running through the whole plan.[30] Above all he gave the new church a twin-tower façade overlooking the river and the landscape. It appears between the symmetrically placed Kaisersaal and library, which are united by a low, transparent wing whose curved front gives the whole complex a pronounced direction. Together, the

11. Karlsruhe, perspective view of the castle and city, from an engraving of 1739.

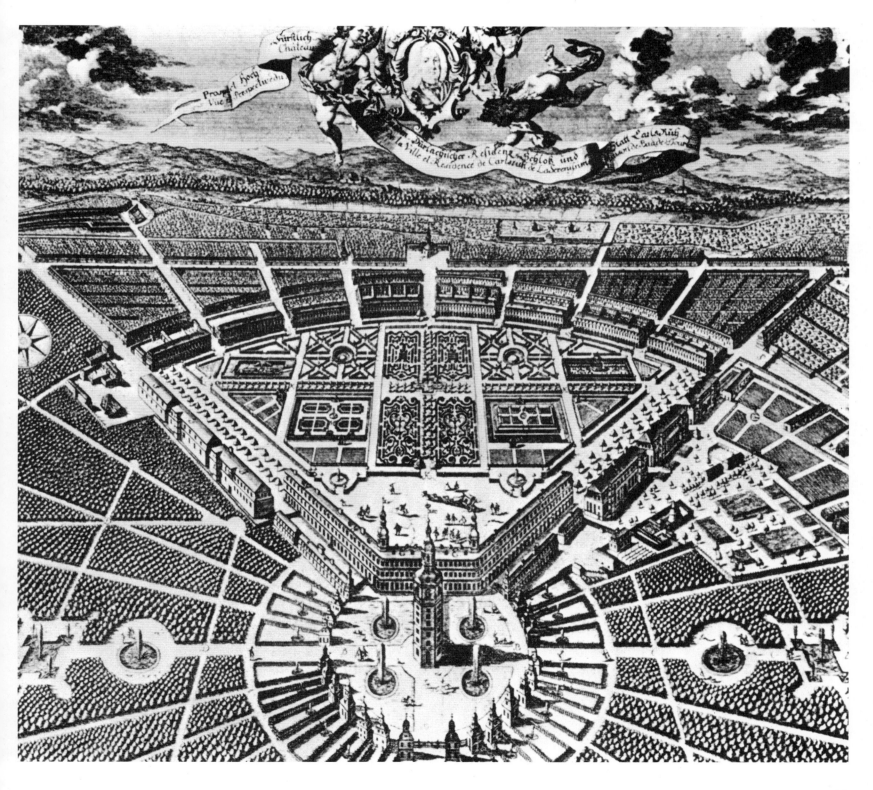

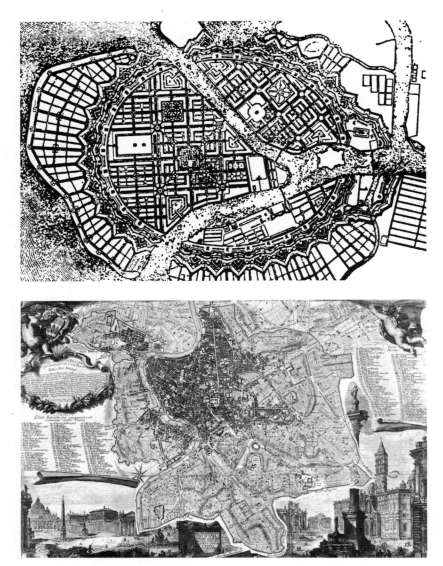

three elements form a triad symbolizing the unity of worldly power, knowledge, and faith. In fact, the Abbot of Melk, Berthold Dietmayr, had in 1706 been elected rector of the University of Vienna. Melk, thus, represents the last great European synthesis, and its active, persuasive form has the full power of Baroque art.

Among the many other large religious institutions of the epoch, we may single out an Italian example, the Superga near Turin (1715). The building was an offering by Vittorio Amedeo II in thanksgiving for his victory over the French in 1706. The characteristic choice of a high hill dominating the whole of Turin and the surrounding landscape satisfies the basic intentions of the period, and the architect Filippo Juvarra gave the project a magnificent architectural form. As in Melk, we find an elongated convent preceded by a tall, dominant church. The classical Italian background is seen in its centralized plan and grand dome, as well as in its tetrastyle portico. The latter, however, is unusually deep, and mainly serves the purpose of giving emphasis to the longitudinal axis. The result is a building that communicates with the landscape by its horizontal extension, while at the same time its vertical axis represents a dominant focus.

The Late Baroque sanctuaries were widely visible, and effectively suggested "nature's infinitude controlled by men in the service of God."[31] Toward the close of the eighteenth century, secularization brought an end to the world they represented, but the sacred landscape they dominated still remains a living reality in many parts of Europe.

During the first half of the eighteenth century a new conception of landscape was being formed. As early as 1709 Lord Shaftesbury wrote that the "genuine order of nature" ought to replace the "mocking of princely gardens," and he was supported by writers such as Joseph Addison and Alexander Pope. The English landscape garden, however, only became a reality two decades later—thanks to the original genius of William Kent.[32] During the 1730s he designed the gardens of Chiswick, Stowe, and Rousham, in all three of which the symbolic geometry and zoning of Le Nôtre was abandoned altogether. Instead Kent aimed at a slightly stylized nature which was intended to look more natural than nature itself. The soft and undulating hills of England were an ideal point of departure for such a conception. Kent's basic desire was to return to an original, paradisiacal condition, throwing overboard the artificial systems of the Baroque Age, as well as their spatial manifestations.[33]

It is beyond the scope of this book to give a detailed analysis of the landscape garden. A few characteristic properties, however, ought to be mentioned, as they allow us a better understanding of the Baroque conception they were to replace.[34] Chiswick House (designed by Lord Burlington and Kent) is built in the Palladian style. Its classical character obviously represents the new enlightened man who puts himself

14. *Rome, port of the Ripetta, plan.*
15. *Rome, port of the Ripetta, perspective reconstruction.*

16. *G.B. Piranesi: view of the Piazza di Spagna in Rome.*▷

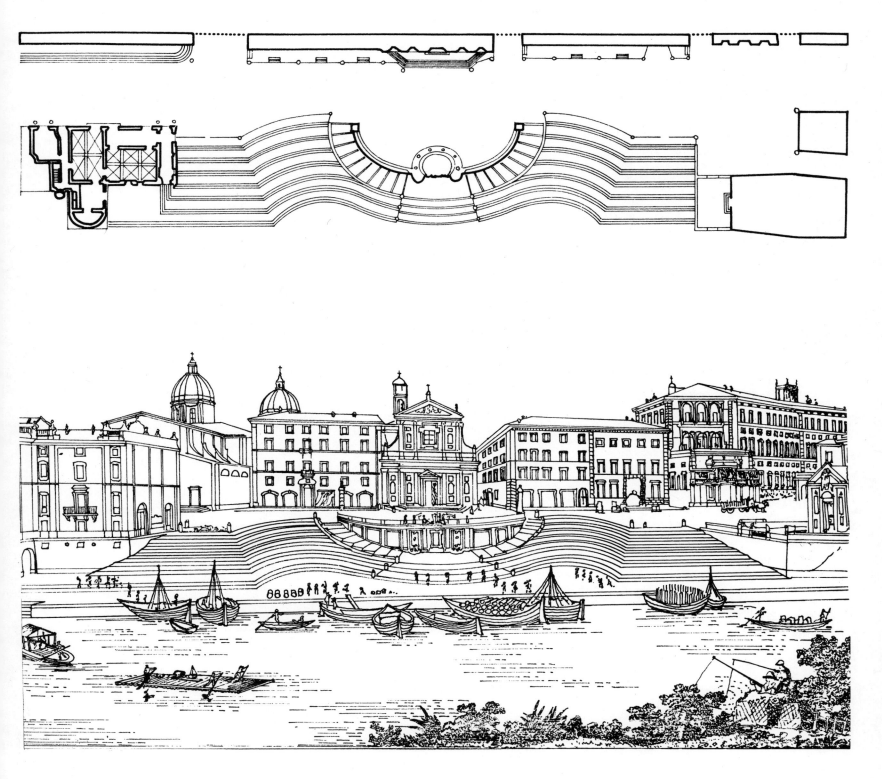

◁ 17. *Rome, Spanish Stairs.*
18. *Rome, Spanish Stairs, plan.*
19. *Rome, Piazza S. Ignazio, plan.*

20, 21. *Rome, Piazza S. Ignazio.*

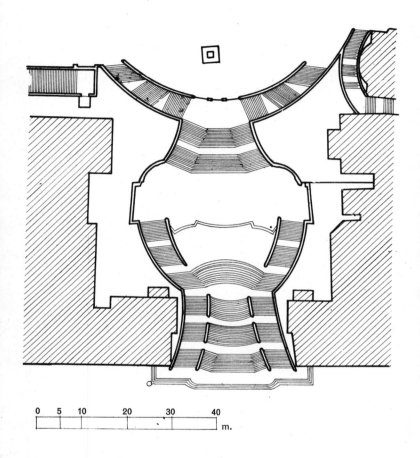

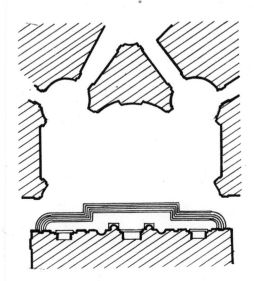

22, 23, 24. Rome, Trevi Fountain.

in front of the natural world of the garden. Rather than imposing himself actively on this world, however, man remains a perceiving spectator. In the Baroque layouts the relationship was basically different. Here the building expressed an attitude of dynamism and conquest, and nature was fully organized by an *a priori* world system. In this case a building and its environment formed a continuous spatial totality, whereas the new environmental ideal of the English garden separated the two aspects. A new symbolic fusion, however, was indicated by the introduction of artificial ruins, which better than any other characteristic express the nostalgic wish for the past. Fusion with nature, hence, only became possible through the death of architecture.[35] The ideal of the landscape garden became generally accepted, and most of the Baroque layouts were transformed, entailing immense expenses. Only today have some of them been brought back to their original state.

The City

The Baroque idea of an infinitely extended, systematized space found its main manifestation in the seventeenth-century concept of the capital city.[36] The capital city was the center of forces extending far beyond its borders. It became the reference point for a whole world, and thereby reduced many smaller centers to a provincial status. The prototype, naturally, was Rome, which already in ancient times had functioned as the *caput mundi.* During the Counter-Reformation its old role was restored, and Pope Sixtus V planned a thorough systematization of the urban texture. Basically he tried to integrate the main religious foci by means of a system of straight streets, thereby imbuing the whole area of the city with ideological value. The dynamic and open character of the capital city, thus, was expressed by its inner structure. During the sixteenth century we also find for the first time that the network of urban streets tends to become integrated with the territorial roads outside. In addition to Rome, the Baroque process of systematization had its most interesting results in Paris and Turin. Whereas the Roman foci were religious monuments, Paris gave this role to squares, the so-called *places royales* whose simple geometric form was centered on a statue of the sovereign. The absolute ruler, thus, is the real focus. Later Le Nôtre introduced his idea of the infinite, radiating perspective, whereby the concept of extension was given precise form. During the reign of Louis XIV the basic structure of Paris had been defined. Its constituent elements were spatial nodes, paths, and regularly programmed districts. The buildings were planned in relation to the spatial system, and therefore do not have any strong plastic individuality. The seventeenth-century planning of Turin also clearly expresses the ideal system of absolute monarchy, and its spatial structure has the French character of a horizontally extended network. The secular system, however, contrasts with the vertical towers of domes

and churches. Turin, thus, represents a singular synthesis of the basic properties of Paris and Rome, and its environment also unites the secular and sacred aspects of the Baroque landscape. But none of the three cities allowed for the full development of a Baroque plan. The existing architectural and topographical circumstances had to be taken into consideration; the results are fascinating compromises, although Turin came close to a total systematization. The ideal city of the seventeenth century, however, is exemplified by Versailles. Here the palace forms the center of two extensive spaces, defined by radiating perspectives: the city on one side and the landscape on the other.

The basic properties of Versailles were repeated in many of the Late Baroque "residence-cities" of the eighteenth century. In Mannheim, Stuttgart, and Würzburg the palace was not situated in the middle of the city proper, but acted as a focus for a larger totality which comprised an ideally open landscape. The most perfect example of this concept is offered by Karlsruhe. The town was founded in 1715 for the Margrave Karl Wilhelm of Baden-Durlach, who perhaps himself designed the plan which was executed by the military engineer Jakob Friedrich von Betzendorf. Here the tower of the palace is placed precisely in the center of a system of thirty-two radiating streets, which, owing to the lack of fortifications, have an infinite extension. Within this regular pattern several spatial relationships are defined. One quarter of the circle is filled in by the regularly planned town. Its fan-like pattern is centered on the palace, from which it is separated by a formal garden and a *cour d'honneur.* The three other quarters are given over to nature. A large circle, however, separates an inner *Thiergarten* and *Fasanengarten* from the surrounding "wilderness." Accentuated orthogonal directions are superimposed on the radiating system. The longitudinal axis is defined by the church and the main entrance of the palace, whereas the transverse axis is differentiated from the other garden paths by the introduction of large fountains. Its direction is repeated in a straight base street which links the town to the neighboring villages of Durlach and Mühlburg. The relationship between this base and the radiating system is the most original and fascinating property of the plan. The base line relates the ideal city to the real world outside and somewhat liberates the plan of its otherwise too theoretical character. The two are integrated by sophisticated details such as the location of the axially placed church on the outside of the base street. The Karlsruhe plan, thus, is more complex than it may seem at first sight. Compared to Versailles, however, it represents a simplification, which mainly consists in the definition of one clearly pronounced center. The persuasive Baroque dynamism based on tensions between centers and directions has almost disappeared and is replaced by a nostalgic manifestation of a world which already belongs to the past. Brinckmann has explained the plan of Karlsruhe as a synthesis of the centralized

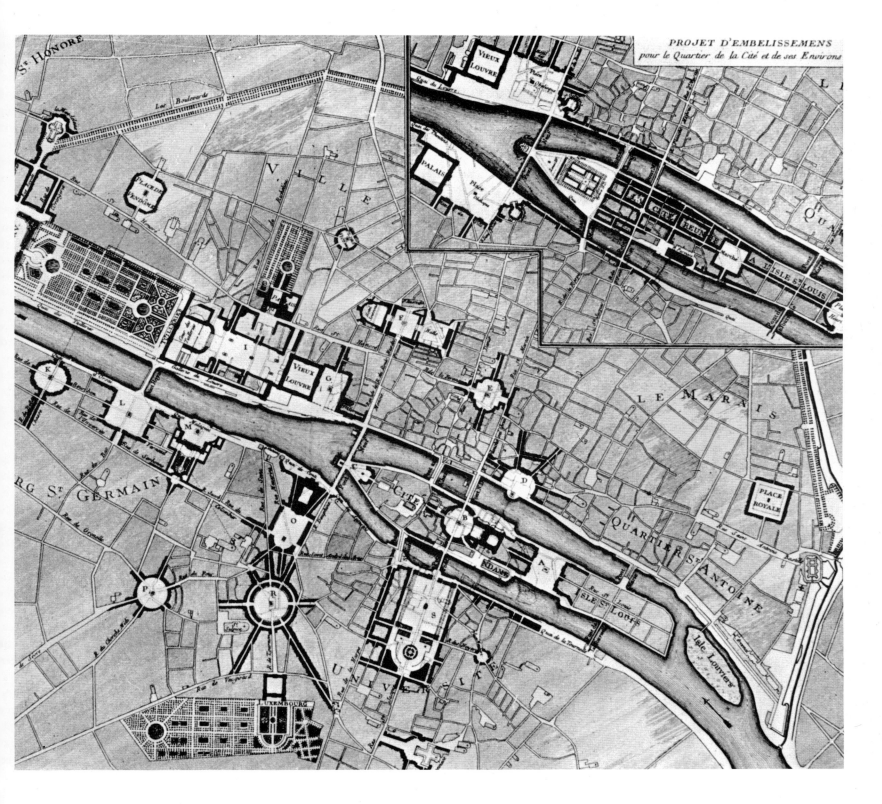

25. *P. Patte: plan of Paris with projects for the Place Louis XV.*

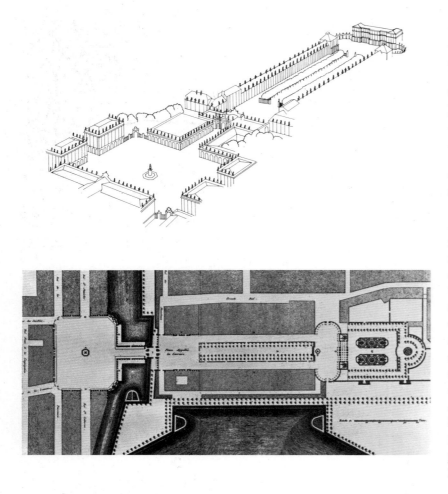

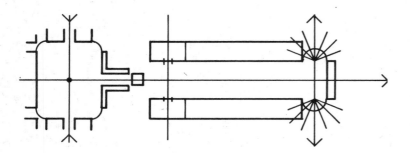

schemes of the Renaissance and the trident of Le Nôtre.[37] We should like to add that Karlsruhe differs from the ideal city of the Renaissance in a more basic way. Whereas the Renaissance city was a perfectly homogeneous organism, evenly distributed around its center, the Baroque focus is placed where city and nature meet. Thus it does not organize a closed civic world opposed to nature, but a synthetic open world composed of different, interacting elements. Seen from this point of view, Karlsruhe becomes the supreme manifestation of the ideal city of the Baroque epoch.

As the most comprehensive urban project of the entire century, however, we may consider the creation of a new capital city for the Russian empire.[38] The city of St. Petersburg was founded in 1703, and in 1712 the Tsar and his family moved there from Moscow, followed by most of the aristocracy. The focus of the new town was the Old Admiralty on the Neva River, from which three main streets branch out. The first of these, the Nevski Prospekt, was planned in 1715. The streets were centered on the tall tower of the Old Admiralty, and they were lined by houses of uniform height and articulation. This system has remained the backbone for the further urban development of St. Petersburg, and we have reason to believe that the idea stems from Peter the Great himself. In 1716 Peter commissioned the French architect Le Blond to make a total plan for the city. The project, however, did not take the actual situation into consideration, and its abstract geometrical pattern in any case expressed an outdated, albeit grandiose, concept of the ideal city. After Peter's death, the development of St. Petersburg was halted and its later urban history falls outside the scope of this book. We ought, however, to mention that the Italian architect Bartolomeo Rastrelli planned a *place royale* with an equestrian statue of the Tsar in front of his Winter Palace (rebuilt 1754–62), next to the Old Admiralty.

The Baroque concept of space also found a continuation in urban creations of a more limited size, such as monumental squares. Some of the most famous examples are found in the three great capital cities of the seventeenth century: Rome, Paris, and Turin.

Roman architecture of the eighteenth century lacked the originality and power of the works of the preceding period. Nevertheless, the numerous buildings contribute in a decisive way to integrating the townscape. The famous plan of Nolli (1748) shows a continuous, dense texture punctuated by great, monumental foci. Some of these date from the eighteenth century, and they add a gay note to the serious rhetoric of the Baroque city. The Spanish Stairs and the Trevi Fountain are among the most popular objectives of any visitor to the Eternal City, whereas the splendid Piazza S. Ignazio is less familiar. The most interesting of all the urban works, however, the port of the Ripetta, was destroyed toward the end of the nineteenth century when the walls along the Tiber

32. *Nancy, Place de la Carrière.*
33. *Nancy, partial view of the Place de la Carrière.*

34. *Nancy, Place Stanislas.*
35. *Nancy, Hôtel de Ville.*

37. *Turin, Quartieri Militari, diagrammatic drawing.*
38, 39. *Turin, Quartieri Militari.*

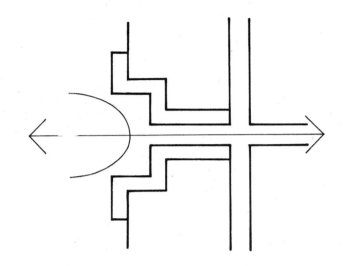

were built. The port was designed by Alessandro Specchi and executed in 1703–5. It showed an interplay of convex and concave curves, expressing a deliberate return to Borrominian principles, after the dry eclecticism of Carlo Fontana which dominated Roman architecture during the last decades of the seventeenth century. Better than most works, the Ripetta demonstrates the unifying force of Baroque architecture. A heterogeneous series of buildings formed the backdrop for the great *scalinata* of Specchi. Fortunately, he found the modest façade of Martino Longhi's S. Girolamo degli Schiavoni approximately in the middle, and could take it as the point of departure for an organizing axis. Along this axis an oval volume protrudes toward the river, flanked on both sides by flights of stairs which indicate a descending movement. To these flights are added larger, concave stairs that receive those who arrive by boat and lead them up to the level of the street above. We find, thus, an interpenetration of two realms: the river-space which enters into the city by means of the concave stairs, and the urban world which protrudes forward. The straight stairs that complete the design on either side obviously have the function of defining the direction of the river itself, thereby giving meaning to the dynamic interplay of curves.[39] The port theme, thus, found a convincing Baroque interpretation, expressing the dialectic of arrival and departure.

The Spanish Stairs were built to unite Via del Babuino (the easternmost of the three main arteries radiating into the city from the Piazza del Popolo) with Via Felice, the first great street planned by Sixtus V (1585). Their junction is crossed at an approximately right angle by Via Condotti, which defines the direction toward St. Peter's and the Vatican. Several projects were made between 1717 and 1720, also by Alessandro Specchi, whose ideas were later assimilated by the chosen architect of the Stairs, Francesco de Sanctis. The very rich and varied solution ultimately employed by De Sanctis (1723–26) is based on a simple doubling in depth of the central theme from the Ripetta: a protruding volume flanked by convex stairs and a straight flight in front. The upper unit presents the theme in its basic form; the lower constitutes an articulate and lively variation. The protruding volume, thus, is somewhat pulled back, leaving a protected, intimate space between the convex, lateral stairs, into which leads a series of concave steps, the so-called "theater." The two units are joined by a complex landing and, along the perimeter, by a continuous undulating wall. As a whole the Spanish Stairs show a rich interplay of rising and falling movements creating a dynamic equilibrium that invites relaxed enjoyment rather than quick passage. The composition is dominated by the axis of the church of Trinità dei Monti, in front of which stands an obelisk to mark the meeting of the various directions. The solution well expresses the change of attitude from the more abstract rhetoric of High Baroque axial layouts toward the sensuous

interpretation of an empirical problem characteristic of the eighteenth century.[40] As early as 1726 Cardinal de Polignac wrote of the Spanish Stairs: "When it is very hot, the whole city of Rome loves to pass the night out of doors, and this place is more frequented than any other because of its freshness and beauty."

The small Piazza S. Ignazio (1727–28) has a different character. Rather than forming a node within the given context of historical Rome, it appears as a fragment of a different kind of city, based on a continuous, undulating movement of interacting spatial cells. In fact, the Piazza S. Ignazio represents the only urban application of the principles of Borromini and Guarini, as expressed theoretically in the latter's *Placita Philosophica.*[41] It is quite surprising that the mediocre Filippo Raguzzini was able to conceive a solution of such importance and originality as this, and we may suspect the influence of Juvarra, who had been awarded the position of architect for St. Peter's in 1725. The composition is generally described as consisting of three oval spaces, a large one in the middle flanked by two smaller ones that form a transition to the streets behind. The lateral palaces, however, are perfectly symmetrical and indicate similar oval spaces at either end. Due to the existence of **Alessandro Algardi's façade for S. Ignazio (1649)**, only two of the four ovals thus defined could be carried out. Rather than representing an adaptation to the church, the piazza constitutes an open system which is interrupted by the church. The lateral ovals are defined by the walls of three different buildings. These walls join optically to define the space in front, freeing themselves from the building behind, at the same time that each of them forms part of the continuous boundary of the building. A singular integration of mass and space results, both being clearly defined by ambiguous surfaces. It would certainly have been interesting to see a larger city district organized along these lines. In spite of this strict system, the Piazza S. Ignazio has the lightness and playful sensuousness of Rococo architecture.[42]

The last urban masterpiece of Roman eighteenth-century architecture to be cited, the Trevi Fountain, was designed by Nicola Salvi in 1732, though finished by Giuseppe Pannini in 1762. It appears as a great *Gesamtkunstwerk* of natural, sculptural, and architectural elements, the architectural parts being the weakest. As a typical manifestation of Baroque rhetoric, it represents "the splendid swansong of an epoch which owed all its vital impulses to one great artist, Bernini."[43]

In Paris building activity waned during the later decades of the reign of Louis XIV when attention was centered on Versailles, but after 1715 Paris again became the true capital city of France, and began to flourish anew. City districts were increasingly developed, notably the Faubourg St-Germain with its numerous private hôtels. A year after the Treaty of Aix-la-Chapelle, a competition was organized among the architects of

Paris for the creation of a square honoring Louis XV. Of over forty projects, the more important were published in 1765 by Pierre Patte in his *Monuments érigés en France à la Gloire de Louis XV*. Basically, they represent a continuation of the Baroque ideas of integrating the townscape by means of axes and *rond-points*, ideas which here have become the object of academic virtuosity. The most grandiose project, developed by Patte himself, shows a unification of the Île de la Cité and the Île St-Louis into one symmetrical island. The Place Dauphine has been torn down and in its place we find a new, immense cathedral where a Latin cross is inscribed within the colonnades of a classical temple. To complete the symmetry Patte also proposed to destroy the Institut de France in favor of a pendant to the Louvre on the other side of the river. The only one of the many projects to be executed, however, was the Place Louis XV, the present-day Place de la Concorde. In 1750 the King gave the land to the city, and in 1753 Ange-Jacques Gabriel was the winner of a new competition, in which nineteen architects took part.[44] The square was constructed from 1755 to 1763. The Place de la Concorde forms part of the great axis of Le Nôtre running from the Tuileries through the Champs Élysées toward infinity. The square, therefore, could not have a normal architectural definition. Instead Gabriel planned a large platform circumscribed by a deep trench and centered on an equestrian statue of Louis XV. On one side the space is defined by the two symmetrical Gardes Meubles (1757–75), whose articulation is clearly derived from the Louvre façade, manifesting the French classical tradition. On the opposite side the square touches the Seine. Thus it forms the transition and link between four realms: the city, the tamed nature of the Tuileries gardens, the free nature of the Champs Élysées, and the natural waterway of the river. Between these realms the Place de la Concorde forms a subtle mean. Instead of the rhetorical *Gesamtkunstwerk* of the seventeenth century we simply find an open space which has meaning through its location. Marc-Antoine Laugier recognized the novelty of the conception and wrote: "Surrounded by gardens and groves, it looks like a pretty promenade in the middle of a smiling countryside. . . ."[45] Although it is clearly inspired by the platforms preceding French châteaux such as those at Vaux-le-Vicomte and Chantilly, the Place de la Concorde was a highly original achievement which better expressed the spirit of the epoch than the more monumental but rather conventional projects shown in the plan of Patte. Today the square has lost much of its character due to the filling-in of the trench (1854).

Among the other urban projects of eighteenth-century France, recognition must be given to the Place Stanislas in Nancy, designed in 1752 by Emmanuel Héré de Corny for Stanislas Leczinski, Duke of Lorraine and father-in-law of Louis XV. In reality the project consists of a succession of three spaces: the Place Stanislas proper, the long Place de la Car-

◁ 44. *Prague, Charles Bridge.*

45. *Prague, Charles Bridge, diagrammatic drawing.*
46. *Bath, plan of the city.*
47. *Bath, plan of the Royal Crescent and the King's Circus.*

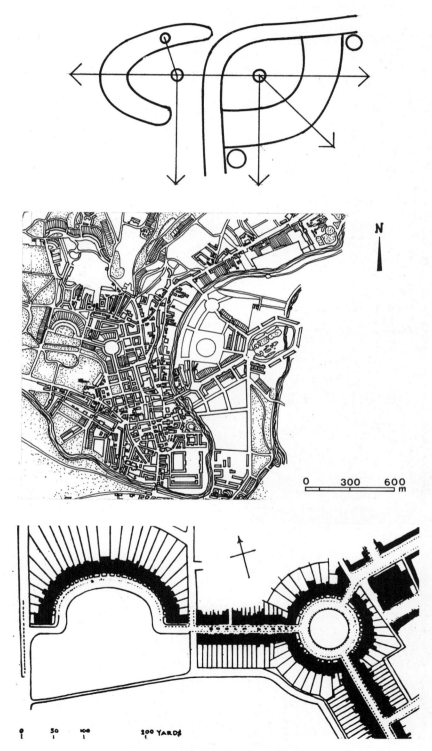

rière, and the Hemicycle in front of the Palais du Gouvernement. Urbanistically, the spaces had the function of joining together the medieval part of the town (containing the Ducal Palace) and the large, regularly disposed Renaissance extension, which were separated by a moat. The Place Stanislas, thus, was planned as a rectangular *place royale* on the outskirts of the Renaissance town. Rather than being an independent unit, however, it was connected with the former tournament field of the court on the other side of the moat, the present Place de la Carrière, which had been bounded on one side by Boffrand (1715). Héré completed the boundary and added the Hemicycle, a rectangle with semicircular colonnades at both ends. In general, the scheme consists of a *place royale*, a long *avant-cour*, and a *cour d'honneur* joined together. A triumphal arch mediates the transition between the two principal parts. The basic spatial relationships within the layout are quite complex and consist of juxtaposed directions, contractions, and extensions. A dominant longitudinal axis, however, runs from the town hall at one end to the government building at the other. The composition is enriched by sensitive detailing. The Place Stanislas, for example, has rounded corners defined by openwork grilles in gilded wrought iron, designed by Jean Lamour. The almost Borrominian continuity of the space boundary, however, is subtly contradicted by the variations in height of the surrounding buildings. Thus the transition toward the Place de la Carrière is mediated by omitting the main stories above the rusticated ground floor, depriving the *place royale* of its traditionally uniform centralization. The Place de la Carrière has the character of a regular, longitudinal promenade, whereas the Hemicycle is unified by a continuous colonnade which also comprises the ground floor of the palace. Its transparent semicircular ends create a spatial opening which makes the square an in-between realm where civic environment and nature fuse.[46] In general, the squares of Nancy form a worthy conclusion to the development of Baroque urban space, and they are scarcely surpassed anywhere else.

In Turin eighteenth-century building activity concentrated on a further development of the general trends of the seventeenth century. The orthogonal system introduced by Ascanio Vittozzi and Carlo and Amedeo di Castellamonte (father and son) was completed by a third city extension toward the west (begun 1706) under the direction of Juvarra.[47] Juvarra continued the Roman street pattern of the adjacent old town, and created a *place royale*, the present Piazza Savoia, as a local center. Within the regular district he erected the elaborate Palazzo Martini di Cigala (1716–19) and later the splendid Chiesa del Carmine (1732–36). He terminated the east-west axis with an *exedra*, the Quartieri Militari (1716–28), following the example given at the termination of Via Po by Amedeo di Castellamonte. Juvarra's *exedra*, however, does not have the usual semicircular form. Rather it appears as half a rectangular *place*

48. *Bath, aerial view.*

royale, indicating the ideally open character of the urban structure. The solution forms a convincing transition between the urban environment and the landscape beyond, and was repeated by Juvarra himself in the Porta Palazzo (1729). The Quartieri Militari have a strong, masculine expression based on a free use of Doric elements. They exemplify Juvarra's extraordinarily appropriate characterization of the individual building type. The Baroque construction of Turin was completed by some important modifications in the old Roman core, such as the opening of two main thoroughfares, the Via Dora Grossa (today Via Garibaldi) and the Via di Porta Palazzo (today Via Milano), running east-west and north-south respectively (1736). Next to the point where they meet, the lovely Piazza Palazzo di Città was created by Benedetto Alfieri in 1756. Thereby the old town also received a worthy center. The façades of Alfieri are still based on the themes introduced by Vittozzi a century and a half before, giving testimony to the remarkable continuity in the urban development of Turin.

Many other residence-cities of Central and Northern Europe received a monumental focus during the eighteenth century, mostly by the construction of a place royale. Particularly interesting is the Amalienborg Square in Copenhagen, which functioned as the focus of a new district, the Frederiksstaden. In 1749 King Frederik V initiated its development, using Niels Eigtved as his architect. Situated north of the old town, the new district forms a long rectangle along the harbor, divided into four sections by two orthogonally disposed streets. Where they intersect, a large octagonal square is left free. It was intended as a true place royale, with a statue of the King in the middle. The shorter axis of the layout was given primary importance by the introduction of a large domed church at its end.[48] The octagonal shape and the articulation of the Amalienborg Square has predecessors in French city planning, but the erection of large semi-detached palaces on the diagonal axes is a very original and convincing idea. The palaces (1750–54) were built by Eigtved for four leading members of the court. Today they house the royal family itself. The buildings have the rusticated ground floor, the tall bel-étage, and the low attic prescribed for all buildings in Frederiksstaden, and thus form the most splendid variation on a general theme. The addition of lower wings on both sides of the main corps-de-logis creates an interesting tension between the masses on the diagonals and the openings on the main axes. Undoubtedly, the ensemble represents one of the most convincing achievements of the European eighteenth century, combining the strict system of absolute monarchy with the charm and commodity of Rococo architecture.

Whereas the capital cities of the absolute monarchies were focused on monumental squares, the main cities of the regions dominated by the Catholic Counter-Reformation show a somewhat different structure. Here

52. *Salzburg, Dreifaltigkeitskirche, interior of the dome.*
53. *Salzburg, Dreifaltigkeitskirche, detail of the interior.*

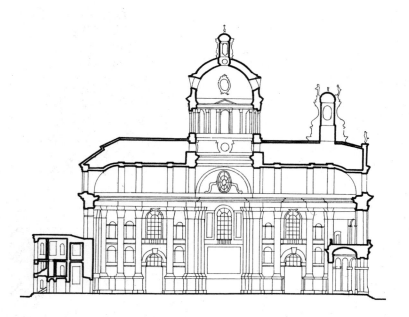

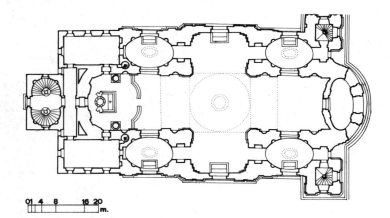

01 4 8   16 20
m.

the townscape is still dominated by the domes and towers of the churches, and the squares are usually centered on Marian columns rather than equestrian statues of sovereigns. As an exceptionally rich and well-preserved example, we may mention Prague, which is usually characterized as a Baroque city, although it shows no trace of real Baroque city planning. Its three main districts—the old town (*staré mesto* or *Altstadt*), the new town (*nové mesto* or *Neustadt*), and the little town (*malá strana* or *Kleinseite*)—have a medieval street pattern, and even the squares were defined long before the Baroque epoch. During the seventeenth and eighteenth centuries, however, Prague became saturated with Baroque elements: churches, palaces, houses, and statues. Nowhere else is the Counter-Reformatory unity of past and present more evident; the integrated medieval cosmos is restored with Baroque persuasive rhetoric. The character of Prague is first of all determined by its beautiful situation. The softly undulating Bohemian landscape is here condensed to form a curved ridge along the large arc of the river Vltava (the Moldau). Inside the arc, a wide plain made a natural place for settlement, protected by two smaller hills at either end. Between the plain and the ridge a ford made the conditions for the development of a town complete. Thus, Prague grew on both sides of the river and the connecting element, the Charles Bridge (also called the Karlsbrücke or Karlův Most), always had primary importance. The bridge existing today was built by Peter Parler in 1357 by order of Emperor Charles IV.[49] As it was partly constructed on the remains of an older bridge, it does not run in a straight line from one end to the other, but rather seems to form a continuation of the crooked streets on both sides. In 1683 the Baroque sculptural decoration of the bridge was initiated with the erection of a statue of St. John Nepomuk, cast after a model by Mathias Rauchmüller. The example was to be imitated on innumerable bridges all over Central Europe, especially after the canonization of the saint in 1729.[50] During the first two decades of the eighteenth century the Charles Bridge was embellished with numerous statues by Mathias Braun, Jan Brokoff, Ferdinand Max Brokoff, Matej Jäkl, and others,[51] whereby it was transformed into a "sacred path" leading from the old town toward Kilian Ignaz Dientzenhofer's Cathedral of St. Veit (1737–53) on the ridge over the little town.[52] The bridge wends its way to the beautiful Mostecká or Brückengasse, which is lined by Late Baroque façades and leads toward the great dome and bell-tower of St. Nicholas on the Kleinseite. Together the two vertical elements dominate the town, appearing in continuously changing juxtaposition as the beholder moves about. In Prague religious persuasion by means of dynamic architecture and sculpture reaches its culmination: the whole town becomes a plastic mass from which the vertical accents gradually but forcefully liberate themselves.

The examples mentioned above demonstrate how the urban ideals of

58. *Salzburg, Kollegienkirche, interior.*
59. *Salzburg, Kollegienkirche, interior.* ▷
60. *Salzburg, Kollegienkirche, detail of the apse.* ▷

the Baroque lived on during the eighteenth century. Simultaneously, however, a new concept of the city came to the fore. This development took place mainly in England, and found its greatest manifestation in the town of Bath. Bath was neither a capital city nor a religious center, but simply a bathing resort built for the entertainment of an anonymous and mixed society. "It attracted the aristocracy, artists, men of letters, and—as Oliver Goldsmith relates—types still more various: 'Clerks and factors from the East-Indies, loaded with the spoils of plundered provinces, planters, negro drivers from our American plantations, agents who have fattened in two successive wars, brokers and jobbers of every kind, men of low birth.'"[53] This new bourgeois society found its congenial interpreter in the dilettante architect and builder John Wood the Elder, who combined great vision with a practical sense and economic shrewdness. In 1725 he planned an extension to the old town, and between 1728 and 1734 he built the first unit of the new Bath, Queen Square, which is clearly related to the great London squares of the time. More original was his next step, the King's Circus, started in 1754 and finished by his son (John Wood the Younger) in 1758. Here Wood obviously wanted to revive the splendor of ancient Bath, known to the Romans as *Aquae Sulis*. The idea of a forum "for the exhibition of sports," however, hardly fitted the place and the times, and the solution turned into a monumentalized row of residences. The result is a kind of "inverted Colosseum,"[54] articulated by three superimposed orders of coupled columns. The basic unit is the ordinary townhouse, whose origin goes back to the Middle Ages. In general it has a narrow frontage to the street, rooms back and front on each floor, and a long court or garden at the rear. Wood's essential contribution lies in his having used this unit for the planning of extensive neighborhoods, treating it as a type that may be varied. In fact, Wood devised houses of different size and degree conforming to six definite standards which he classified as ranging from first-rate to sixth-rate. The topography contributed further to the rich variety that is experienced within the planned unity of Georgian Bath. John Wood the Younger continued the work initiated by his father, building the beautifully varied Brock Street (1765) which connects the King's Circus with his masterpiece, the Royal Crescent (1767–74). Whereas the King's Circus has the character of an enclosed space, the half-oval Royal Crescent opens onto the landscape. It expresses a new concept of living in contact with nature, even as its great Ionic colonnade reflects the ideals of Neoclassical architecture. The solution was to have considerable influence on the subsequent development of residential building. In Bath itself it inspired the long serpentine line of Lansdown Crescent and Somerset Place, built by John Palmer and John Eveleigh between 1789 and 1793. Baroque centralization has disappeared in this town, and the idea of extension has been given a new interpretation. In-

61. *Kappel, pilgrimage church, plan.*

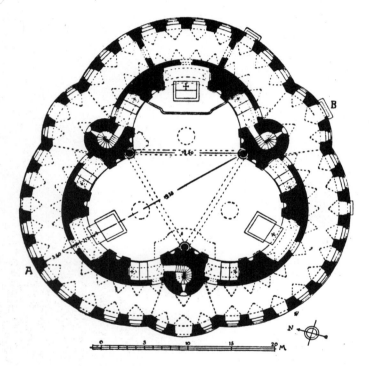

62. *Kappel, pilgrimage church, section.*

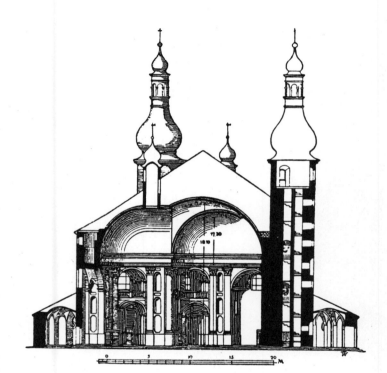

63. *Kappel, pilgrimage church, exterior.*

stead of an infinite and absolute geometrical system, we find an empirical use of a theme that is varied according to the circumstances. Within the basically open totality, however, characteristic places are formed, such as the King's Circus and the Royal Crescent, which enable the individual to identify with his neighborhood and to arrive at an image of the whole town. In general Bath represents the beginning of a new "democratic" architecture, where everybody finds a place within a flexible totality. But we may add that this achievement only became possible by utilizing the spatial experiences of Baroque architecture.

The Church

In the past certain building types were significant because they aimed at expressing the common cultural values on which the form of life in question was founded. The church and the palace played this role throughout the centuries. From the end of the eighteenth century new major types appeared. Interest was directeed in turn toward the landscape garden, the monument, the museum, the theater, the exhibition hall, and the factory.[55] In the seventeenth century the church was generally the main form, and in Catholic countries it retained this role during most of the eighteenth. It also served as an urban focus according to the principles previously established by Alberti and Palladio. Seventeenth-century ecclesiastical architecture took the traditional longitudinal basilica as well as the centralized church of the Renaissance as a point of departure. The former was preferred by the clergy because it satisfied the Counter-Reformatory demand for a congregational building, whereas the latter had been recommended by architectural theorists because its form was believed to represent the abstract harmony of the cosmos. As a result, the two types tended to fuse, the larger churches becoming centralized longitudinal buildings, and the smaller ones elongated central buildings. In Early Baroque churches the two types were combined rather than integrated,[56] but during the seventeenth century leading architects aimed at the creation of truly synthetic types. This was achieved by introducing two axes of symmetry in a longitudinal organism, arriving thereby at what may be called bi-axial space, by making the spatial elements mutually interdependent or by emphasizing the continuity of the space boundary. In the inspired buildings of Borromini all three possibilities are exploited, whereas his follower Guarini studied the grouping of interpenetrating or otherwise interdependent spatial cells.[57] In the works of these two masters the Baroque demands for synthesis and systematization were satisfied, mainly by making space the real constituent element of architecture. The church also became more actively related to its environment. By emphasizing the longitudinal axis as well as the vertical axis through the center, it could serve as a focus both to its neighborhood and to the city as a whole. The Baroque church represented the stability

of the basic dogmas, and at the same time its dynamic forms aimed at persuasion and participation. Bernini was the great inventor of the illusional decoration and the dramatic light of the epoch, and the persuasive dynamism of his architecture is primarily created by these means, whereas Borromini and Guarini made architectural form itself the carrier of the expressive content. In the Late Baroque architecture of Central Europe and Piedmont the two approaches were fused into a last exuberant synthesis. We will return to the problem in more detail in the next chapter, but should here illustrate the general trend with a few examples.

The Italian concepts were introduced into Central Europe during the seventeenth century by traveling Italian architects. None of them, however, arrived at truly original contributions. The situation changed when Johann Bernhard Fischer von Erlach returned from Rome and Naples in 1686 after having studied and worked in Italy for fifteen years. Fischer brought back direct knowledge of the works of Bernini and Borromini, and his projects also show the influence of Guarini. His two main churches in Salzburg, planned in 1694, clearly demonstrate his background. The Dreifaltigkeitskirche (Trinitätskirche) forms the central part of a large complex comprising a house for priests and the Collegium Virgilianum. Fischer here introduced a general symmetrical disposition which was repeated in most of the great monasteries of the eighteenth century. The plan of the church is a longitudinal oval, following a basic Roman type, whereas the concave façade, with flanking *campanili* and an oval landing in front, repeats the general disposition of Borromini's S. Agnese in Agone in Rome.[58] The articulation is an interesting synthesis of Borrominian surface continuity and Berninesque definition of the individual volumes. Thus, the ground floor has continuous stylized rustication and uniform windows, while above the church liberates itself from the flanking buildings. The general character is determined by the relationship between flat, concave, and convex surfaces. The Kollegienkirche (Collegiate Church) is a much larger and more important building. Its foundation-stone was laid in 1696 and it was consecrated in 1707. Here Fischer adopted the bi-axial plan that had been introduced by Rosato Rosati in S. Carlo ai Catinari, Rome (1612). The spatial character, however, is quite different. The longitudinal and vertical axes are strongly emphasized and create a directed rather than a centralized space. Particularly impressive are the tall proportions of the nave, resembling those of a Gothic church. To achieve this effect Fischer put a colossal order on plinths which are fourteen feet high. The slender dome contributes to the general verticality, yet the simple articulation of the walls is truly Roman, whereas the bi-axial plan with four domed chapels between the arms of the cross has its origin in Byzantine architecture. The façade shows a strongly projecting oval volume between two *campanili*, a variation on the theme of the Dreifaltigkeitskirche, but here the plastic

body of the church proper is separated from the towers by recesses, an idea Bernini had introduced in a sketch for the completion of the façade of St. Peter's in Rome. The unity is secured by a continuous giant order of pilasters. The strong front interacts successfully with the narrow Universitätsplatz, and it introduces with true Baroque rhetoric one of the most monumental spaces of the epoch. Although the Kollegienkirche has its predecessors and in general expresses the Baroque desire for synthesis, its character is highly personal. Again we encounter Fischer's wish for an "historical architecture," in which Byzantine, Roman, and medieval concepts fuse to form a new and original unity. Fischer's achievement, however, does not constitute a type, nor does the Kollegienkirche represent any general methodology of spatial composition, such as the *ars combinatoria* of Guarini.[59]

Guarini's ideas were made generally known when his projects were published in 1686, but two years earlier Georg Dientzenhofer had already started building the Kappel shrine near Waldsassen, where the problem of composing with spatial cells is approached in an original way. The unusual plan of the church is obviously due to a conscious desire to symbolize the Holy Trinity; the region of Franconia and Bohemia had a long tradition in the use of symbolic plans. The solution here, however, goes far beyond the mere application of a geometrical figure. In general, the church appears as a centralized structure without a façade. The picturesque silhouette unites Eastern, Slavic, and Gothic elements, whereas the naked walls are related to simple folk architecture. The church, hence, synthesizes an architectural inheritance of a much wider range than the elements of the classical tradition. More important, however, is the basic formal structure, which may be described as a juxtaposition of cells within an enveloping membrane-like wall. The lack of a façade makes the constituent role of the spatial elements evident. Kappel, thus, appears as a particular case of a more general spectrum of spatial compositions, and was, in fact, the first of a long series of varied buildings designed by members of the Dientzenhofer family, all consisting of juxtaposed cells enclosed by a secondary wall. Although Kappel may be considered an original achievement, the knowledge of Guarini's works was to have a decisive influence on further developments.

To make a composition with spatial cells effective, it is essential that the primary structure be reduced to a skeleton; that is, the walls should not constitute the spaces, but rather play the role of secondary panels that may be put in or taken away at will. Such a system comes close to the structure of Gothic architecture. In Guarini's works the skeletal character is very pronounced, although he usually maintains a continuous horizontal entablature. In the Early Baroque architecture of Germany, however, attempts were made to transform the wall into a skeleton by adapting the local tradition of *Wandpfeiler*, or wall-pillar, construction.

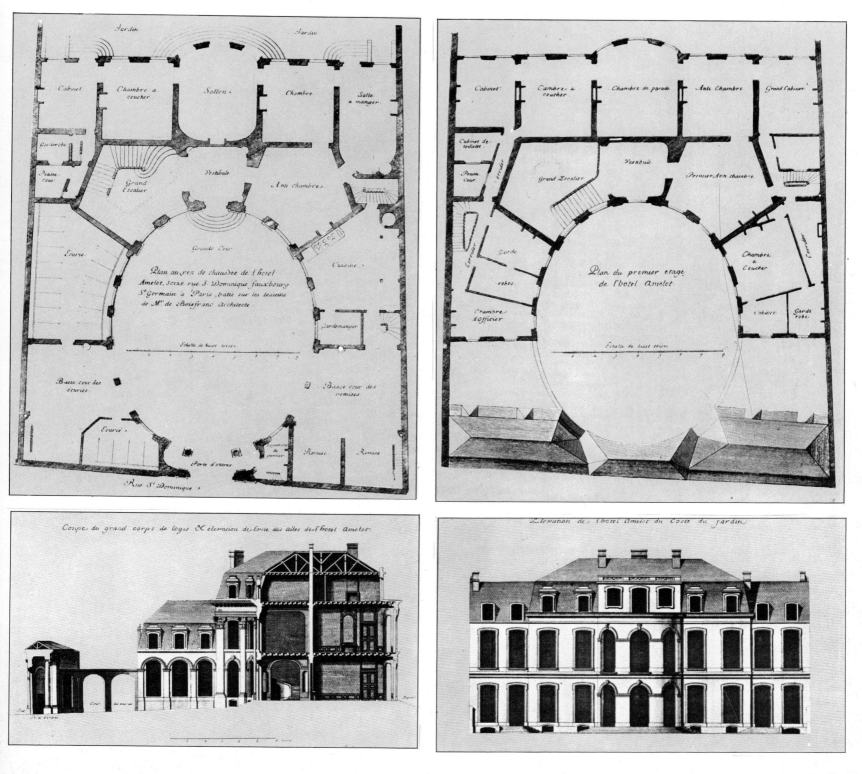

74. *Paris, Hôtel Amelot de Gournay, elevation of the courtyard façade.*
75. *Paris, Hôtel Amelot de Gournay, courtyard façade.*
76. *Paris, Hôtel Amelot de Gournay, detail of the courtyard façade.* ▷

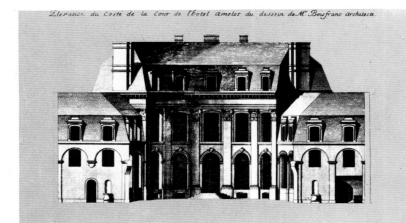

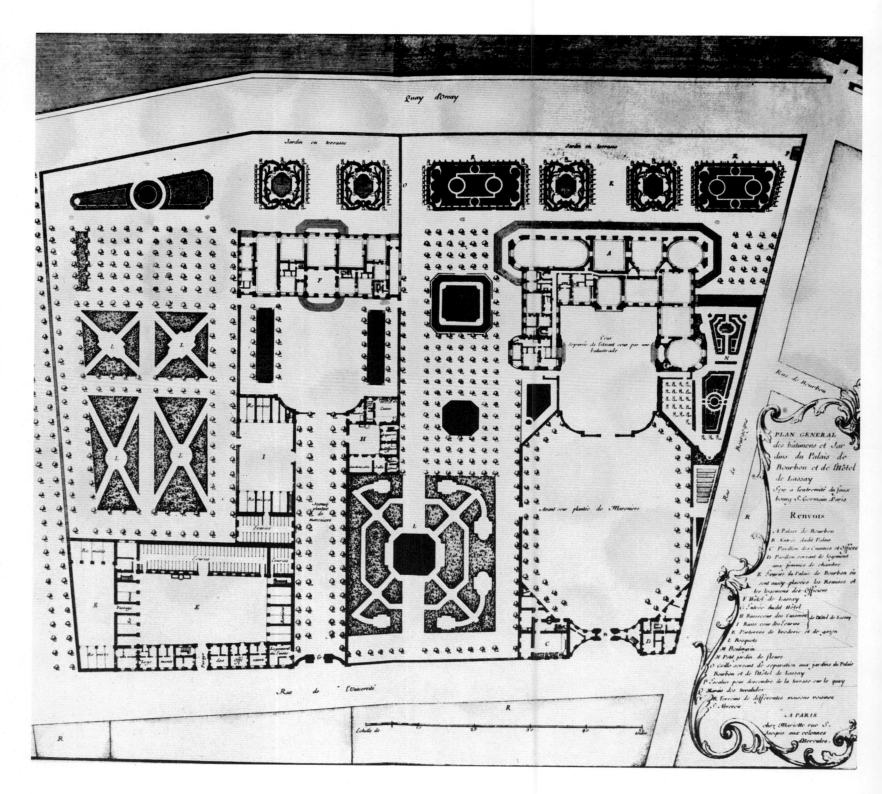

78. *Vienna, Althan Palace, from an eighteenth-century engraving.*
79. *J.B. Fischer von Erlach: project for a Lustgartengebäude.*

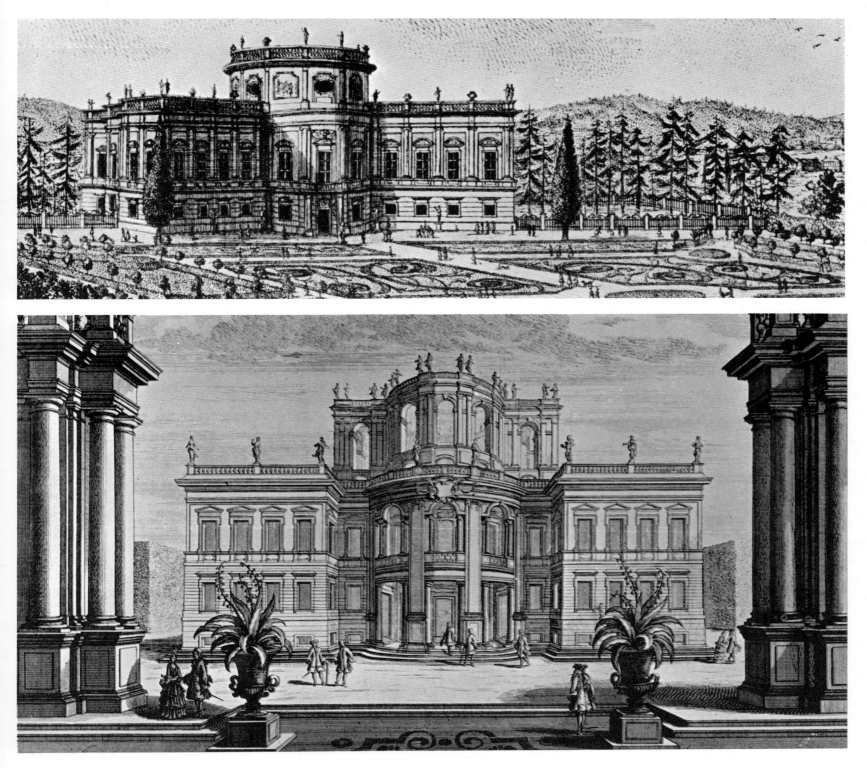

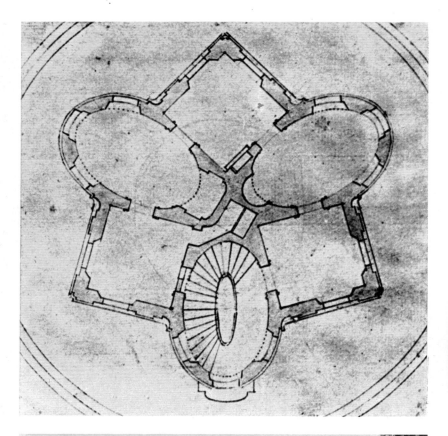

80. *J.B. Fischer von Erlach: project for the Gartenhaus of Klesheim.*
81, 82. *Klesheim, Gartenhaus.*

83. *L. von Hildebrandt: project for a Gartenhaus for the Mansfeld-Fondi Palace in Vienna (diagrammatic drawing).*
84. *J.B. Fischer von Erlach: sketch for a Lustgartengebäude in Vienna.*
85. *Turin, Palazzo Madama, façade overlooking Piazza Castello* ▷

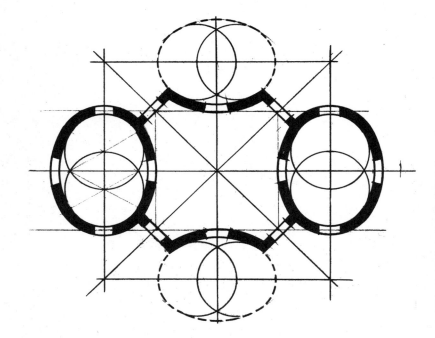

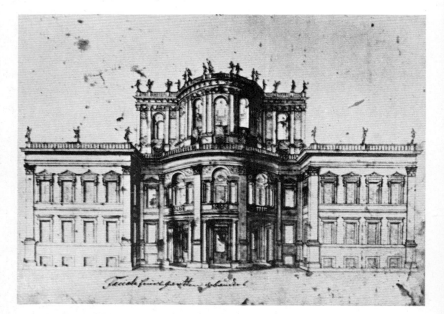

Wall-pillars are Gothic buttresses, placed inside instead of on the exterior of the building, connected by a thin non-supporting wall.[60] An early use appears in the church of St. Michael in Munich (1583), the type being fully developed by Hans Alberthal between 1610 and 1620. The Thirty Years' War stopped its further evolution. Toward the end of the seventeenth century, however, the builders from the Vorarlberg region of Austria made a new start, and created a clearly defined type of Baroque wall-pillar church, known as the *Vorarlberger Münsterschema*. The first important example is the pilgrimage church at Schönenberg near Ellwangen, built by Michael and Christian Thumb and Franz Beer between 1682 and 1695. At Obermarchtal the same architects arrived at a still clearer definition of the system (1686–92). Here the horizontal entablature is reduced to small fragments on which the transverse arches rest. Between them tall windows penetrate into the vault. The Vorarlberg builders, however, did not know the spatial ideas of Guarini, and applied their structural system to rather conventional longitudinal halls or, in some later churches, to bi-axial organisms.[61]

It is probable that Georg Dientzenhofer's younger brother Christoph visited Turin about 1690, where he could see the works of Guarini.[62] In any case, the ideas of Guarini were introduced into Bohemia by Johann Lucas von Hildebrandt, who started the construction of the church of St. Lawrence in Gabel, northeast of Prague, in 1699. Hildebrandt had grown up in Italy and spent the years 1695–96 in Piedmont.[63] His plan for the church in Gabel is clearly derived from Guarini's S. Lorenzo in Turin (indeed, Hildebrandt's church is dedicated to the same saint). The most important difference is the addition of an oval narthex, corresponding to the presbytery, whereby the open character of Guarini's system becomes evident. The exterior is defined as a continuous enveloping surface which even comprises the bell-towers. The approach, thus, is related to Kappel rather than to the apparently more similar Kollegienkirche in Salzburg. The spatial elements of the Gabel church do not interpenetrate, but are related according to the Guarinian principle of pulsating juxtaposition.[64] When one space expands, the adjacent one contracts, and a pulsating effect results. A similar disposition is found in Hildebrandt's contemporaneous Piaristenkirche in Vienna (1698). Hildebrandt, however, did not know the wall-pillar system, and his spaces maintain the traditional character of general enclosure. It was left to the Dientzenhofers to fuse the *ars combinatoria* of Guarini with the wall-pillar system, whereby the last great flourishing of Baroque ecclesiastical architecture was made possible.

The Palace

In the absolute monarchies of the seventeenth century the royal palace came to replace the church as the leading form of building. This change took place mainly in France, where the traditional château and hôtel made up of loosely linked wings around a spacious courtyard developed into a symmetrical U-shaped organism whose strongly emphasized longitudinal axis made the building appear as the focus of an infinitely extended landscape. The block-shaped Italian palazzo, however, also survived in many countries as the typical city dwelling. Thus, in Vienna the well-to-do usually possessed a city-palace, as well as a garden-palace outside the city walls.[65] The character of the Italian palazzo is basically that of a family seat, a private place which hides its inner structure behind massive walls. The development of the French hôtel is related instead to the growing centralization of absolutist power, which interfered with the private character of the city-palace. The hôtel, in fact, is subordinated to a general systematized space, of which, however, it dominates a part, reflecting the structure of a particular kind of hierarchical society.

Functionally, the palace is much more complex than the church. A true spatial integration, therefore, is hardly possible, and the Guarinian methodology was never really assimilated in palace architecture. The form of the Baroque palace may rather be understood as a synthesis of the epoch's particular functional demands and the general desire for systematization. It is commodious as well as representative and dominant. The desire for convenience came to the fore mainly in France, where the *appartement double* was introduced to allow for a more practical distribution of rooms than the *enfilades* of the old-fashioned *appartement simple*. In the *appartement double* the different rooms are disengaged so that most of them can be reached without going through the others, while at the same time they form a practical group rather than a simple row.[66] The desire for convenience also brought about a stronger differentiation of the spaces, according to their use. In the Italian palazzo all the main rooms generally have the same shape and size, whereas the French introduced a multitude of specialized spaces, such as the *antichambre, chambre de parade, salon, chambre à coucher, salle à manger, cabinet, garderobe*, and *galerie*. The plan, thus, became divided into many relatively small units. In general, this was already happening during the seventeenth century, but the aim also characterizes the first decades of the eighteenth, when a further differentiation of rooms took place. As a typical example we may cite the Palais de Bourbon in Paris, designed by Pierre Lassurance about 1720. Whereas the Italian palazzo has a relatively small enclosed interior courtyard, the U-shaped French hôtel is more conveniently connected with the street by means of a semi-open *cour d'honneur*. The *cour d'honneur* makes the functions of coming and going a representative part of public life, and it became a standard feature in the major residences of the eighteenth century. A certain experimentation with the shape of the courtyard took place; Boffrand, for instance, designed an oval court in the Hôtel Amelot de Gournay (1710–13). Half of the oval belongs to the *corps-de-logis*, and the other half to the entrance and the stables, whereby the two elements become truly integrated. The Hôtel Amelot de Gournay also shows a characteristic tendency to increase the size of the windows. The "French window" had already been introduced by the seventeenth century. It gives emphasis to the contact between interior and exterior space, and reduces the wall to a kind of transparent skeleton. Jules Hardouin-Mansart still used the classical orders as constituent elements of the skeleton, whereas the architects of the first half of the eighteenth century employed a skin-like wall which is perforated by large openings. Here we recognize one of the basic formal properties of Régence and Rococo architecture.[67] We may trace the origin of this revolutionary emancipation of the surface back to Borromini, and we may also relate it to the membrane-like walls introduced into ecclesiastical architecture by the Dientzenhofers. In the Hôtel Amelot de Gournay we still find a colossal order in the courtyard, whereas the garden façade demonstrates the new approach.

In Austria, Italian and French patterns were unified to form an exceptionally versatile form of palace architecture. Again we encounter Fischer von Erlach as the great protagonist of the transition from the seventeenth to the eighteenth century. His early projects for garden-palaces abound in original and fertile ideas. Already in 1688, two years after his return from Italy, Fischer planned the extraordinary *Lustgartengebäude* for Count Althan in the Rossau outside Vienna.[68] A rotunda with attached wings is a basic motif in Baroque palace architecture, but the diagonal disposition of the wings found in the Althan Palace is highly original.[69] It forms a natural combination of centralization with extension, and was soon adapted by the leading French and Italian architects, Boffrand and Juvarra. The articulation of the Althan Palace had an Italian character although the tall windows reflect the French desire for openness. In a series of projects for garden-pavilions Fischer continued his research on centralized organisms with radiating spaces, one of which was built in the park of Klesheim Castle near Salzburg (1700–9). In his larger projects he returned to an orthogonal disposition, maintaining, however, the theme of the central rotunda, which he usually characterized as a transparent volume. His researches culminated with the project for a large *Lustgartengebäude*, designed toward the end of 1698 and reproduced in the fourth book of his *Entwurff einer historischen Architektur in Abbildung unterschiedener berühmter Gebäude des Altertums und fremder Völker*. The façade appears as a condensed version of Bernini's first project for the Louvre, whereas the plan shows the bi-axial symmetry found in some of the châteaux of Salomon de Brosse and Louis Le Vau.[70] In some of his projects Fischer approaches the problem of juxtaposed spatial elements. His cells, however, are added together without being truly in-terdependent. It was Hildebrandt who was to introduce the Guarinian idea of pulsating juxtaposition in his project for a garden-pavilion for the Mansfeld-Fondi Palace in Vienna (1697), transferring the system of S. Lorenzo in Turin to a secular building.[71] With the exception of some attempts by Kilian Ignaz Dientzenhofer, the idea had no following; by and large, eighteenth-century palace architecture continued along more conventional lines.

Conclusion

The preceding sections have presented an introduction to the basic spatial and typological problems of Late Baroque and Rococo architecture. Whereas these, in general, form a continuation of seventeenth-century intentions, the epoch treated in this book is also characterized by a new pluralism of expressive means. We must distinguish here between two currents. Firstly, we find the wish for an historical synthesis which is already evident in the works of Borromini and Guarini, and which culminates with Fischer's *Entwurff einer historischen Architektur*. The book, in fact, is the first comprehensive history of architecture, and it ends with his own synthetic projects. Secondly, we encounter a general attempt at giving each building, and every room within it, an individual characterization. Although buildings have always differed according to the practical and symbolic functions they have had to fulfill, eighteenth-century pluralism is something essentially new, pointing toward the historicism of the nineteenth century. As a particularly successful representative of the pluralistic approach we may mention Filippo Juvarra, whose activity comprises all the main building types of the epoch. Instead of thinking in terms of abstract systems, Juvarra gave each type an individual character, to which he first gave a general definition in brilliant sketches, which show an extraordinary sensitivity for the function of the building as well as for the site in question. The church of La Superga (1715), for instance, is primarily intended as a vertically directed focus in relation to the landscape. Its restrained classical forms and elevated position give it the pure, spiritual appearance of a shrine which gives confirmation to the strength and integrity of belief. The large, inviting portico echoes the forms of a Roman temple, while the *campanili* add a note of Baroque rhetoric. The Superga, thus, is a true piece of historical architecture, but the elements are more intimately fused than in the compositions of Fischer. In fact, Juvarra transcends the level of persuasive allusion and arrives at a true psychological synthesis that expresses the range of the human mind. In his great façade and staircase for the Palazzo Madama in Turin (1718–21), Juvarra defines the exterior in terms of representative monumentality, approaching the character of French classical architecture. In the interior, however, the forms become plastically alive and accompany the festive movement of the splendid stairs.

89. *Turin, Chiesa del Carmine, interior.*

90. *Turin, Chiesa del Carmine, interior.*

93. *Paris, Hôtel de Soubise, ceiling of the oval salon.*

The public dignity of the façade, thus, is transformed into a more intimate, albeit grandiose, Baroque interior world full of surprises and expressive details. In the Chiesa del Carmine (1732–36) we encounter a different world, one permeated by mystical religious feeling, whose character is achieved by means of light filtered down between tall wall-pillars—a solution so far unknown in Italy, and whose most probable source of inspiration is Gothic architecture. Juvarra's range of expression becomes evident if we recall the power and seriousness of the nearby Quartieri Militari (1716–28).[72] Although Juvarra is still conscious of the classical tradition, his achievement is mainly based on a free exploitation of plastic and spatial form. In this expansion and conquest of Vitruvian architecture, he comes close to the Rococo.

Many words have been used to draw a demarcation line between Late Baroque and Rococo architecture. In general, we may say that the Late Baroque conserved the belief in a great comprehensive synthesis, while the Rococo takes differentiation and individuality as its point of departure. As a consequence, the latter tends to abolish the classical orders and replace their tectonic quality with figured ornaments on a neutral wall-surface.[73] In reality, however, it is hardly possible or necessary to make a clear distinction. The German sacred architecture of the eighteenth century certainly represents a last great synthesis, although its treatment of wall, ornament, and color to a large extent has a Rococo character. Even in France it is hard to point to a pure example of Rococo architecture. The "inventor" of Rococo forms, Juste-Aurèle Meissonier, did not leave any concrete achievement behind, and we must turn to the old master Germain Boffrand to find what is generally considered the masterpiece of French Rococo interior decoration. In Boffrand's oval salon in the Hôtel de Soubise in Paris (begun 1735) a continuous wall of large windows (or mirrors) alternates with narrow panels. The wall is united with the richly adorned ceiling by means of a series of freely shaped paintings by Charles Natoire. In general, the space seems to fuse indoor and outdoor characters. An ambiguous character is also found in the high altar of the pilgrimage church of Vierzehnheiligen, one of the few examples of a three-dimensional *rocaille* (designed by Johann Jakob Michael Küchel, 1744–63). Built without any tectonic substance, it expresses a total dissolution of classical form. In relation to the strong spatial and skeletal system of Neumann's church, however, the altar appears as an expression of a meaningful extreme of human sentiment.

The dissolution of the classical tradition also took place as a Neo-Gothic current. It is particularly visible in England, where it had already appeared in Sir Christopher Wren's Tom Tower at Christ Church in Oxford (1681–82). The movement culminated with Nicholas Hawksmoor's All Souls' College in Oxford (1716–35) and with his towers for Westminster Abbey, completed by John James (1734–45). Indepen-

dently of the English development, we find quite an interesting Gothic current in Bohemia. As early as 1703 Johann Santini Aichel (Giovanni Santini) rebuilt the large church of the Cistercian abbey in Sedlec near Kutná Hora, which had been destroyed during the Hussite wars, and in 1712 he took charge of the reconstruction of the Benedictine abbey in Kladruby.[74] In both cases he was requested to build *more gotico* ("in the Gothic manner") to revive the monastic tradition of the Middle Ages. He solved this problem in a very personal way: the splendid system of interlacing ribs that is used to articulate the vaults of the two churches has no structural function; it is purely decorative. In reality the buildings consist of continuous surfaces on which lines are drawn. They lack classic plasticity as well as a true Gothic skeleton, and the result is of an almost surreal character.

Although apparently different, the Neo-Gothic buildings thus have important formal properties in common with the contemporary Régence and Rococo. And both styles are basically nostalgic and irrational in character. The Rococo is a play on the transitory and perishable, while the Neo-Gothic current turns to surreal abstractions, creating thereby an expression of frigidity and alienation—two manifestations, therefore, of the dissolution of the anthropomorphous classical tradition. No wonder that man again sought new security through a Neoclassical revival. The new classical architecture, however, did not solve the problem. Rather than arriving at a true human synthesis, it put together devaluated fragments by means of academic rules and considerably narrowed the range of expression attained by Baroque architecture. Being an architecture of "reason," it did not sufficiently take the psychological need for a meaningful environment into consideration. The split between basic form and expressive decoration found in Rococo and Neo-Gothic architecture was not conquered, but was succeeded by a one-sided emphasis on rational structure. The last organic style in the history of European architecture, therefore, is the Late Baroque of the eighteenth century.

Introduction

The most important manifestations of Late Baroque and Rococo sacred architecture are found in Central Europe. After the Thirty Years' War a great Catholic restoration took place, which in many respects represented a continuation of the Counter-Reformation. Architecture, therefore, must be understood as part of a missionary activity, and until the end of the epoch, about 1770, it maintained its Baroque persuasive rhetoric. To accomplish its object, it had to arrive at a synthesis of local and Roman elements. The medieval tradition, which had been interrupted by the Reformation, had to be revived, and its Gothic forms fused with the classical importation. So it is natural that the Central European architects were particularly open to those Italian works which have an affinity to Gothic architecture, that is, the architecture of Borromini and Guarini. But the general aim of persuasion also made them adopt the illusional means of Bernini's *theatrum sacrum*. The Late Baroque of Central Europe, therefore, represents an exceptionally rich synthesis.

It has already been mentioned that Hildebrandt and the Dientzenhofers played a decisive role in the process of symbiosis, whereas Fischer von Erlach aimed at a more general historical synthesis in the service of the imperial Austrian state. After Hildebrandt had made his early attempt to assimilate Guarinian principles, he abandoned his pursuit and created instead a personal version of the Austrian *Staatskunst*, giving prime importance to secular building projects. The further development of ecclesiastical architecture, therefore, was left in the hands of Georg Dientzenhofer's younger brothers, Christoph and Johann.[1] It seems that the Dientzenhofers settled in Prague about 1675, to which Christoph returned in 1686 after spending a period with Georg in Waldsassen. Johann probably studied in Prague, and after a sojourn in Italy worked in Fulda, Bamberg, and Würzburg. Their works demonstrate a close affinity, but Christoph was the first to emerge as a mature artist. Due to the early victory of the Catholics on the White Mountain in 1621, Prague had a lead on the other capital cities in Central Europe, and provided the young Dientzenhofer with favorable working conditions.

Longitudinal Integration

About 1700 a group of admirable churches were built in Bohemia. We refer here to the convent church in Obořiště (1699 – c.1712), the chapel of the castle in Smiřice (c. 1700–13), St. Nicholas on the Kleinseite in Prague (1703–11), St. Clare in Cheb (1707), and the church of St. Margaret at Břevnov near Prague (1709–15). All these buildings present formal analogies, and their author is generally recognized as Christoph Dientzenhofer.[2] From Obořiště to Břevnov we can follow a logical development in the use of Borrominian and Guarinian principles, and in all the churches we find recurring characteristic details, such as a large segment gable on columns or pilasters, also known as the "Dientzenhofer motif."

The church in Obořiště is the most immature of the group. The plan is clearly derived from S. Maria dell'Immacolata Concezione in Turin by Guarini (1673), which must have been known to Christoph. Subdivisions and axes are identical, and even the positions of the pilasters and the breaks in the entablature are repeated. In both churches a square presbytery is added to the nave, but in Obořiště a corresponding narthex is attached, creating a complete bi-axial organism. A more important difference, however, is seen in the treatment of the central bay, where Dientzenhofer introduces a concave entablature to enhance the general continuity of the wall. The geometrical system is also somewhat different. In Obořiště the cells of the nave are not circular but of a more complex form, and the space cannot easily be interpreted as consisting of interpenetrating cells. Dientzenhofer is seeking a stronger plastic and spatial integration, but the church does not yet have fully developed wall-pillars, although the outer walls are treated as neutral surfaces. The exterior is less pronouncedly Guarinian. The central *risalto* of the façade is of Borrominian derivation, projecting diagonally forward on both sides and forming a concave curve in the middle.[3] The bell-tower is most successfully integrated with the façade by means of coupled pilasters which secure the vertical as well as the horizontal continuity. The large segment gable over the entrance had already appeared in the works of Georg Dientzenhofer, and it is repeated by Christoph in St. Nicholas on the Kleinseite, a double-curved version of Obořiště.

In the chapel at Smiřice Dientzenhofer takes the decisive step of combining Guarini's ideas of spatial juxtaposition with the Central European system of wall-pillars. The plan is inspired by S. Lorenzo in Turin. It consists of an elongated octagon with internally convex sides. On the longitudinal axis secondary oval spaces are added, whereas the transverse axis is closed by neutral walls filled in between the slightly projecting wall-pillars. The diagonals are extended by lens-shaped recesses. Thus the space has been treated as an open system where cells may be added at will, according to the principle of pulsating juxtaposition. The chapel is the first true example of what H. G. Franz has called a "reduced central church." The reduction represents a general answer to the desired synthesis of centralized and longitudinal space. The structure of the centralized space is intact, but by means of reduction it is transformed into a longitudinal organism. The desire for longitudinality is also expressed by the splitting of the center. The reduction was made possible by the introduction of wall-pillars, which make the walls become neutral panels that may be added or taken away at will. The exterior presents itself as a bi-axial organism enveloped in a continuous, undulating surface. The potential openness of the main axes, however, is indicated by large

99. *Obořiště, convent church, plan.*
100. *Obořiště, convent church, interior.*
101. *Smiřice, chapel of the castle, plan.*

102. *Smiřice, chapel of the castle, diagrammatic drawing.*
103. *Smiřice, chapel of the castle, interior*
104. *Smiřice, chapel of the castle, exterior.* ▷

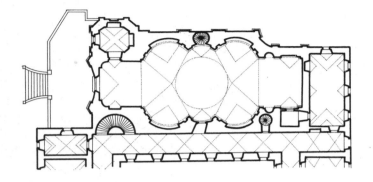

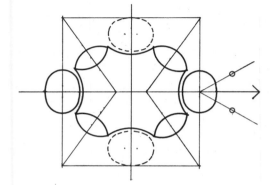

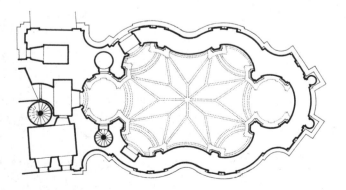

segment gables. The chapel in Smiřice has a rare organic unity with a convincing complementary relationship between interior and exterior. Undoubtedly, it represents one of the most original and germinal achievements in the history of Baroque ecclesiastical architecture.

In St. Nicholas on the Kleinseite in Prague we confront a much more complex building, although the basic layout is related to Obořiště and Smiřice. In all three churches the nave consists of three bays with secondary cells added at both ends. The space in St. Nicholas may actually be understood as a more systematized version of Obořiště. In the later building deep wall-pillars are introduced, between which we find chapels and galleries. The chapels are treated as centralized baldachins with neutral panels filled in along the perimeter. On both sides of the narthex two larger chapels are added, one of which shows a continuous, undulating wall treatment analogous to the exterior of the Smiřice chapel. The system of the nave has an ambiguous character. It may be understood as a series of three interpenetrating ovals defined by obliquely placed pilasters and, in the original project, by double-curved transverse arches. Because of the interpenetration, the spaces defined by the transverse arches expand over the pilasters and contract over the lateral chapels. The normal bay system is thus contradicted by the spatial definition drawn by the arches on the surface of the vault, and the two spatial definitions are displaced in relation to each other in such a way that it becomes meaningless to talk about cells. The principle employed may be called "syncopated interpenetration" and represents an original and important invention by Christoph Dientzenhofer.[4] In St. Nicholas he created, by means of the new principle, a space that is highly articulate but at the same time more convincingly integrated than in any previous building. Its impact is extraordinary, and it must be counted among the greatest achievements of Baroque architecture. The exterior also represents a further development of ideas from Obořiště. The elevations are united by means of a continuous entablature and uniform windows. In the main façade the system is transformed into an interplay of undulating curves, without, however, losing its continuity. The solution is of Borrominian derivation and has some relation to Hildebrandt's façade in Gabel, but the general character is truly original. Together with Smiřice, the façade of St. Nicholas introduces a note of organic dynamism, which seems to have fitted the Bohemian spirit particularly well.

The spatial disposition of St. Clare in Cheb comes very close to Obořiště. It consists of two transverse ovals separated by a narrower intermediate section. In Obořiště the horizontal continuity is still intact, whereas the later works preserve only small fragments of the entablature, so as to make the secondary character of the outer wall evident. In St. Clare the intermediate bay is united by one piece of entablature, and is thus characterized by a wide wall-pillar. The two oval spaces are covered by

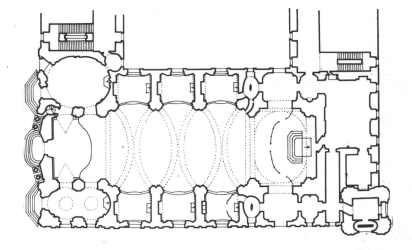

107. *Prague, St. Nicholas on the Kleinseite, detail of the façade.*
108. *Prague, St. Nicholas on the Kleinseite, section of the original project.*
109. *Prague, St. Nicholas on the Kleinseite, plan of the original project.*

110. *Prague, St. Nicholas on the Kleinseite, interior.*
111, 112. *Prague, St. Nicholas on the Kleinseite, details of the interior.*

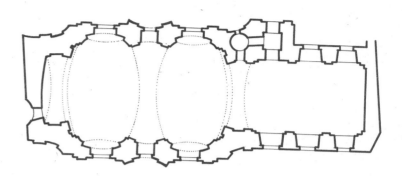

wide "Bohemian caps," whereas the vault contracts over the intermediate bay. In this way the spatial composition is not based on the syncopated interpenetration encountered in St. Nicholas, but is rather a case of pulsating juxtaposition. As the two ends of the church are joined to the convent of which it formed a part, the entrance is placed in the middle of the longitudinal wall. It is spatially articulated by a concave *risalto* of the type from Obořiště. In general, St. Clare shows a desire for simplification, and the result is truly monumental.

A similar mature simplification is found in Christoph's last masterpiece, the church of St. Margaret in Břevnov. Here he returns to the syncopated interpenetration explored in St. Nicholas, so that the vault contracts where the space below expands, and vice versa. The expansive, lens-shaped sections of the vaults are furthermore characterized as open by means of illusional painting, whereas the intermediate sections (which correspond to the pairs of adjacent arches in St. Nicholas) are treated as structural parts. In Břevnov the nave is reduced to two transverse ovals, but smaller ovals which participate in the system are added at both ends. The bi-axial organism encountered in Obořiště has thus become fully integrated. The lateral chapels of St. Nicholas have been omitted in accordance with the simpler nature of the building, illustrating the basically open character of the system. The walls in Břevnov therefore appear as a succession of tall wall-pillars filled in by secondary neutral surfaces.

The space thereby defined is simultaneously rich and simple. Its formal structure is complex and irrational, but the general effect has a liberating clarity and strength. The same may be said of the exterior. A single colossal order of Ionic pilasters keeps the whole volume together. The relationship with Smiřice and Cheb is evident. Instead of a continuous envelope, however, we find a more elaborate characterization of the different parts. The two oval spaces which constitute the nave proper are united to form a straight *risalto*, whereas the secondary ovals at both ends are indicated by convex wall sections. At these points the entablature is broken and the deep recesses thus formed are flanked by full columns. It is as if the outer envelope is split apart to make the interior system visible. And, in fact, here we find the entrances to the church, so that a convincing relation between outside and inside is established by means of a meaningful articulation of the plastic form. Undoubtedly, St. Margaret in Břevnov is one of the most organic creations in the whole of Baroque architecture.

Nová Paka

In the small Bohemian town of Nová Paka we find the church of the Ascension of the Holy Virgin, which shows the same characteristics. It was built after 1709, and consists of a succession of transverse ovals related by syncopated interpenetration. The somewhat crude details of the

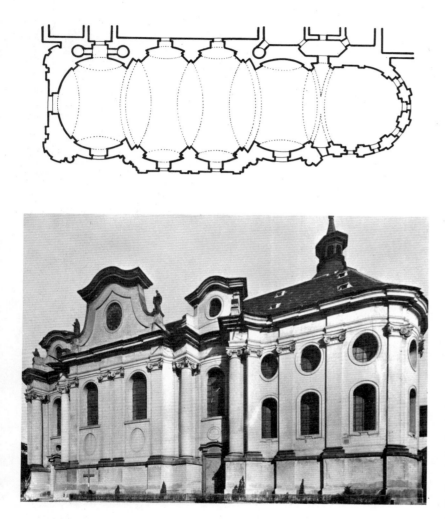

interior make the architectural historian H. G. Franz believe that a second architect was responsible for the design. The ingenious solution, however, forms a natural sequel to Břevnov, and we therefore prefer to propose the authorship of Christoph Dientzenhofer. The large, undulating segment gable of the façade is also truly Dientzenhoferian. It should be pointed out too that the church naturally prepares for the simple succession of baldachins found in Christoph's last works, the church of Our Lady of Loreto on the Hradčany (façade, 1717–23) and the first project for St. John Nepomuk (the church of the Ursulines) later built by his son.

A close acquaintance with the buildings analyzed above convinces one that they are products of the same creative mind. Their character is entirely different from that of the works of Johann Santini Aichel, whom some scholars have suggested as their possible author.[5] An analysis of the works definitely attributed to the latter contradicts such an assumption. Whereas the wall is the constituent element of Santini Aichel's buildings, Christoph Dientzenhofer gives the wall only a secondary role within a primary system of interdependent baldachins. The works described above also form a natural part of the production of the entire Dientzenhofer family. In the buildings of Johann we encounter, in fact, the same basic intentions, while Kilian Ignaz brought some of them to their natural conclusion.

The first great church by Johann Dientzenhofer, the Cathedral of Fulda (1704–12), is a somewhat conventional building.[6] Erected on the foundations of a previous Carolingian church, it has a Latin-cross plan with aisles and a domed crossing. The rhythmically disposed nave shows a certain affinity with Borromini's S. Giovanni in Laterano. The two lateral chapels which are added to the façade, however, are covered by Dientzenhoferian baldachins and the Marienkapelle on the right side of the presbytery shows unexpected interruptions of the entablature. Moreover, the main entrance to the church is framed by the characteristic segment gable on columns (the "Dientzenhofer motif"). After his hesitant start in Fulda, Johann emerged as a mature artist with his splendid Benedictine abbey church in Banz (1710–13; consecrated 1719). The plan is based on the scheme of Obořiště and Cheb: two transverse ovals are connected by a narrower intermediate section. As in Cheb, the latter is defined as a large wall-pillar. Similar sections are added at the extremes of the nave, creating the same rhythmical succession of narrow and wide intervals we encountered in Fulda. In Banz, however, this rhythm forms a counterpoint to the spaces defined by the double-curved transverse arches. These spaces expand over the narrow intervals and contract over the wide ones as in St. Nicholas and Břevnov, according to the principle of syncopated interpenetration. As a paradox, we could also say that the spatial units simultaneously contract and expand. The nave

is accompanied by oval chapels which interpenetrate with the main transverse ovals. Their interaction is expressed by undulating galleries. Because of the intervals added at both ends of the nave, Johann could do without the secondary ovals used by his brother in Břevnov. A deep presbytery is joined to the nave by the simpler principle of pulsating juxtaposition. The abbey church in Banz, thus, exploits all the spatial possibilities developed by Christoph Dientzenhofer, and must be considered the most mature work of the entire group of buildings. The façade also has the character of restrained maturity. Basically, it consists of one continuous tripartite wall with a convex central section. A characteristic "Dientzenhofer motif" is the most important distinguishing feature.

After Banz, Johann Dientzenhofer was mainly occupied with the planning and construction of the great palace at Pommersfelden, and later he participated in construction of the Residenz in Würzburg. Toward the end of his life, however, he made two projects for the abbey church in Holzkirchen (c.1724).[7] In both, the point of departure is a large rotunda defined by coupled columns on the diagonal axes. In one case the rotunda is contradicted overhead: its vault is "eaten away" by the secondary spaces—circular on the main axis and lens-shaped on the transverse. The rotunda of the other is intact and secondary spaces are added by means of pulsating juxtaposition. The projects thereby state in the clearest possible terms the two basic principles of spatial organization defined above.

An analysis of the works of Christoph and Johann Dientzenhofer demonstrates how they intentionally employed spatial interpenetration and pulsating juxtaposition to make the spatial elements interdependent. The formal integration they achieved surpasses anything done by their predecessors. In particular, the organizing principles were used to satisfy the traditional desire for a true synthesis of the longitudinal and the central plan. Such a synthesis may be possible on a smaller or larger scale, and the one or the other of the two aspects may dominate, as expressed in the terms "centralized longitudinal church" and "elongated central church." The principles developed by the Dientzenhofer brothers represent a general open method that may satisfy all these cases. Their work was continued by Kilian Ignaz Dientzenhofer and Balthasar Neumann, the first adopting pulsating juxtaposition as his basic method, the second interpenetration.

Multilateral Systematization

After a period of studies in Vienna, probably with Hildebrandt, Kilian Ignaz Dientzenhofer returned to Prague in 1717.[8] During the following years he collaborated with his father on the completion of Our Lady of Loreto, but in 1720 he also initiated his first two independently designed churches, St. John Nepomuk on the Hradčany in Prague (for the Ursu-

123. *Banz, Benedictine church, façade.*

124. *Banz, Benedictine church, plan.*
125. *Banz, Benedictine church, interior.*

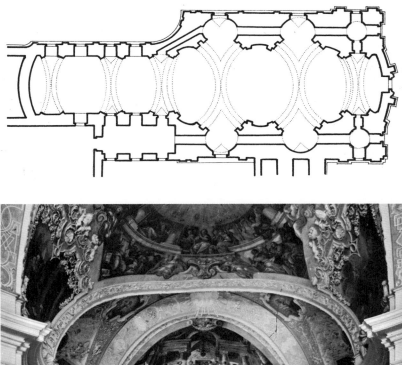

126. *Banz, Benedictine church, detail of the interior.*
127. *Banz, Benedictine church, detail of the vault.* ▷

128. *Banz, Benedictine church, detail of the interior.*

129. *Graphic representation of the principles of spatial interpenetration and pulsating juxtaposition.*
130. *Holzkirchen, abbey church, plan, first project by J. Dientzenhofer.*
131. *Holzkirchen, abbey church, plan, second project.*

nes) and the pilgrimage church in Nicov. Both repeat the general dis- position of Hildebrandt's church in Gabel, but the Guarinian composi- on with interdependent cells has been replaced by a simpler system adjacent spaces. As the continuity of the entablature is interrupted ev- ywhere, these spaces are defined as baldachins, and the whole interior ust be interpreted as a group of such. We recognize, thus, a wish for nifying the reduced Greek-cross plan of Hildebrandt with the wall-pillar stem of Christoph Dientzenhofer. More fundamental, however, is the tempt at composing a complex organism by means of centralized open lls. Shaped as baldachins, the cells seem freely placed within a contin- us, extended space. This is particularly evident in Nicov, where a spa- us gallery runs behind the main pillars which carry the dome. In fact, icov represents the first successful attempt at creating what is generally own as *Zweischaligkeit*, that is, the double delimitation of the main ace. The use of light contributes to the effect of a spatial continuum nich surrounds the interior. The open character of the system is indi- ed by the outer walls, which are treated as secondary and neutral sur- es, whereas the continuous horizontal gallery helps to hold the differ- t parts together visually. The façade varies the theme used in Obořiště, proaching more closely the original Borrominian version.[9] St. John epomuk is in general simpler than Nicov, but in some details more vanced. Particularly interesting is the narthex, where Kilian Ignaz in- oduces the pulsating juxtaposition used by Hildebrandt in the project the garden-pavilion of the Mansfeld-Fondi Palace. This small space presents the key to a great part of Kilian Ignaz's future development.

In his next main work, in fact, Kilian Ignaz employs pulsating juxta- sition as the organizing principle. The splendid church of the monas- y of St. Edwige at Wahlstatt in Silesia (1723–31) is clearly derived m the chapel in Smiřice. The main space, however, is an elongated xagon. Its internally convex sides reflect the expansion of the surround- g cells: oval on the main axis and lens-shaped on the diagonals.[10] e organism is constituted by a skeleton of slender columns and arches, ed in by "Bohemian caps" decorated with grandiose frescoes by smas Damian Asam, and neutral wall-surfaces. The church thus ap- ars as a single complex group of baldachins which are organized accord- g to the principle of pulsating juxtaposition. In general the plan is per- tly integrated and represents a convincing synthesis of longitudinal and ntral plans. Nevertheless, Kilian Ignaz did not employ the solution ain. The reason is probably that the organism is closed (except along main axis) and therefore did not contain the possibilities of variation sought. Before we return to this question, we should, however, say ew words about the exterior. The convent has a symmetrical layout, th the church in the middle as a dividing axis. Its façade has a close inity to Banz, but the restrained scheme of Johann Dientzenhofer has

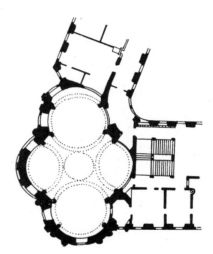

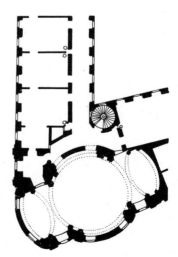

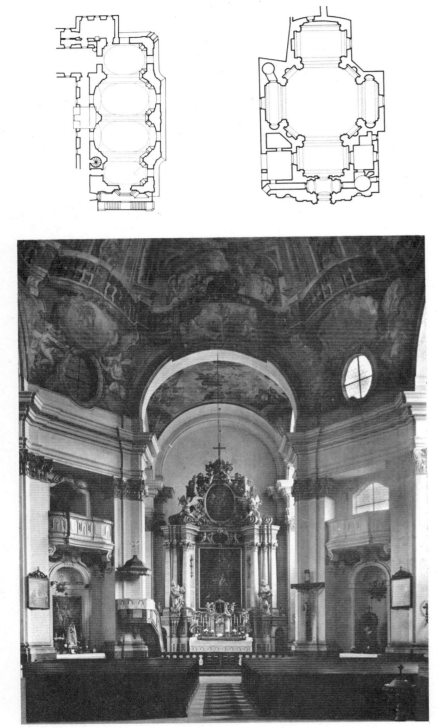

been transformed into a violently dynamic essay in Baroque rhetoric. The basic theme is the gradual liberation of the forms in vertical direction. While the lower story has a simple tall Ionic order, the upper is articulated by bundles of pilasters, and its entablature is broken as if under the influence of rising forces. A dominant "Dientzenhofer motif" has an integrating effect. The side elevations of the church, which are visible from the courtyard of the convent, are treated as continuous envelopes, although they do not undulate as in Smiřice.

With the large complex in Wahlstatt, Kilian Ignaz Dientzenhofer emerged as one of the most talented and original architects of his generation. In 1724 he started the construction of another church that plays a more important role in his oeuvre, although it is much smaller and apparently less significant: for St. Adalbert in Počaply, he based the whole plan on the Hildebrandtian scheme he had employed in the narthex of St. John Nepomuk on the Hradčany. The main space is an octagon with longer, internally convex sides on the main axes. A longitudinal direction is created through the addition of transverse ovals on two opposite sides. But the two other sides are also curved in the same way; other ovals could have been added, and the organism must be characterized as a reduced or elongated central church. The system therefore contains the multilateral freedom which was lacking in Wahlstatt. The principle of pulsating juxtaposition secures the interdependence of the spatial elements. In Počaply we also find a more conscious treatment of the exterior plastic articulation, which from now on is mainly used to express the spatial structure of the organism. The transverse axis, thus, is characterized as open through an interruption of the architrave and frieze, and a gable marks the portal thereby created. The neutral, provisory character of the wall that closes the opening is expressed by a large chasuble-shaped window which naturally has an analogous function when seen from the inside.

The basic theme defined in Počaply was repeated in several smaller and larger projects during the following years.[11] Most important is the church of St. John on the Rock in Prague (project 1729; construction 1730–39), which is probably the best known of Kilian Ignaz's works and often considered the Bohemian Baroque church *par excellence*. In no other building is the plastic dynamism and dramatic quality so dear to the country expressed with more ability and conviction. The church's position on a rock accentuates the effect, and the staircase in front enhances the vertical movement of the façade. In spite of its dramatic character, the church is based on a most rigorous composition. The plan repeats the general layout from Počaply, but the greater importance of the later building is emphasized by the addition of a twin-tower façade and a circular sanctuary. The central octagon is slightly elongated, but almost equilateral. A regular series of arches over the entablature contributes to

135. *Nicov, pilgrimage church, plan.*
136. *Nicov, pilgrimage church, detail of the façade.*
137. *Nicov, pilgrimage church, detail of the interior.*

138. *Nicov, pilgrimage church, section.*
139. *Nicov, pilgrimage church, interior.*

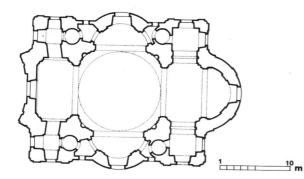

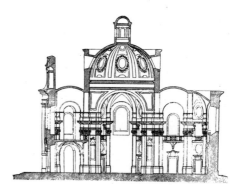

140. *Wahlstatt, monastery church, plan.*
141. *Wahlstatt, monastery church, section.*

142. *Wahlstatt, monastery church, diagram.*
143. *Wahlstatt, monastery church, diagram.*
144. *Wahlstatt, monastery church, façade.* ▷

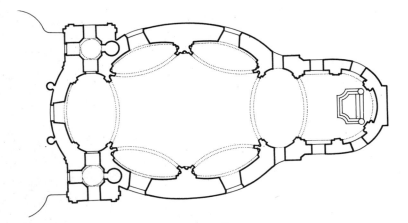

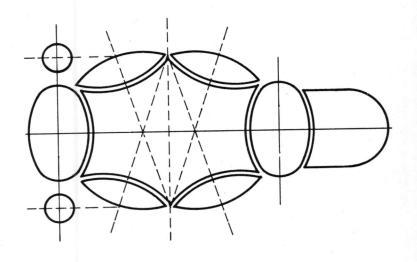

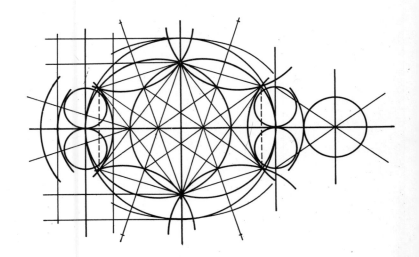

the creation of a rotunda-like impression. Both the centralization and the longitudinal movement are thus strengthened. A general effect of double delimitation is created by the introduction of a "Dientzenhofer motif" on the diagonal axes, whereas the transverse axis is closed by characteristic neutral walls perforated by large chasuble-shaped windows. The entablature is interrupted where the system is open, but continues from the main space into the secondary ovals for a better integration of the cells. The structural system is fully articulated, as the vaults and the arches rest on independent sets of pilasters. Because of the arches which penetrate into the vaults and the windows placed within them, it seems as though the baldachins are immersed in a much higher luminous space. The plastic form of the exterior corresponds to the interior organization. St. John on the Rock, in fact, constitutes an unsurpassable example of complementary correspondences between inside and outside. Even the diagonally placed *campanili* are integrated in the general spatial disposition. An order of Tuscan pilasters circumscribes the entire building, and the continuity is enhanced by an uninterrupted cornice. The architrave and frieze, however, are broken to indicate the spatial openings. The main entrance is further accentuated by a strongly pronounced "Dientzenhofer motif." The bell-towers are integrated into the horizontal system without losing anything of their strong vertical movement, which is enhanced by particularly rich steeples. It would be hard to point out another Baroque church as formally integrated as St. John on the Rock, or one in which the details are treated in an equally meaningful way.

In 1733 Kilian Ignaz Dientzenhofer started the construction of the slightly smaller village church of St. Clement in Odolená Voda, where certain characteristics first seen in St. John on the Rock are further developed. Again the central space has internally convex sides on the main axes, whereas the diagonals are concave, strengthening the effect of rotunda-like centralization as well as vertical continuity. The double delimitation of the main space is also carried a step further by the addition of shallow secondary spaces on all axes. The aim obviously was to create the impression of one large baldachin within a continuous envelope.

The architect's series of elongated central churches culminated with St. Mary Magdalen in Karlovy Vary (Karlsbad), built between 1733 and 1736 (project 1732). A preliminary project shows a general disposition very similar to St. John on the Rock, but with secondary spaces added on all axes. The inner faces of the wall-pillars between them are articulated by columns, which carry a star-like system of vault-ribs,[12] so that the general effect would have been of a centralized skeleton surrounded by a luminous secondary zone. The final solution maintains this concept, which is strengthened by the transformation of the main space into an oval. Simultaneously, however, the longitudinal axis is emphasized by the introduction of internally convex zones of transition between the

147. *Počaply, St. Adalbert, diagram.*
148. *Počaply, St. Adalbert, exterior.*

149. *Počaply, St. Adalbert, section.*
150. *Počaply, St. Adalbert, interior.*
151. *Prague, St. John on the Rock, exterior.* ▷

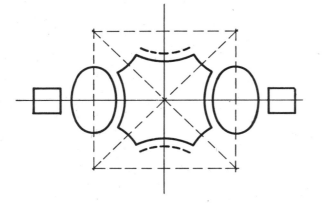

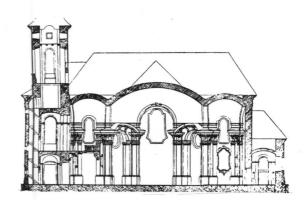

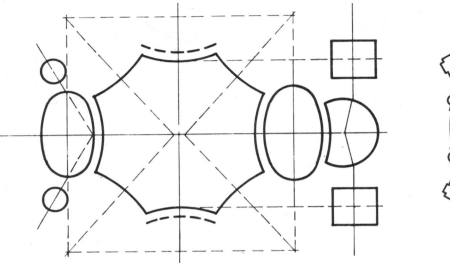

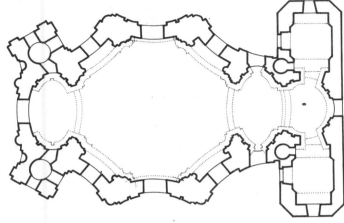

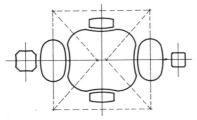

main and secondary ovals (narthex and presbytery). The open charact[er]
of the system is thereby maintained and the organizing principle is, [as]
usual, pulsating juxtaposition. To prevent the optical disintegration [of]
the diaphanous system, an undulating gallery is carried all around th[e]
space. The gallery also contributes considerably to the dynamic charact[er]
of the interior. The church in Karlovy Vary is a complex organism base[d]
on multiple definitions. First and foremost it shows a completely deve[l]
oped *Zweischaligkeit*, which enriches the splendid synthesis of centraliz[ed]
and longitudinal space. The solution also comprises a suggestive use [of]
light and color. The exterior is related to St. John on the Rock bu[t]
as a logical consequence of the plan, the *campanili* are frontally dispose[d.]
The plastic form complements the interior organization, and the mai[n]
axes are marked by breaks in the entablature and by characterist[ic]
"Dientzenhofer motifs." In all, the church may be ranked as the mo[st]
important architectural achievement of Kilian Ignaz Dientzenhofer.

All the churches described above may be characterized as elongate[d]
central buildings. In some cases Kilian Ignaz also tackled the proble[m]
of the centralized longitudinal organism. Most important is the Jesu[it]
church of St. Francis Xavier in Opařany, built between 1732 and 1735[.]
The nave repeats the scheme of Cheb, but a narthex and presbytery hav[e]
been added by means of pulsating juxtaposition. The solution also show[s]
a stronger definition of the structural system by the introduction of co[l]
umns which carry the arches, while the vaults rest on independent pilas[-]
ters. The skeleton, thus, is plastic, whereas the baldachins appear a[s]
surfaces. This double system is closed off by the usual neutral walls perf[o]
rated by large chasuble-shaped windows. The church in Opařany, togethe[r]
with St. Mary Magdalen in Karlovy Vary, represents a stage of consum[-]
mate maturity.

In 1734–35 Kilian Ignaz Dientzenhofer made two projects for th[e]
great church of the convent of the Ursulines in Kutná Hora. One of hi[s]
projects repeats the disposition of Opařany in monumentalized form wit[h]
secondary spaces added along the perimeter. The final version, howeve[r]
shows the growing interest of the architect in the development of a dom[-]
inant central rotunda: the main space has become circular and [is]
crowned by a drum and dome. The pulsating juxtaposition has disap[-]
peared, but the *Zweischaligkeit* is fully developed. We see how the devel[-]
opment of Kilian Ignaz leads from the open system of interdependen[t]
cells toward the vision of a unitary, seemingly infinitely extended space[,]
in which a great baldachin is immersed. The church in Kutná Hor[a]
would have been the crowning achievement of the architect; unfortunate[-]
ly, it was never built and only a fragment of the large convent was com[-]
pleted.

160. *Karlovy Vary, St. Mary Magdalen, plan of a preliminary project.*
161. *Karlovy Vary, St. Mary Magdalen, diagram.*
162. *Karlovy Vary, St. Mary Magdalen, interior.*

163. *Karlovy Vary, St. Mary Magdalen, exterior.* ▷

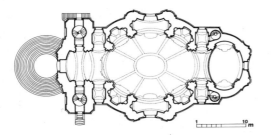

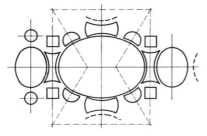

Kilian Ignaz, however, built another centralized structure which manifests similar intentions. In St. Nicholas in the Altstadt in Prague (1732–37) we find a dominant octagonal dome that forms a counterpoint to a strongly emphasized longitudinal axis. The two spatial elements are unified by means of a very pronounced *Zweischaligkeit*. Here again the primary skeleton seems immersed in an infinitely extended space. As with St. Mary Magdalen in Karlovy Vary, a continuous gallery creates horizontal coherence. The main space is characterized by a strong vertical movement. The exterior represents a tour de force of plastic articulation. Again the basic theme is the gradual liberation of the forms in a vertical direction, so that the tripartite façade is united by a continuous basement, while the main story is split apart and the bell-towers rise freely toward the sky. The characteristic Baroque increase in plasticity toward the middle of the façade contrasts with the linear treatment of the dome, which appears as light and distant. In general, the exterior may be interpreted as an inversion of the interior. While the interior appears open and infinite in the lower zone and united by the vaults above, the exterior has inverse properties. As a result, St. Nicholas in the Altstadt is the most intensely expressive of Kilian Ignaz's buildings.

In the exposition above we have treated only the major works of Kilian Ignaz Dientzenhofer. However, his systematic method of spatial combination also allowed for the solution of such simpler organisms as parish churches and chapels. The latter are usually solved by means of a single centralized spatial cell. The parish churches may consist of a fairly large, elongated cell, or, in his later years, be solved as a longitudinal succession of simple baldachins.[13] After a relatively short initial period when Dientzenhofer defined his most general aims, he concentrated on a versatile experimentation with the method of pulsating juxtaposition. In the later works, however, he returned to a simpler approach, elaborating in a more systematic way the skeletal character already manifest at Nicov. His most original inventions are the pulsating works of the middle period, whereas the late works have a basic affinity to general Late Baroque intentions which we will also encounter in the churches of Balthasar Neumann, Johann Michael Fischer, Dominikus Zimmermann, and Bernardo Vittone. Hardly any of his contemporaries, however, showed the same versatility and none adopted the systematic approach of Guarini to the same extent. His combination of circumstantial freedom and systematic organization may be compared with another great achievement of the epoch: the *Well-Tempered Clavier* of Johann Sebastian Bach. The churches of Kilian Ignaz Dientzenhofer, therefore, represent an ideal synthesis of the *esprit de système* of the seventeenth century and the *esprit systématique* of the eighteenth.

164. *Karlovy Vary, St. Mary Magdalen, interior.*
165. *Opařany, Jesuit church, plan.*
166. *Opařany, Jesuit church, diagram.*

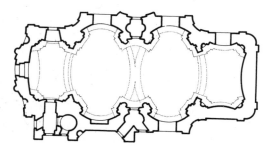

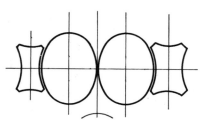

The Dominant Rotunda

A great number of architects contributed to the incredibly rich ecclesiastical architecture of the eighteenth century in southern Germany.[*] Among them Johann Michael Fischer and Dominikus Zimmermann a[re] distinguished by true creativity. Whereas the first left countless building[s] behind, the latter spent a large part of his life creating two magnificen[t] *Gesamtkunstwerke*. Both men had their roots in the traditions of loc[al] crafts, and did not belong to the international world of Fischer von E[r]lach, Hildebrandt, and Neumann. Together with the Dientzenhofer[s,] however, they realized a truly popular form of church architecture whic[h] represents an essential contribution to the sacred landscape of Centr[al] Europe.

Johann Michael Fischer started his professional activities in 1718 i[n] Munich as a *Maurermeister*, after some years of travel and study in Bohe[] mia and Moravia.[15] His first independent churches stem from the year[s] 1726–27, and clearly demonstrate his Bohemian background. Thus, th[e] great Premonstratensian abbey church at Osterhofen (1726–29) is d[e] rived from Christoph Dientzenhofer's St. Nicholas on the Kleinseite i[n] Prague, although the spatial system is considerably simplified. Fische[r] did not attempt any definition of cells but interpreted the nave as a uni[] fied space permeated by an undulating movement which corresponded t[o] the expansive lateral chapels (pulsating juxtaposition). It should also b[e] pointed out that the wall-pillar system is treated as a skeleton closed o[ff] by neutral wall-surfaces. In general, the space is impregnated with [a] pronounced Baroque dynamism, heightened by the splendid decoration[s] by the Asam brothers. A related approach is found in the contemporar[y] St. Anna-am-Lehel in Munich (1727–33), for which Christop[h] Dientzenhofer's chapel in Smiřice obviously served as the point of depar[] ture. Again the systematic definition of spatial elements gives way to [a] more general integration, although the presbytery is joined to the mai[n] space by simple interpenetration. Between the tall wall-pillars we fin[d] a continuous succession of deep niches. Whereas the niches in Smiřic[e] show a clear separation between vault and wall, to characterize the wal[l] as a secondary surface within an open system, Fischer's niches are struc[] turally unified and close off the spatial organism.[16] The church wa[s] bombed during World War II and lost most of its interior decoration.

In 1727 Fischer also started the reconstruction of the Benedictin[e] church in Rinchnach. The interesting bi-axial layout may be understoo[d] as a variation on the theme of St. Anna-am-Lehel. The transverse axi[s] is strongly emphasized by wide flanking wall-pillars of the type used b[y] Christoph Dientzenhofer in Cheb, and the walls between them ar[e] treated as neutral surfaces perforated by large chasuble-shaped windows[.] We see, thus, how Fischer had absorbed characteristic elements of th[e] Dientzenhoferian language.[17]

In 1730–32 Fischer built the small parish church of Unering, where he introduced the theme which was to remain his major preoccupation thereafter: the octagon with unequal sides. Again we find a surprisingly close relationship to Bohemian models, this time to Kilian Ignaz Dientzenhofer's first church, St. John Nepomuk on the Hradčany (1720–28); in Unering the diagonals are shaped as wide skeletal wall-pillars, and the neutral walls between them are perforated by large, freely shaped windows. We realize that Fischer adopted a particular interpretation of the octagon: it is understood as a simple baldachin placed within an "infinite" space. In Unering the baldachin is closed off directly, but the *Zweischaligkeit* of his later works is already potentially present.[18] Compared with the dynamism of his earlier churches, Unering is marked by classical simplicity.

The theme stated in Unering could be developed in different ways. We have seen how Kilian Ignaz Dientzenhofer chose to use the octagon as a point of departure for open multilateral groups of interdependent spatial cells. Fischer, instead, settled on the more general problems of *Zweischaligkeit* and the introduction of a longitudinal axis. In 1735 he simultaneously designed three important churches which offer interesting answers. The church of St. Michael in Berg am Laim near Munich (1735–44) still shows a close connection between baldachin and walls, although the perforated pendentives add to the potential *Zweischaligkeit*.[19] The complex movement of the entablature belongs to Fischer's early "Baroque" phase, and gives the solution a somewhat undecided general character. It has, however, the purpose of unifying the nave with the presbytery and the sanctuary, resulting in an interesting combination of centralization and longitudinality.

The Franciscan church of St. Mary in Ingolstadt (project 1735; construction 1737–39) represented a more mature approach to the octagon with double delimitation. The great innovation was the complete hollowing-out of the corner pillars.[20] Large oval chapels with galleries above made the structural members appear on a luminous background. The wall-pillars as such disappeared optically, and a splendid baldachin resulted, consisting of a huge "Bohemian cap" on slender supports, interpenetrated by alternating wide and narrow arches. The corner spaces were related to the main space by means of pulsating juxtaposition, as in Osterhofen. A longitudinal axis was introduced by a large, centralized presbytery shaped as a simpler variation on the theme of the main space. The church in Ingolstadt undoubtedly was one of Fischer's most convincing achievements, and its destruction represents a tragic loss.[21]

A somewhat similar building is preserved, however, in the contemporary pilgrimage church of Maria Schnee (project 1735; construction 1736–51) in Aufhausen near Regensburg. Here the skeletal character is still more pronounced. Between slender supports, the wall is com-

168. *Kutná Hora, Ursuline convent, initial project.*

169. *Kutná Hora, Ursuline convent, final project for the upper story.*
170. *Kutná Hora, Ursuline convent, final project.*

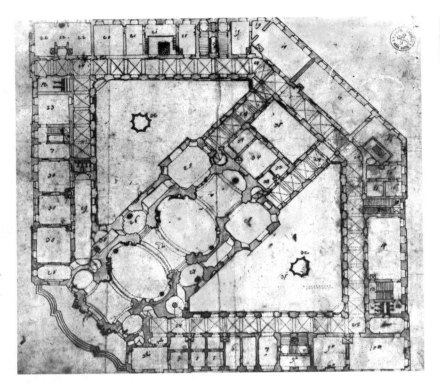

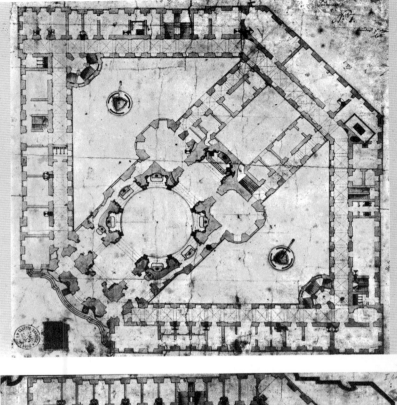

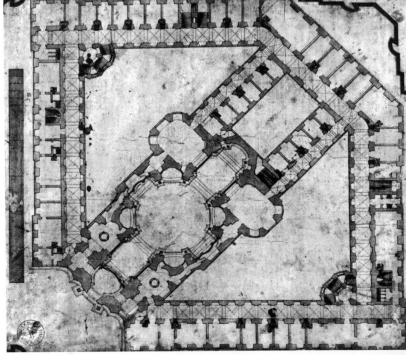

tely opened, and a splendid effect of *Zweischaligkeit* results. The plan,
 fact, shows a completely regular distribution of secondary spaces, and
e addition of a square narthex makes the organism approach bi-axiality.
e undulating entablature found in Fischer's early works has disap-
ared completely; the short fragments still present are straight and
ve the purpose of indicating the main spatial directions.

Aufhausen very closely approaches the disposition of Fischer's last, and
rhaps greatest, masterpiece, the Benedictine monastery church of St.
arinus and St. Arianus (1759–66) in Rott am Inn near Wasserburg.
ere the bi-axial layout is complete, so that the main space appears as
dominant rotunda within a longitudinal organism.[22] The supports are
ll more slender than in Aufhausen, and the corner chapels are larger,
hancing the effect of *Zweischaligkeit*. The main rotunda has a very light
d regular character, and Baroque dynamism has been succeeded by a
ling of luminous, tranquil extension. The members and details have
st their former plasticity; even the parapets in the corners are straight.
 this connection we may mention its late date of construction and
e approach of Neoclassicism.)

After his splendid achievement in Rott, one should perhaps expect no
rther contributions from Fischer. In the Benedictine monastery church
 the Brigittines in Altomünster (1763–73) he returned once more
 the theme of the octagon with double delimitation, and in certain
spects arrived at a further simplification. The secondary zones have
en reduced to a narrow corridor which runs all along the longitudinal
quence of spaces that makes up the building. If anywhere, the word
veischaligkeit is appropriate in Altomünster. The articulation of the oc-
gon is somewhat rigid, while the presbytery consists of a particularly
egant and unified baldachin.

In the discussion above only the interiors of the churches have been
eated. Fischer, actually, did not give much attention to the exteriors,
d his façades are usually simple and somewhat clumsy. His buildings
e determined from within, and the outer wall is conceived as a distant,
latively inarticulate element. Better than anything else, this fact illus-
ates the difference between his approach and the complementarity of
ilian Ignaz Dientzenhofer. We may find therein a desire to turn away
om Baroque persuasive rhetoric.

In addition to the churches already mentioned, Fischer had a few com-
issions that required a more conventional solution. In the Kollegien-
rche at Diessen (project 1731; construction 1732–39) and at Zwiefal-
n (1741–52) he had to continue two churches already begun by local
uilders, and solved the problem by means of a standard wall-pillar
stem. In both cases, however, he added a flat dome as a counterpoint
 the longitudinal movement. The Benedictine abbey church of Zwiefal-
n is a very large building, measuring 104 yards in length. Its strong

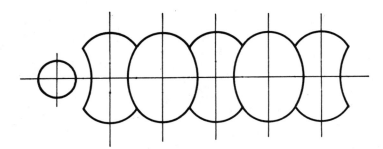

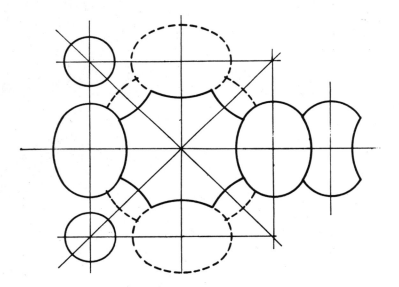

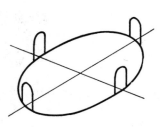

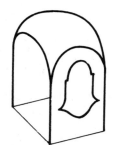

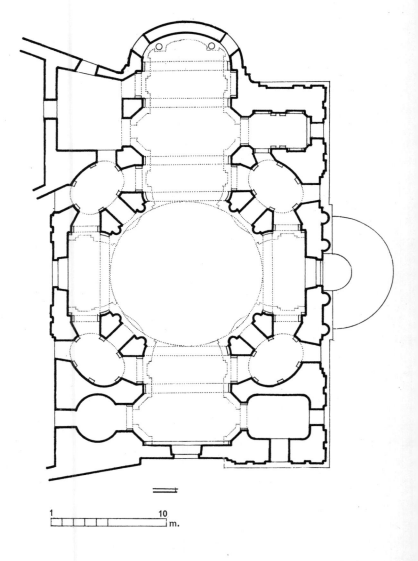

movement in depth still has a truly Baroque rhetoric, which may explain why Fischer gave the façade an exceptionally powerful form. The convex center is emphasized by double columns plus a pilaster on either side, a most successful variation on the triple columns introduced by Martino Longhi in his SS. Vincenzo ed Anastasio a hundred years before. The broad wall is unified by a beautifully articulated undulating gable. The dynamism of the façade is repeated in the interior, where convex galleries penetrate into the main space between the wall-pillars. The latter, however, are articulated by coupled columns which give the long nave a regular, strong rhythm. Zwiefalten undoubtedly represents one of the most convincing interpretations of the Vorarlberg system.

The building that is usually considered Fischer's *magnum opus*, the Benedictine abbey church in Ottobeuren (1748–66), also falls outside his general development. The construction had been initiated in 1737 by Simpert Kraemer, and when Fischer succeeded him in 1748, he had to accept the general layout, which showed a cross plan with nave and presbytery of approximately equal length and a deep transept. Fischer simplified and strengthened the composition, widening the pillars of the crossing considerably and transforming nave and presbytery into similar baldachin units. The general disposition, therefore, approaches the solution in Rott, although Fischer could not develop a full rotunda in the middle. As Kraemer's plan included aisles, a certain *Zweischaligkeit* along the main axis was possible. By means of a strongly emphasized order of columns and pilasters, Fischer unified the different spatial zones. The interior of Ottobeuren combines simplicity and monumentality, so that the church is one of the most easily appreciated of the whole epoch. It does not, however, represent any original contribution to the development of Late Baroque typology. The exterior closely follows the disposition of the plan and is characterized by a pronounced voluminousness. The convex, powerful façade is accompanied by two tall bell-towers which emphasize the Baroque character of the building.

Whereas Johann Michael Fischer had to find his way through years of spatial experiments, Dominikus Zimmermann started the construction of a mature masterpiece as early as 1727: the pilgrimage church of Steinhausen (1727–33). Being the leading stuccoist of his time, Zimmermann shaped his buildings with his own hands, so to speak, and usually spent several years on each building site. His churches, therefore, show a rare perfection.[23] The plan of Steinhausen is a simple longitudinal oval, but Zimmermann has transformed the seemingly banal organism into something quite novel. The best description of the solution is that of a centralized *Hallenkirche*. We might also call it a centralized wall-pillar church with perforated wall-pillars. The system, thus, is truly Gothic, but the oval space and the members employed stem from the classical tradition. The solution not only represents a new and very convincing

answer to the question of integrating centralization and longitudinality, but also satisfies the traditional need of the pilgrimage church for an ambulatory.[24] As a particular feature of the disposition we may notice the blocking of the transverse axis whereby the longitudinal movement (*i.e.*, the pilgrimage) is emphasized. The slender pillars end in plastically rich, but light and playful, pieces of entablature on which a regular series of arches rests. Thus the general impression is that of a great baldachin that is sunk down within a thin outer shell, perforated by large freely shaped windows. The relationship to certain of the basic intentions of Kilian Ignaz Dientzenhofer, Neumann, and Johann Michael Fischer is evident, but Zimmermann has given these typical ideas his own original interpretation. Nobody who has visited Steinhausen can ever forget the luminous white interior with its rich, early eighteenth-century decoration. The great vault fresco was painted by Dominikus Zimmermann's brother Johann Baptist, who thus completed the magnificent *Gesamtkunstwerk*. And under the organ gallery we find the signature of the master himself: *DOMINICUS ZIMERMAN. ARCHIT. E STUCKADOR LANDSBERGENSIS.* The exterior appears as a large volume enclosed by thin membrane-like walls. A number of gables over the roof somewhat contradict the general organization, indicating a cross-shaped plan. In his later churches Zimmermann did not repeat this questionable feature. The tall tower is integrated with the façade, although not in the convincing manner of Neumann's smaller churches.

The theme of Steinhausen is repeated in more elaborate form in Zimmermann's second masterpiece, the Wieskirche (project 1744; construction 1745–54).[25] Its site was the goal of a very popular pilgrimage, and the church was built with the active participation of the local population. It actually represents the culmination of Late Baroque popular church architecture and still transmits a particular kind of fascination—a quality heightened by its singular position at the foot of the Bavarian Alps. The volume of the church seems to repeat the shape of the hills behind and appears as a kind of humanized and spiritualized natural element. In few places do landscape and architecture interact in such a deeply moving way. The exterior treatment is simpler than in Steinhausen, and the walls really appear as a light membrane. Numerous freely shaped windows indicate the large volume inside, and the columns that are attached at the western end have only an expressive function. The bell-tower is removed from the façade and is used as a joint between the church and the small convent behind, so that not a trace of Baroque rhetoric is left. The building does not appear as an active center of radiating forces; instead it represents a goal wherein we may discover the essence of our existence. The plan repeats the oval disposition and the double delimitation of Steinhausen. The organism, however, is more complex, due to the accentuation of the main axes and the addition of

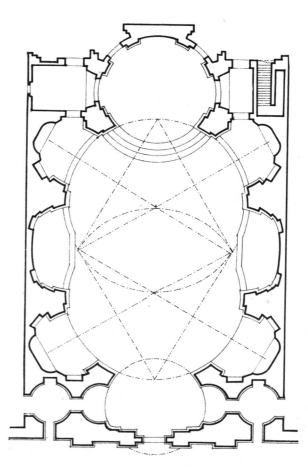

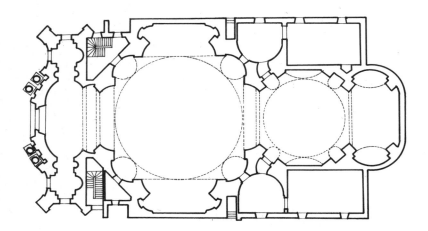

186. *Ingolstadt, Franciscan church, plan.*
187. *Ingolstadt, Franciscan church, interior.*

188. *Rott am Inn, Benedictine church, plan.*
189. *Rott am Inn, Benedictine church, façade.*

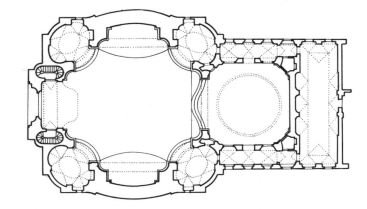

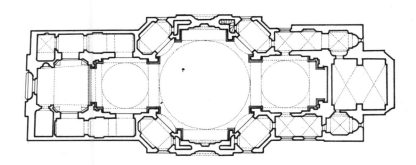

190. *Rott am Inn, Benedictine church, interior.*
191. *Altomünster, Brigittine church, interior.*

192. *Zwiefalten, Benedictine church, exterior.*

193. *Ottobeuren, church of the Benedictine abbey, plan.*
194. *Ottobeuren, church of the Benedictine abbey, aerial view.*

195. *Ottobeuren, church of the Benedictine abbey, façade.* ▷

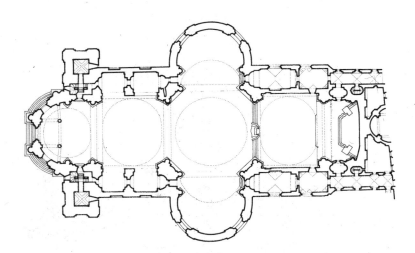

the deep presbytery. A lighter and more elegant character is achieved by the splitting of the pillars into pairs of slender columns whose linear character is emphasized by gothicizing shadow edges. The decoration is fully Rococo and gives the space an exuberant expression of rejoicing and fulfillment. The deep presbytery appears as a Rococo interpretation of the royal chapel at Versailles, and is one of the few truly tri-dimensional pieces of Rococo architecture in existence. The shallow galleries and the hollowed-out and perforated lower part of the vault produce the most splendid example of *Zweischaligkeit* of the entire period. Wies, indeed, is one of the great masterpieces in the history of Baroque architecture.

Only once was Zimmermann given the opportunity to apply his concepts to a large building. In 1732 he was asked to make a design for the church in Ottobeuren, and worked out a plan consisting of a spacious oval rotunda to which narthex and presbytery are added by means of pulsating juxtaposition. The long organism shows a fully developed double delimitation of all the main spaces, and is, like Steinhausen and Wies, articulated with great mastery.

Synthesis

Balthasar Neumann is usually considered the most important architect of the German Late Baroque. Equally active in ecclesiastical, secular, and military architecture, he produced work that is exceptionally rich and varied, his great churches of Vierzehnheiligen and Neresheim representing the culmination of the Late Baroque research into spatial problems.[26] Born at Cheb in Bohemia, Neumann must have known Christoph Dientzenhofer's church of St. Clare in his native town. His visits to Vienna and northern Italy after 1717 brought him into direct contact with other pioneer works of Late Baroque architecture. In 1719 he was employed as court architect by Count Johann Philipp Franz von Schönborn in Würzburg, where he began the planning of the great Residenz. In 1721 he took over the construction of the Schönborn Chapel in the same town. During his first years of professional activity, Neumann worked in close contact with Johann Dientzenhofer, and the plan of the Schönborn Chapel represents, in fact, a variation on the theme we have encountered in the latter's projects for Holzkirchen. A central rotunda is flanked by two secondary oval spaces. Rather than syncopated interpenetration or pulsating juxtaposition, the organizing principle is the simple interpenetration introduced by François Mansart in his Parisian Church of the Visitation almost a hundred years before. The main rotunda is fully developed, whereas the secondary spaces are incomplete. The rotunda is interpreted as a baldachin with freestanding coupled columns on the diagonal axes. An unbroken entablature circumscribes the secondary ovals, but is interrupted behind the altar to leave the main axis open. A sophisticated tension is thereby created between the longer but closed

196, 197. *Ottobeuren, church of the Benedictine abbey, interior.*

198. *Steinhausen, pilgrimage church, exterior.*

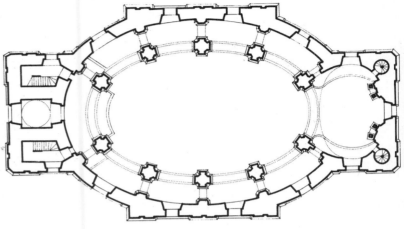

199. *Steinhausen, pilgrimage church, plan.*
200. *Steinhausen, pilgrimage church, interior.*
201. *Steinhausen, pilgrimage church, interior.*▷

202. *Wies, pilgrimage church, plan.*
203, 204. *Wies, pilgrimage church, exterior.*
205. *Wies, pilgrimage church, interior.* ▷

transverse axis and the shorter but open main axis. In the Schönborn
Chapel the main theme of Neumann's ecclesiastical buildings is already
present: a central rotunda that dominates a linear or multilateral succession of spaces. We also find a conscious desire to integrate the spatial
elements. In general the chapel shows a surprisingly mature treatment
of proportions and details.

After the death of Johann Dientzenhofer in 1726, Neumann took over
the planning of the church in Holzkirchen. A simple circular space is
inscribed within an octagon. The rotunda is defined by an unbroken entablature resting on eight composite columns, a solution inspired by the
corner chapels of Jules Hardouin-Mansart's Dôme des Invalides in Paris,
which Neumann had seen when visiting Paris in 1723. Through a sophisticated treatment of the window niches, however, Neumann gives
new life to the somewhat dry scheme. In the contemporary church at
Wiesentheid (1727–32) Neumann for the first time approached the
problem of integrating bell-tower and church façade, thereby giving new
life to a traditional type of Central European parish church. As in the
churches of Kilian Ignaz Dientzenhofer, the problem is solved by a
combination of vertical and horizontal continuity.

In 1727 Neumann also started the construction of the Benedictine
church of Münsterschwarzach near Kitzingen.[27] Here, for the first
time, he could tackle the problem of a large ecclesiastical building. The
solution shows a rather conventional basilica with a twin-tower façade.
A characteristic dominant rotunda, however, is inscribed. Like that in
the Schönborn Chapel, it is defined as a baldachin by means of freestanding coupled columns under the pendentives. Thus Münsterschwarzach introduces in a somewhat hesitant way the basic type that was to serve
as the point of departure for Neumann's later churches. Similarly tentative is the general layout of the pilgrimage church of Gössweinstein
(1729–39). Here, however, the architect takes the important step of
employing a true wall-pillar system.

A trip to Bohemia in 1730 must have had a liberating effect on
Neumann. He probably knew the church of Banz before, but in Prague
he could see the large basilica of St. Nicholas on the Kleinseite with its
interdependent spatial units. His new acquaintance with the works of the
Dientzenhofers is clearly reflected in his splendid plan for the Hofkirche
in Würzburg (1731–32). The history of the planning is somewhat complicated. Preliminary projects by Maximilian von Welsch, Robert de
Cotte, and Germain Boffrand had been discarded. About 1730 Hildebrandt also made a design, and he later collaborated on the interior decoration of the chapel. Without doubt, however, the general solution is
due to Neumann, and it represents one of his greatest achievements. The
chapel is inserted in the rectangular southwestern wing of the large Residenz. Within the simple box-like volume Neumann placed a succession

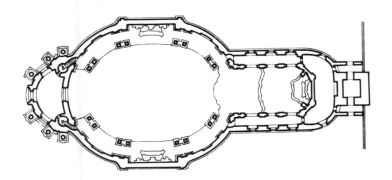

of interpenetrating oval spaces. The general scheme is bi-axial and the center is emphasized by a characteristic rotunda that has the shape of a longitudinal oval. Wide, transverse ovals at both ends define the zones of narthex and presbytery. These spaces, however, are integrated by two other narrower transverse ovals that define clearly pronounced transverse axes. The latter ovals are strongly emphasized by freestanding columns. In the ceiling, however, they contract between the expansive vaults of the primary spaces, so we have two contradictory spatial definitions according to the Dientzenhoferian principles of syncopated interpenetration. The solution comes fairly close to that for Banz, but Neumann separates the system of baldachins completely from the outer walls, introducing freestanding columns. And, above all, he gives the space a true center. The ingeniously articulated and richly decorated interior of the Hofkirche certainly is one of the masterpieces of Late Baroque architecture.

During the 1730s Neumann also reconstructed the church of St. Paulinus in Trier, destroyed by the French in 1674. The integration of tower and façade attempted in Wiesentheid is here achieved with great simplicity and conviction. The interior is a longitudinal hall articulated by a succession of shallow wall-pillars between which tall "medieval" windows penetrate the vault.

About 1740 Neumann got the opportunity to return to his main theme: the integration of a dominant rotunda in a longitudinal organism. In the three parish churches at Heusenstamm, Etwashausen, and Gaibach we encounter variations on the same theme. The point of departure is a traditional Latin cross, but in all three buildings the crossing is strongly emphasized, resulting in the effect of centralized spaces. Heusenstamm (1739–56) is the least mature, showing a solution that may be characterized as a simplified version of Gössweinstein. The crossing is defined by freestanding columns and covered by a "Bohemian cap" into which the vaults of the nave and transept penetrate. In Etwashausen (1740–45), the main space is a true baldachin-rotunda resting on coupled freestanding columns. The vault is again interpenetrated by the nave and transept. Several preliminary projects are preserved, which show that Neumann experimented with a succession of baldachins on columns within a continuous skin-like outer wall. The final solution is a more conventional elongated Greek cross, but the exterior remains a beautiful example of plastic integration. Spatially, Gaibach (1740–45) is the most interesting of the three churches. Here we encounter an attempt at employing the principle of syncopated interpenetration to integrate the different parts of a cross plan; the central baldachin-rotunda is surrounded by secondary ovals which are contradicted in the vault, creating the effect of a most original kind of multilateral open organism. This character is emphasized by the consequent interruption of the entablature. The solution fails somewhat where the more conventional nave is added to the

207. *Würzburg, Hofkirche, plan.*
208. *B. Neumann: longitudinal section of the Hofkirche at Würzburg.*
209. *B. Neumann: transverse section of the Hofkirche at Würzburg.* ▷
210. *Würzburg, Hofkirche, interior.* ▷

centralized part. To our knowledge, Gaibach is the only building in which the syncopated interpenetration of Christoph Dientzenhofer has been used in connection with a fully developed cross plan.

In 1742 Neumann drew up plans for four large churches: the Jesuit churches of Mainz (consecrated 1746; razed 1805) and Würzburg (never built), the church for the monastery of Langheim (never built), and the pilgrimage church of Vierzehnheiligen (consecrated 1772). All the projects show a preoccupation with the basic theme of the three preceding parish churches. The larger dimensions, however, bring about both new problems and new possibilities. The introduction of aisles and galleries makes a fully developed *Zweischaligkeit* possible, and the intentions indicated in the Hofkirche and in the radical preliminary designs for Etwashausen are thus further developed. The Jesuit church in Würzburg would have had a splendid wall-pillar hall with a gallery running all around the space. The continuity of the system is extraordinary, although variations in proportion and instrumentation characterize the different zones. The transverse oval rotunda, thus, appears as an expansion of the continuous space boundary. It is interpenetrated by the barrel vault of the nave so that a certain syncopation results. In general the project offers a convincing solution to the problem of *Zweischaligkeit*. The Jesuit church in Mainz represents a still more mature stage of development, and certainly was one of Neumann's greatest achievements. The general system has the clarity of French classical architecture, and the tall gallery may recall the royal chapel at Versailles. Through the introduction of a dominant rotunda, however, the organism is changed into a truly Late Baroque synthesis. The transition between nave and rotunda is ingeniously solved by means of syncopated interpenetration.[28] Hardly any other project by Neumann offers the same ideal combination of richness and clarity. The church for the monastery at Langheim is seemingly more conventional. The basilical nave has no galleries and is divided into bays by transversely placed coupled columns. The aisles continue behind the rotunda, creating an outspoken *Zweischaligkeit*. The result would have been a very interesting synthesis of the characteristic longitudinal oval of Baroque architecture and a basilica reduced to its essentials. The latter component is probably due to French influence.

The features developed at Langheim appear in simplified form in Neumann's first project for Vierzehnheiligen (1742).[29] A drumless dome was to be supported by coupled columns forming a continuation of the columns of the nave, so that again we find a skeletal system placed freely within an outer envelope. In a preliminary project Neumann had experimented with a series of adjacent baldachins, but the chosen solution shows a simple addition of three spatial units plus apses.[30] The construction was started on April 23, 1743, with Neumann's rival Gottfried Heinrich Krohne as a supervisor. Krohne, however, was not faithful

Balthasar Neuman

Christlicudenant

Inv. et fecit. d. 26. Jan.

to Neumann's design, and construction was suspended in December of the same year. As Krohne had built the foundations of the presbytery further to the east than planned, the sacred place of the fourteen saints no longer coincided with the crossing of Neumann's basilica. Therefore a new plan had to be made, and in 1744 Neumann arrived at the ingenious solution that makes Vierzehnheiligen the most original of all Late Baroque churches.

The pilgrimage church occupies a beautiful position over the river Main, opposite the monastery of Banz. Its restrained exterior has the form of a Latin-cross basilica with an impressive twin-tower façade. Upon entering the building, however, a different world is revealed. Within a seemingly infinite, luminous space a series of oval baldachins are placed. The rich and dynamic effect is structured by a regular system of colossal columns and pilasters. The longitudinal axis is emphasized by the large main altar in the presbytery, but equally strong is the center, marked by the splendid Rococo altar of the fourteen saints. An analysis of the spatial composition shows that two systems have been combined: a bi-axial organism basically similar to the Hofkirche in Würzburg, and a conventional Latin cross. As the center of the bi-axial layout does not coincide with the crossing, due to the unfortunate (or perhaps fortunate) error of Krohne, an exceptionally strong syncopation results. Over the crossing where the center of the church ought traditionally to be, emphasized by a dome, the vault is eroded by four interpenetrating spaces.[31] Instead we find the true center at the very middle of the longitudinal axis, in evident contradiction to the Latin cross. Compared with the Hofkirche, the succession of ovals organized here by means of syncopated interpenetration is enriched by secondary ovals and circles on the transverse axes, the latter creating the effect of a transept. The solution is suggested in Banz, but whereas Banz combines only simple longitudinality and restrained bi-axiality, Neumann also incorporates a dominant center defined by an oval rotunda as well as the Latin cross. Vierzehnheiligen, thus, unites all the basic concepts of Baroque church architecture into a singular synthesis. It ought to be pointed out that this achievement was possible only by means of the Dientzenhoferian method of syncopated interpenetration.

After Vierzehnheiligen, Neumann returned to his former, less ambiguous combination of rotunda and longitudinal axis. His project for the Hofkirche in Vienna (1746) again shows a great transverse oval between two smaller circular baldachins. The clear differentiation between primary and secondary structural elements and the beautifully planned *Zweischaligkeit* make the project one of Neumann's most convincing designs. Another alternative shows a solution more closely related to the Hofkirche in Würzburg.

In 1747 Neumann finally got a commission in which he could carry

◁ 212. *Würzburg, Hofkirche, interior.*
213. *Etwashausen, parish church, exterior.*
214. *Etwashausen, parish church, interior.*

215. *Gaibach, parish church, plan.*
216. *Gaibach, parish church, interior.*

217. *Trier, St. Paulinus, exterior.*

out his basic scheme on a monumental scale: the great Benedictine church of Neresheim.[32] Whereas Vierzehnheiligen remains a particular solution, Neresheim represents a typical integration of dominant rotunda and pronounced longitudinality. In the preliminary projects Neumann was undecided whether he should again employ the Dientzenhoferian integration of the spatial units or return to the simpler concepts of Langheim.[33] Fortunately, he adhered to the method of spatial interpenetration and thereby created a truly organic solution.[34] The disposition consists of five ovals in a row. The central longitudinal one is considerably larger and is defined as a baldachin on freestanding columns. It is accompanied by smaller lateral ovals that indicate a transept. The nave and presbytery are covered by two expansive vaults each, whereas the thin walls are divided into three equal bays. The middle one is contradicted by the vault, and again we recognize the principle of syncopated interpenetration. Similar bays of transition are introduced between nave, central rotunda, and presbytery, so that a continuous pulsating movement in depth is created, resembling the pulsating organisms of Kilian Ignaz Dientzenhofer. The lower part of the complex system of interpenetrating baldachins is defined as a transparent skeleton which is placed freely in front of a luminous outer wall. The exterior, in fact, shows a neutral surface pierced by numerous large windows, except for the main façade, which is a wonderfully restrained variation on the theme of Banz. Whereas Vierzehnheiligen represents a total synthesis, Neresheim expresses a Late Baroque interpretation of the eighteenth-century ideal of unifying Gothic structure and classical elements.[35]

Our discussion of Neumann's churches shows that he worked with a few basic themes which he tackled in various ways. Most important was the old problem of the dominant center within a longitudinal organism, a problem which found some of its finest solutions in his projects. Secondly, we encounter pronounced interest in the double delimitation of interior space, whereby the structural skeleton becomes clearly distinguished from the neutral outer wall. In Neumann's most important works the spatial problems are solved by syncopated interpenetration, but obviously he did not consider this the only possible method. Neumann did not have the particular inventive spirit of Christoph Dientzenhofer, nor did he adopt the systematic approach of Kilian Ignaz. His churches also lack the Bohemian dynamism which is typical of the works of these architects. Rather they are distinguished by a singularly harmonious monumentality that seems to unify all the basic aspirations of the epoch.

The Luminous Center

Piedmont is the only region outside Central Europe where we find Late Baroque churches comparable to the examples described in the preceding sections. Next to Filippo Juvarra, Bernardo Vittone was the most prolific

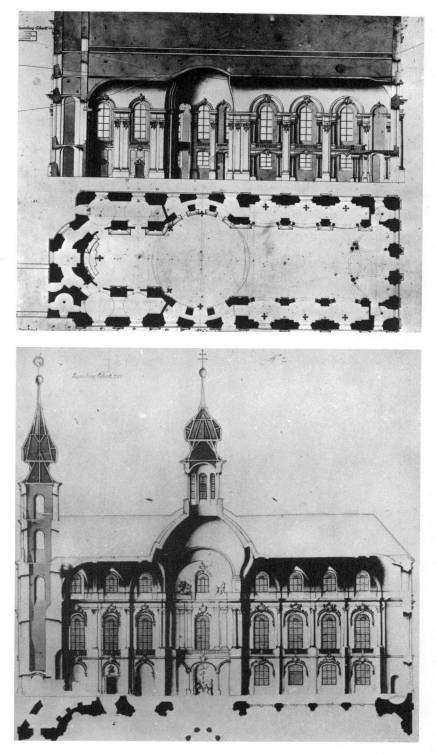

220. *B. Neumann: project for the pilgrimage church of Vierzehnheiligen, plan.*
221. *B. Neumann: project for the pilgrimage church of Vierzehnheiligen, section.*

222. *B. Neumann: project for the pilgrimage church of Vierzehnheiligen, elevation.*
223. *Pilgrimage church of Vierzehnheiligen, exterior.* ▷

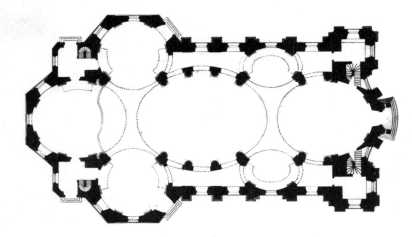

224. *Pilgrimage church of Vierzehnheiligen, axonometric drawing.*

225, 226. *Pilgrimage church of Vierzehnheiligen, views of the interior.*

227, 228. *Pilgrimage church of Vierzehnheiligen, views of the interior.*

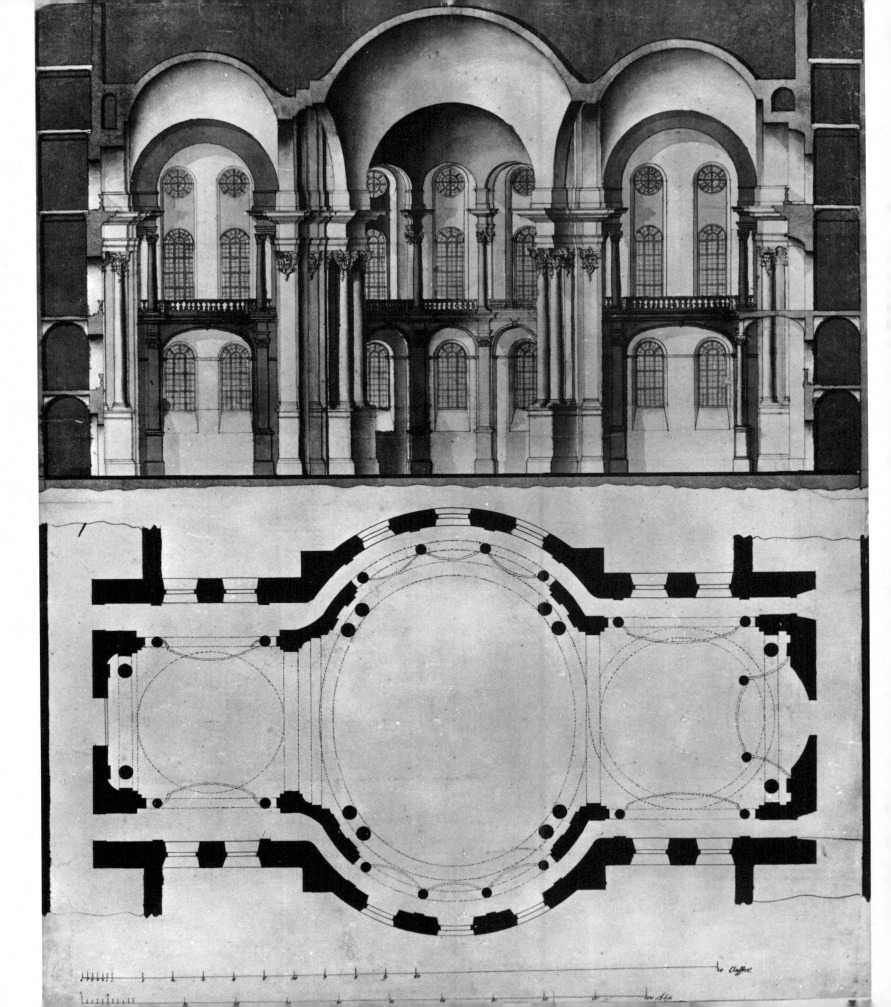

Piedmontese architect of the eighteenth century, and he was the only one to carry out a systematic research into the problems of ecclesiastical architecture. The general scope and thematic unity of his achievement is only equaled by the works of Kilian Ignaz Dientzenhofer and Johann Michael Fischer. As he was trained in Rome and lived in Turin in daily contact with the buildings of Guarini, we may expect that Vittone's churches should deviate from the general typology outlined above.[36] In fact, he does not show much interest in the longitudinal church, which because of medieval tradition and Counter-Reformatory purposes always remained of basic importance to Central European architects. Instead he concentrated his attention on the problems of the centralized organism, and in particular on its vertical development, as well as the relationship between space and light. While his contemporaries used to define their complex spatial organisms by means of relatively simple baldachin-shaped domes, Vittone perforated pendentives and vaults and surrounded his center by systems of light-chambers.[37] We could also say that he gave a vertical dimension to the theme of double spatial delimitation.

Even in his earliest major work, the pilgrimage chapel of the Visitation at Vallinotto near Carignano (1738–39), Vittone's intentions are clearly expressed.[38] In general, the plan is derived from Borromini's S. Ivo, but the vertical development is completely different. Instead of carrying the complex concave-convex movement of the ground plan into the dome, Vittone introduces a regular system of arches which rest on the six primary supports, creating thereby a regular hexagon. Behind the arches light is admitted through perforations in the semi-domes that close off the apses. The light comes from chambers which surround the lower part of the dome and which also give light to large openings over the arches. These arches therefore seem to span freely through space. Instead of a conventional dome we find a system of interlacing ribs, through which we look into another "infinitely distant" space. The idea of free arches is obviously derived from Juvarra's Chiesa del Carmine, whereas the diaphanous dome is a typical Guarinian concept. The structure of the chapel may in general be characterized as a centralized skeleton immersed in an extended and luminous space. Vittone himself has given us a key to its interpretation, saying: "The interior [of the chapel] consists of one main room, surmounted by three vaults, one above the other, which are perforated and open; the visitor's eye travels through the spaces created by the vaults, and, with the help of the light that enters through windows invisible from the interior, it can enjoy the variety of the hierarchies [of angels] which rise, in a growing crescendo, up the vaults to the very top of the lantern, where one finds the representation of the most Holy Trinity."[39]

We see, thus, that Vittone from the very beginning was perfectly conscious of his ends and means. The exterior of the Vallinotto chapel ap-

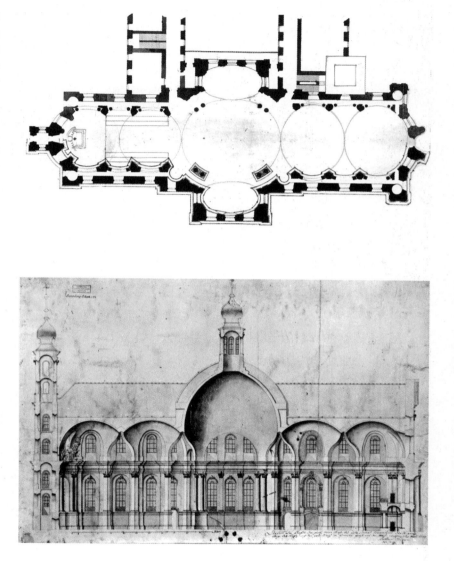

234, 235, 236. *Neresheim, Benedictine church, details of the interior.*

237. B. Vittone: *section and plan of the pilgrimage chapel of the Visitation at Vallinotto.*

238. *Vallinotto, pilgrimage chapel of the Visitation, exterior.*
239. *Vallinotto, pilgrimage chapel of the Visitation, interior.*
240. *Corteranzo, chapel of S. Luigi, exterior.* ▷

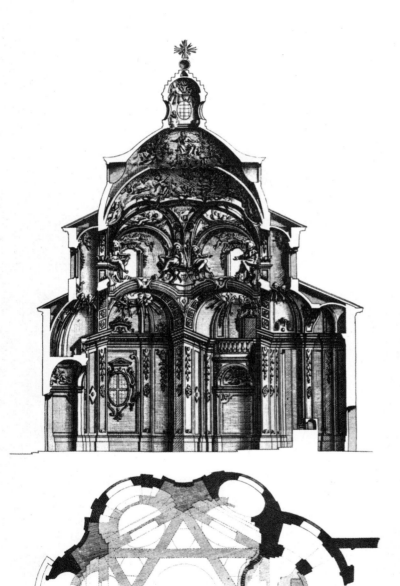

241. *Corteranzo, chapel of S. Luigi, plan.*
242, 243. *Corteranzo, chapel of S. Luigi, details of the interior.*

244. *Chieri, S. Bernardino, exterior of the dome.*
245, 246. *Chieri, S. Bernardino, interior of the dome.*

pears as a pagoda-like volume which corresponds to the disposition of the interior space. The dome is hidden behind two superimposed rings of light-chambers, whereby the crowning lantern also receives a fundamentally new character. Although the outer surface is permeated by a continuous undulation, we cannot talk about an active relationship between the building and its surroundings. The undulation is clearly determined from within. Seen from a distance, however, the chapel appears as a vertical axis which gives a halt to horizontal extension.

The ideas of the Vallinotto chapel were repeated in the small cemetery church of S. Luigi Gonzaga at Corteranzo, probably built about 1740.[40] Here the spatial organization is simpler: three secondary ovals surround the main space according to the principle of pulsating juxtaposition. Vittone does not try, however, to give identity to the individual cells; again the organism appears as a skeleton immersed in a continuous space. The exterior also repeats the basic properties of the Vallinotto chapel in simplified form. The chapel is situated in the flat Po valley, but the Corteranzo church lies among the hills of the Monferrato. In both cases, however, the vertical axis is capable of giving structure and meaning to the surrounding landscape.

In 1740 Vittone was also commissioned to complete the church of S. Bernardino in Chieri, begun by Quadro. The conventional Greek-cross plan did not prevent Vittone from carrying out his characteristic intentions. Again we find that the perforated vaults of the apses and even the pendentives have been opened up to admit light, which enters from tall light-chambers around the drum. The latter, which appears as a diaphanous skeleton, has a cross-shaped plan because of the chambers, and this determines the complex exterior. The ingenious idea of superimposing light-chambers on the cross arms is repeated on a monumental scale in the architect's project for a *grande chiesa parrocchiale*. This seemingly conventional design, which probably stems from Vittone's early period, also contains other radical innovations, such as a continuous ambulatory around the skeletal arms of the Greek cross—in other words, a fully developed *Zweischaligkeit*.

Smaller but more mature is the splendid church of S. Chiara in Brà (1742), which may be considered the masterpiece of Vittone's early period. Again the building appears as a vertical volume and the dome is hidden behind a ring of light-chambers. The corner position between two streets emphasizes its function as vertical axis in the townscape. The plan shows a circle interpenetrated by four secondary ovals, together forming a kind of Greek cross. The interpenetration is clearly shown in the floor by means of steps, but otherwise the spaces fuse optically and form a continuum. The interior appears as a very high centralized hall surrounded by a luminous zone. The effect is splendid and may very well be compared with the best contemporary interiors in Central Europe.

The height is functionally motivated by large galleries which serve the adjacent convent. These galleries span freely between the main pillars, and are shaped like the intermediate arches of Juvarra's Chiesa del Carmine. The solution, thus, may be characterized as a centralized version of the Carmine, and also shows a close affinity to the wall-pillar structures of Central Europe. Again Vittone lets light filter in everywhere; even the surface of the dome itself is perforated. The skeletal effect is pronounced, and the general luminosity is thrilling.

Shortly afterward Vittone applied the same basic system to a longitudinal oval in the church of S. Gaetano in Nizza.[41] The oval is interpenetrated by six secondary, approximately circular spaces whose outline is indicated by double curved arches, whereby the main vault is reduced to an internally convex hexagon.[42] The *Zweischaligkeit* that results contributes to the creation of a very dramatic and fascinating space whose boundaries dissolve in a play of light and shadow. A convincing structural coherence, however, is achieved by the introduction of a giant order of pilasters.

The system employed in the Carmine, with tall arches that penetrate into the vault, was repeated by Vittone on several occasions. A particularly beautiful example is provided by the hexagonal church of S. Chiara in Vercelli.[43] The very high space has two superimposed orders between which characteristic Carmine-type arches are spanned. The ground floor shows alternating niches like those at Vallinotto, whereas the upper level expands only over the entrance, and the other intervals are closed off by neutral flat walls. The system, thus, is interpreted as a spatially open skeleton, which can be filled in with curved or flat walls according to need. The vision of a diaphanous space from the first works has here found a precise structural formulation which offers the necessary freedom for spatial extensions and varied treatment of the illumination. The solution may be compared to the open baldachins of Kilian Ignaz Dientzenhofer, although Vittone never used the skeleton to imply an extended system of interacting cells.

Several years before the construction of S. Chiara in Vercelli, Vittone had studied similar problems in connection with an octagonal space with unequal sides. S. Chiara in Turin, in fact, has a ground plan which resembles the mature works of Johann Michael Fischer.[44] As in the buildings of Fischer and Kilian Ignaz Dientzenhofer, the corners are hollowed out, with the purpose of achieving a complete double spatial delimitation. The main space is surrounded by an ambulatory whose horizontal movement contrasts with the vigorous vertical continuity of the structural members.[45] The latter are treated as Gothic ribs rather than as plastic, classical elements. Although the indirect illumination of the early works has been replaced with large windows in membrane-like walls, the general effect of an open skeleton is very pronounced. The plan

247. B. Vittone: section and plan of S. Chiara, Brà.

248. Brà, S. Chiara, exterior.
249. Brà, S. Chiara, interior of the dome.

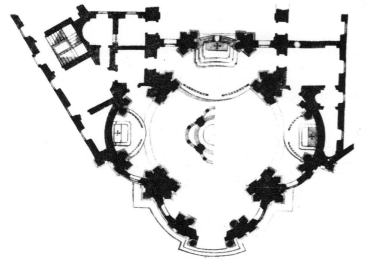

250. *B. Vittone: plan of S. Gaetano, Nizza.*
251. *B. Vittone: section of S. Gaetano, Nizza.*
252. *Nizza, S. Gaetano, interior.* ▷

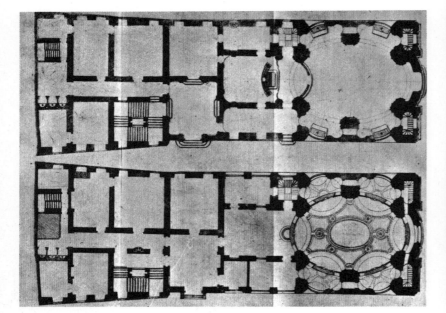

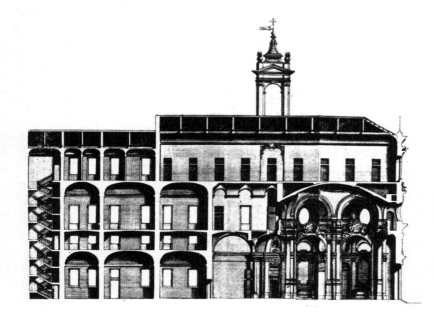

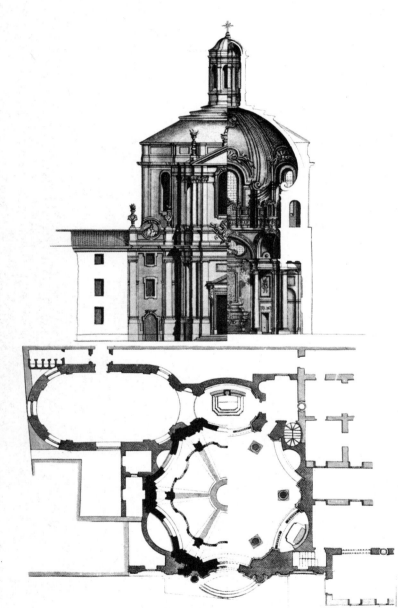

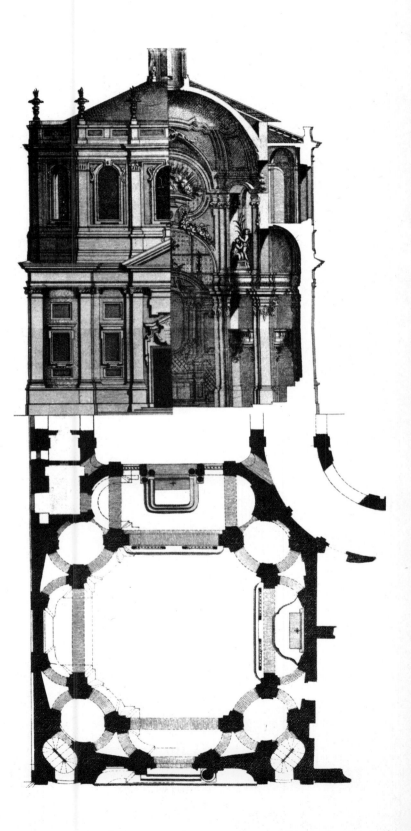

made by Vittone himself for publication shows all the members of the structure projected on the floor, and thus demonstrates that he was perfectly conscious of the properties described above. In S. Chiara in Turin all the traditional parts of a centralized church—dome, drum, pendentives, corner pillars, and arches—have been transformed to constitute a new totality of rare organic coherence. In the oeuvre of Vittone, S. Chiara in Turin represents an ideal mean between the Baroque dynamism of his earlier period and the calmer classicism of some of his later works.

In S. Michele at Rivarolo Canavese (begun in 1758) we encounter a truly surprising Neoclassical interpretation of the theme from S. Chiara in Turin. The general system is basically similar, but all the details at Rivarolo are designed in a style that is somewhat dry yet sensitive. Whereas S. Chiara was the fluid result of a process of modeling, Rivarolo seems to have been made by carpenters. This is not said, however, to deny the extraordinary beauty of the luminous space, for light is still the basic medium that gives life to interior space.

Whereas one basic type of space is the starting point for the mature solutions of Neumann and Johann Michael Fischer, Vittone always worked with several alternatives. With equal interest he tackled the problems of the octagon, the hexagon, the circle, the oval, or the Greek cross. During the 1750s he also built several more complex churches. S. Maria di Piazza in Turin[46] consists of a dome over a square with added half-domes on the longitudinal axis (like Hagia Sophia in Constantinople) plus a smaller octagonal presbytery of emphasized verticality. The lower part of the main space has a fully developed double delimitation and the vaults are transformed into diaphanous skeletons. The presbytery is covered by one of the extraordinary domes in which Vittone makes the traditional spherical shell dissolve as if it were eaten away by light. The idea stems from the perforated pendentives of S. Bernardino, but in S. Maria di Piazza Vittone fuses pendentives and drum completely by means of deep concave recesses. The dome appears to be suspended within a larger luminous space.[47]

In S. Croce in Villanova di Mondovì (1755), Vittone approaches more closely than in any other project the kind of synthesis of central and longitudinal space pursued by the Central European architects. The seemingly complex organism, however, reveals itself on closer scrutiny as a Greek cross to which there is added a circular presbytery by means of interpenetration and a transverse monks' choir. The longitudinality is strengthened by an undulating movement along the outer walls. The skeletal effect is very pronounced, and in contrast to most Central European churches of the epoch, it is carried into the dome by a particularly radical version of hollowed-out pendentives. The dome and the supporting structure here merge into an indivisible whole. It is interesting to note that the main arches, which are integrated in the solution, are

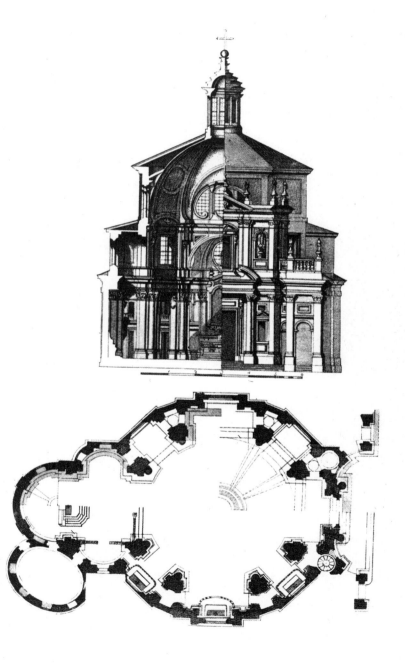

258. *Rivarolo Canavese, S. Michele, interior of the dome.*

259. *B. Vittone: section, elevation, and plan of S. Maria di Piazza, Turin.*

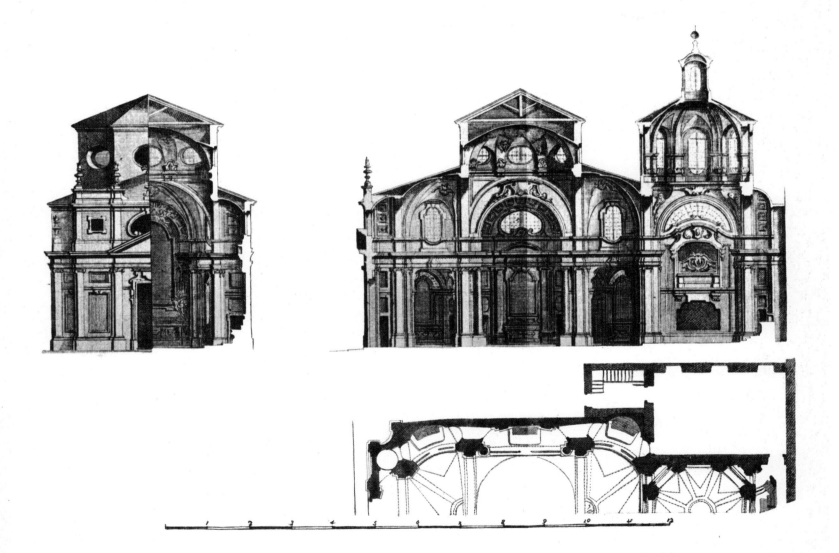

260. *Turin, S. Maria di Piazza, interior of the dome.*

shaped like the free Carmine-type arches, indicating the skeletal character of the system. The church of Villanova certainly conveys the effect desired by Vittone's client: "A vase endowed with novelty and light-hearted charm."

Among the numerous churches by Vittone, there are two which embody his basic intentions in a particularly straightforward way. The parish church of the Assunta in Grignasco stems from his middle period (begun 1750), whereas the parish church in Borgo d'Ale was begun in the last year of his life (1770).[48] Both are based on the idea of a diaphanous rotunda, and both show a hexagonal disposition of the active vertical members. There are also, however, important differences. In Grignasco the hexagon still appears as such, while Borgo d'Ale unifies the six intervals into a true circular rotunda. The desire for unification is also apparent in the treatment of the niches. In Grignasco their emphasized perspective makes the space expand along the six axes, whereas the round apses of Borgo d'Ale unite the space within a continuous undulating contour. In the vertical direction we find a corresponding difference. The primary columns in Grignasco stop at the height of the entablature of the niches, so that the space is divided horizontally into two zones. In Borgo d'Ale the columns are colossal and continue above the arches. Light-chambers between the arches and the vault make a last sophisticated variation on the Carmine-type motif. Borgo d'Ale is a space of rare strength and unity, and may be understood as Vittone's architectural testament. As a "Late Baroque Pantheon," it concretizes basic classical principles in a much more convincing way than most Neoclassical buildings.

Our analysis of Vittone's churches shows that they may be interpreted as variations on a simple theme. Vittone never tried to group individual cells in the Guarinian manner. Although he employed the same geometrical principles, his spatial elements are integrated optically to form indivisible wholes, although not of a static and finished character. His spaces are structured by skeletons, while the walls have only secondary importance. These skeletons are imbued with an active upward movement toward the light from above. Together the two conquer the amorphous matter of the wall. Vittone did not use light to accentuate a dramatic event as did Bernini; rather he treated it as an abstract element, which is concretized through its meeting with the architectural structure. Vittone's churches, thus, express the archetypal idea of the luminous center, which in this case becomes a christocentric concept. The churches of Vittone are true shrines, foci of a spiritual world which is concentrated but limitless.

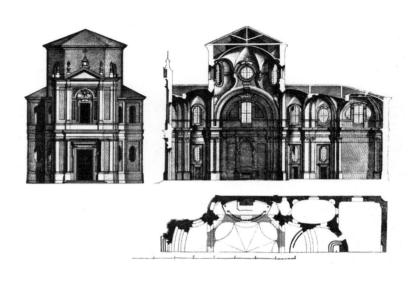

261. B. Vittone: section, elevation, and plan of S. Croce, Villanova di Mondovì.
262. Villanova di Mondovì, S. Croce, interior.

263. *Grignasco, parish church, plan.*
264. *Grignasco, parish church, section.*

265. *Grignasco, parish church, exterior.* ▷

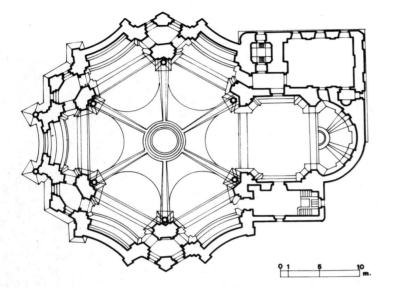

Conclusion

Great themes of architectural history are brought together in the churches of the Baroque. The concepts of center, path, and extension are fused into a last comprehensive synthesis. During the seventeenth century the longitudinal movement had primary importance. The Counter-Reformatory church required this symbol of God's people on their way. The vertical axis represented an ideal center which accompanied the journey, and the apparent infinite extension concretized the spirit of conquest and rapture. The rhetorical and persuasive character of High Baroque architecture was assimilated in Central Europe before the turn of the century, and characterizes the works of Christoph and Johann Dientzenhofer as well as the early creations of Kilian Ignaz Dientzenhofer. The buildings of these architects form part of a profound and popular renewal of religious values. In the early churches of Kilian Ignaz we find an ideal synthesis of centralization and longitudinality within a general, infinitely extended multilateral system.[49] His churches radiate the forces represented by the ideal center, and their undulating walls express this process. Therefore they belong to a truly Late Baroque architecture, and in a certain sense mark the culmination of the Baroque epoch.

After 1730, however, we find a growing interest in turning the movement inward, and the dominant rotunda appears in the works of both Neumann and Fischer. The longitudinal axis, however, remained a necessary component in their projects for large pilgrimage churches. Yet instead of aiming at truly synthetic Borrominian solutions, the architects tried to integrate centralization and longitudinality without sacrificing their individual identity. We find the same tendency in all the great churches of this period.

Buildings of this kind are still Baroque, in spite of Rococo or Neoclassical decoration, but in some cases the longitudinal movement and the feeling of substantial extension are abolished. The movement really turns inward and is concretized in diaphanous, centralized structures. We have seen that this tendency is present in all the great composite buildings which include a dominant rotunda, but in some cases it becomes the single aim. To a certain extent this holds true for the churches of Zimmermann, and certainly for most of Vittone's. To classify such buildings as Rococo is hardly satisfactory. They may have lost the persuasive rhetoric of the Baroque proper, and as a substitute offer a sort of spiritualized sensualism, which certainly is related to the Rococo. But we should understand that this aim can be attained in various ways, from the evident Rococo of the Wieskirche to the somewhat arid classicism of S. Michele at Rivarolo. In Paris we might also cite Soufflot's Ste-Geneviève (project 1757) in this connection. The content of the works of art sometimes lies beyond their stylistic categories.

To conclude, we may point out that the architectural development of

266, 267. *Grignasco, parish church, interior.*

268. *Borgo d'Ale, parish church, exterior.*

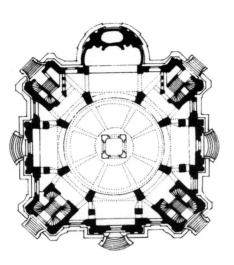

the Catholic church described above arrives at a final solution which ha a certain affinity with the typical Protestant church. The centralized spaces of the latter types also represent a gathering around an inner cen ter (dedicated to the Biblical word), and their bright illumination wa certainly intended, consciously or unconsciously, to be something mor than a mere practical aid for easier reading. The greatest of all Protestan Baroque churches, the Frauenkirche in Dresden by Georg Bähr (begur in 1726), may also be characterized as a diaphanous centralized structure in which the main space is surrounded by a complex system of light chambers.[50] Thus we see here an unconscious ecumenical spirit tha prefigures the Enlightenment.

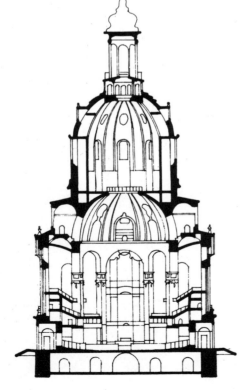

Introduction

In the first chapter we referred to the basic constituent types of eighteenth-century secular architecture: the French hôtel and the Italian palazzo. Both types were fully developed during the seventeenth century. The Late Baroque and the Rococo offer no fundamentally new typological contribution. We find, however, many interesting attempts at combining the main elements of the tradition, as well as a further development of basic intentions, such as the functionally differentiated plan. Particularly important is the new relationship between the inside and the outside found in Régence and Rococo architecture. The dominant, "infinite" axis of the High Baroque, thus, is succeeded by a more intimate contact with the immediate surroundings.

The development followed the social system and way of life of the country in question. We have pointed out that Austria offers a particularly rich palace architecture which reflects the influence of Catholic Rome, as well as the wish to imitate and surpass the forms of the French monarchy. Thus, Austrian state architecture is basically Baroque, although its historical synthesis also expresses the new pluralism of the eighteenth century. The German scene is dominated by the palatial residences of the many small capital cities, which indeed reflect the great model of Versailles. Thanks to the genius of Neumann, some of these buildings are true masterpieces which may be considered the culmination of Baroque palace architecture. In Russia a very colorful Late Baroque palace architecture was created about the middle of the century under the Tsarina Elizabeth. Although an Italian, Bartolomeo Rastrelli, was mainly responsible for it, it has an unmistakably Russian flavor. In England we also find a characteristic Late Baroque architecture, mainly during the reign of Queen Anne. Its great manifestation is Blenheim Palace, built for the Duke of Marlborough by John Vanbrugh.

Because of the many regional variants, it is natural to treat the eighteenth-century palace according to countries. In the following pages, we will take a look at the contributions of France, Italy, Austria, Germany, Russia, and England.

Interior and Exterior

Around the turn of the century French architecture was still under the spell of Jules Hardouin-Mansart's genius. His clear and powerful style represented an ideal manifestation of the absolute state, and was even admired by Voltaire and Rousseau. Although his works were always impregnated with the *grand goût* of the High Baroque, we find toward the end of his career a more fluid and elegant expression and a certain desire for simplification; the traditional straight entablature and semicircular arch are often replaced by the segmental arch, which gives emphasis to the continuity of the wall rather than to the tectonic system.[1]

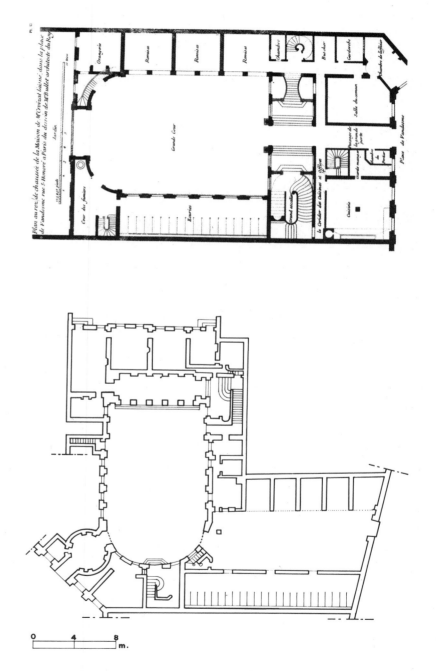

273. *Paris, Hôtel Crozat, plan.*
274. *Paris, Hôtel d'Evreux, plan.*

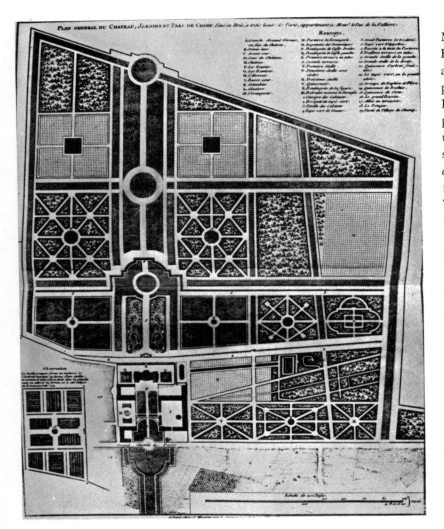

The new direction thereby indicated was also followed by Hardouin-Mansart's contemporary, Pierre Bullet.[2] Being a pupil of Jacques-François Blondel, Bullet took great care in the working out of the details and proportions. What he lacked in original genius, he made up by sophisticated planning and design. His two adjacent hôtels behind Hardouin-Mansart's façades on the Place Vendôme represent important progress in the functional distribution and differentiation of spaces. In the Hôtel Crozat (1700–2) the particular circumstances led to an inversion of the conventional disposition with a *cour d'honneur* in front of the *corps-de-logis*. Instead we find an *appartement double* in which the living rooms face the Place Vendôme and the bedrooms the courtyard behind. The courtyard opens toward a garden, but is defined as such by two curved terraces which also form a transition between the building and the open space behind. The garden façade has no classical order, but is perforated by closely placed French windows. The interior spaces are characterized by fluid continuity and great variety. The adjacent Hôtel d'Evreux (1707) had to be built on a difficult site at the very corner of the Place Vendôme. Very cleverly, Bullet adapted the usual hôtel plan to the circumstances, incorporating a circular *porte-cochère* in the center of Hardouin-Mansart's façade. The beautiful symmetrically disposed court is rounded near the entrance and at the far end has an open portico which gives access to the main *corps-de-logis*. The axis, however, is displaced, as the symmetrical garden façade also comprises one of the wings of the Hôtel Crozat. And the latter occupies one of the bays of the corner façade toward the Place—an ingenious exploitation of the building site.

The aims of Bullet are particularly well expressed in the Château de Champs-sur-Marne, built about 1700 for the rich financier Paul Poisson. The beautifully disposed plan is clearly derived from Louis Le Vau's Vaux-le-Vicomte, but whereas the interior shows a further development in functional differentiation, the exterior has abolished the dynamic plastic articulation of Le Vau. Bullet's sketches demonstrate the gradual development of the final integrated solution, in which the exterior appears as a continuous voluminous shell.[3] Except for a controlled rustication which serves to define the slight projections of the *ressauts* and the slender columns marking the entrance, the walls are like a skin wrapped around the interior. The character is emphasized by the unified volume of the Mansard roof. The large French windows have only flat linear frames and segmental arches on the upper floor. In general, the Château de Champs represents the first mature manifestation of the restrained and sophisticated secular architecture of the eighteenth century, and gives testimony to Bullet's important role as a mediator between the seventeenth and eighteenth centuries.

A related approach is found in the works of Hardouin-Mansart's pupils, Pierre Lassurance and Robert de Cotte. Both architects were

276. *Champs-sur-Marne, château, entrance.*
277. *Champs-sur-Marne, château, view overlooking the garden.*

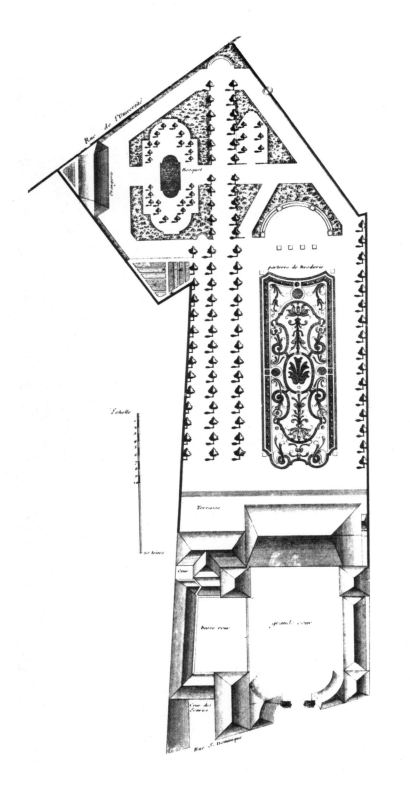

responsible for many of the interiors of Hardouin-Mansart's buildings—a fact that already proves the new direction of interest. Lassurance emerged as an independent architect about 1700 with the Hôtel Rothelin d'Argenson. Here, as well as in the Hôtel Desmarets (1704),[4] the walls are treated as a relatively simple skin, although the main axis is still strongly emphasized by means of columns, and the volume is split into units by divisions in the roof. A more advanced approach is found in the Hôtel de Roquelaure, initiated by Lassurance in 1722, and finished by Jean-Baptiste Leroux in 1736. Here the *corps-de-logis* has a very simple uniform façade. The blocked longitudinal axis is not marked by a *ressaut*, but only by vertical rusticated bands, and lateral entrances are placed in the corners. The windows are the same throughout the whole back wall, and the smaller segmented ones on the upper floor also appear on the projecting wings that define the inner part of the *cour d'honneur*. These wings, however, have rusticated arches on the ground floor, which form a continuation of the lateral walls of the court, achieving a sophisticated integration of *corps-de-logis* and service buildings.[5] In the Hôtel de Lassay (1722) Lassurance also stressed the continuity of the surface, whereas the Palais de Bourbon (1720–22) shows a return to the skeletal architecture of Hardouin-Mansart's Grand Trianon, probably because of the special character of the building.[6]

Robert de Cotte played a considerable role in the development of the decorative style of the Régence, and was widely in demand as a consultant abroad, for instance at Schleissheim, Brühl, and Frankfurt (Thurn und Taxis Palace, 1727).[7] His first important independent work in Paris was the Hôtel du Ludes (1710). The plan is neither innovative nor interesting, but the wall-articulation shows the actual wish for simple continuity. More important are the Hôtel d'Estrées (1713),[8] which had a simple, unified design, and the rebuilding of François Mansart's Hôtel de la Vrillière for the Count of Toulouse (1713–19). The latter clearly illustrates the change in taste. Whereas Mansart's disposition was based on a dominant longitudinal axis and a centralized vestibule that connected the court and the garden, De Cotte blocked the axis and created a new vestibule and *grand escalier* to the left. We see, thus, how representative and symbolic symmetry gave way to a more commodious and differentiated plan. The most important preserved work of De Cotte, however, is the Palais de Rohan in Strasbourg, built between 1728 and 1742. Here we encounter the simple, voluminous character and the sophisticated articulation introduced by Bullet in the Château de Champs. A half-oval space precedes the Doric gate, a motif already employed in the Hôtel d'Estrées and even earlier by Delamair in his hôtels. The longitudinal movement through the *corps-de-logis* is blocked, but an organizing axis of symmetry is still present, defined by a slightly projecting *ressaut*. The entrances are found in both corners, following the example of the

Hôtel de Roquelaure, although here they are emphasized by columns within the general continuity of the wall. On both floors the large windows have segmental arches, which introduce a note of lightness and elegance. The garden façade, which here faces the river Ill, shows a perfectly regular distribution of windows, but as a surprise four giant columns are added to accentuate the three central bays. In spite of its emblematic function, the motif contradicts the shell-like character of the structure.[9] In general, however, the Palais de Rohan well represents the *noble simplicité* of the Rococo palace.

Simultaneous with De Cotte we find a whole generation of younger architects who exploited all the different possibilities of the period. Gilles-Marie Oppenord and Jean Courtonne contributed in a significant way to the development of the Rococo, the former mainly as a decorator. Pierre-Alexis Delamair carried out a few very sophisticated hôtels without giving up the basic character of the French classical tradition, whereas Ange-Jacques Gabriel combined that tradition with a Rococo sense of volume and surface. Germain Boffrand, finally, mastered the whole range of expressive means, and may be considered the most prolific architect of the first half of the century. Let us take a brief look at some of their main works.

It is natural to start with the meticulous Delamair. With the Hôtel de Soubise (1704–9) and the Hôtel de Rohan (1705–8), he created two of the major monuments of the eighteenth century in Paris.[10] The famous courtyard and façade of the Hôtel de Soubise consist of a two-story *corps-de-logis* and lateral colonnades with coupled columns. The façade, however, does not tell the truth about the building behind. As the solution had to incorporate the remains of the medieval Hôtel de Clisson as well as the Hôtel de Guise from the seventeenth century, Delamair simply added a new façade, hiding a vestibule and a great staircase, at a right angle to the existing structure. He created one of the true masterpieces of French classical architecture. The solution basically consists of two elements: the plain façade proper and the lateral colonnades. A highly sophisticated integration is achieved, as the colonnade continues along the ground floor of the building. Two pairs of columns on either side are simply used to carry statues representing the Seasons, whereas four pairs in the middle define the central *ressaut* with coupled columns on the upper floor as well. The bays of the *ressaut* are considerably smaller but not so narrow as to interrupt the general rhythm around the court. The engirdling continuity is also emphasized by a projecting cornice. The colonnade, thus, is used as a "theme with variations." The façade proper has rusticated arches on the ground floor and relatively distant, rectangular French windows above. The wall therefore does not yet have the shell-like character of the imminent Rococo, but is rather related to the "crystalline" expression of François Mansart. Very delicate

283. *Paris, Hôtel de Matignon, plan.*
284. *Paris, Hôtel de Matignon, detail of the façade overlooking the courtyard.*

285. *Paris, Hôtel de Matignon, façade overlooking the courtyard.*

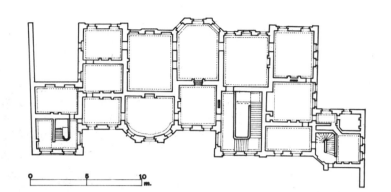

286. *Paris, Hôtel Peyrenc de Moras-Biron, façade.*

287. *Paris, Hôtel Peyrenc de Moras-Biron, plan.*
288. *Malgrange, château, plan of the second project.*
289. *Paris, Hôtel de Rohan, plan.*

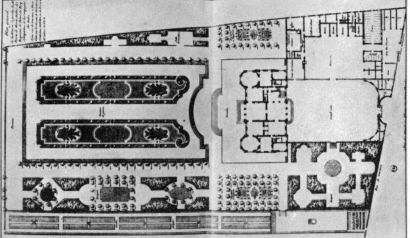

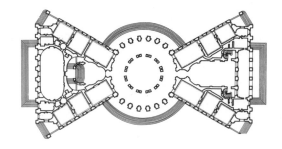

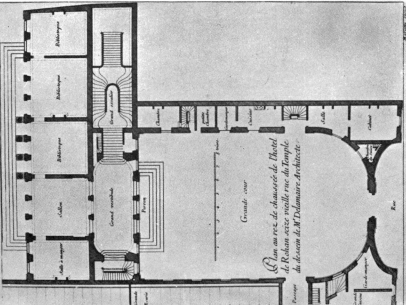

proportions contribute to the extremely pleasing general effect. In the adjacent Hôtel de Rohan, Delamair contented himself with a much smaller courtyard, but designed a particularly splendid staircase. The palace has a displaced main axis because of the customary addition of a lateral base court. The garden façade is quite impressive, although it does not possess the subtle variations in detailing and proportions found in the Hôtel de Soubise. In spite of the numerous large windows, the general expression is still basically tectonic. In both hôtels we find characteristic half-oval spaces on both sides of the entrance gate, a most successful solution to the problem of the transition between urban space and courtyard, which to the best of our knowledge was invented by Delamair.[11]

The hôtels of Jean Courtonne are convincing manifestations of the new taste of the eighteenth century. The Hôtel de Noirmoutier (1720) and in particular the Hôtel de Matignon (commissioned 1721) clearly demonstrate the new way of treating mass and surface. The plan of the Hôtel de Matignon is an ingenious study in the use of a displaced axis, and we notice that the garden façade makes the building appear as a freestanding unit. The walls are treated as continuous surfaces perforated by numerous tall windows. Classical orders are not used; instead we find a sophisticated articulation by means of different openings. Semicircular arches give all three *ressauts* of the court façade a more skeletal appearance, indicating the vestibules behind, whereas the garden façade only has this sort of opening in the very center. All the other windows have the segmental arches typical of the period. The many venetian blinds contribute to the general light and mobile character.

The well-known Hôtel Peyrenc de Moras-Biron (1728–31) by Jacques V Gabriel has a similar character, although the articulation is somewhat more conventional. The axial disposition is marked by pronounced *ressauts*, and the different volumes are indicated by tall old-fashioned roofs. But its general shell-like character is very evident, and still more than the Hôtel de Matignon it appears as a freestanding volume.[12]

A similar desire for defining the building as a unified volume surrounded by a continuous wall also characterizes the works of Jean-Silvain Cartaud, despite a preference for the colossal order which is probably due to his period of studies in Rome. As a characteristic example we may refer to his beautiful Château de Montmorency (begun 1702).

In Germain Boffrand we finally encounter an architect capable of a versatile experimentation with the different possibilities of the epoch. Like De Cotte, he was employed outside Paris and abroad, and his numerous works certainly deserve a thorough discussion.[13] We have already mentioned his original and significant Hôtel Amelot de Gournay (1710–13), and should only add that the free movement of the spaces as well as the skin-like garden façade represent a very early and surprisingly mature example of the style which became usual about 1720. We may also point

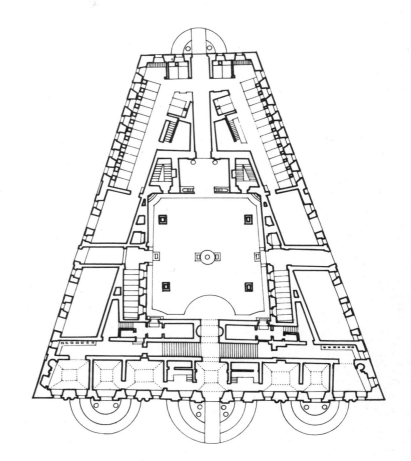

out the sophisticated integration of the main body and the wings by means of uniformly shaped windows (semicircular arches in the skeletal courtyard façade, and segmental ones toward the garden). The garden façade of the Hôtel Seignelay (1718) shows a similar approach, although the plan is more conventional. The same holds true for the large Hôtel de Torcy (1714). In all these buildings we find the use of semicircular and segmental arches as a means of characterization, a device suggested by Bullet and brought to perfection by Courtonne. The creative genius of Boffrand is particularly evident in his two projects for the Château de Malgrange near Nancy (begun 1712). One of them shows a large circular *grand salon* from which four arms branch out diagonally, repeating the basic scheme of Fischer von Erlach's garden-palace for Count Althan (1688).[14] Boffrand's monumentalized version is certainly a reflection of the fact that the palace was planned to serve the Duke of Lorraine. The contrast between the skeletal central rotunda and the closed wings is most expressive, and the interior contains a particularly splendid staircase. The second project is apparently more conventional. At least it represents a decisive step toward the plans of the great Late Baroque palaces of Central Europe, such as the Residenz in Würzburg, for which Boffrand acted as a consultant to Neumann. The original model for the Château de Malgrange is evidently Vaux-le-Vicomte, but the desire to create a unified volume has been carried still further than was the case in the Château de Champs. The great double-height *salle des gardes* flanked by a spacious staircase and a chapel between two inner courts would have created quite a new and impressive spatial continuity in the interior, which must have inspired Neumann's great projects of the following period.

Our discussion of the French hôtel has demonstrated how a new approach became manifest during the first decades of the eighteenth century. We may characterize the general trend by the word *individualization*. Instead of forming part of a superior system, the buildings receive a more intimate individuality. The dominant Baroque axis loses importance and the hôtel instead appears as an independent volume. The Baroque skeleton, which expressed a general spatial extension, was succeeded by a continuous wall perforated, however, by large openings to allow for a more agreeable contact between inside and outside. Above all, the interior spaces were further differentiated, and a rich playful decoration created a feeling of intimate enchantment. The simple sophisticated exteriors form a meaningful counterpoint and reveal how the focus of life had turned inward.[15]

Pluralist Characterization

Toward the end of the seventeenth century Roman palace architecture lost its creative momentum. The buildings from the first three decades

299. *Turin, Palazzo Asinari, detail of the atrium.*
300. *Turin, Palazzo Asinari, atrium.* ▷

of the eighteenth century appear as pale variations on themes from the High Baroque. Only in a few works can we recognize a certain affinity with the lighter, surface-oriented approach of the French architects. This is, for instance, the case in the attractive Palazzo Pichini (1710) by Alessandro Specchi and in the palaces situated on Raguzzini's Piazza S. Ignazio. The more important buildings of the 1730s, however, follow different aims. Undoubtedly the most original creation is the Palazzo Doria on the Corso (1731–33) by Gabriele Valvassori. The rich, vibrating façade abounds in original details and compositional innovations. Although it is very different from the reserved French exteriors of the period, the basic desire for continuity and integration is evident. It is natural that Valvassori was more directly influenced by Borromini, and we find in his work clear references to Borromini's round corners, undulating horizontals, and complex frontispieces. In spite of the general emphasis on the surface, the Palazzo Doria has a truly Roman plasticity unknown in contemporary French architecture. Valvassori also revived the rhythmic grouping of windows introduced by Giacomo della Porta, so as to organize the large wall and to obtain a certain concentration on the middle axis. Particularly interesting is the treatment of the two lower stories. The ground floor appears as an infinitely extended, albeit rhythmical, succession of windows, which are distributed in triplets repeated in the story above. The result is a simultaneous horizontal and vertical integration that is most convincing. The window becomes the protagonist of the composition, rather than an order of pilasters, as was still the case in Borromini's Palazzo di Propaganda Fide. The sophisticated articulation and detailing give the Palazzo Doria a unique position within the Roman Late Baroque,[16] although Valvassori in fact created his masterpiece when a strong Neoclassical movement was becoming manifest.[17]

Ferdinando Fuga, who was less original but more prolific than Valvassori, built several large palaces in Rome during the 1730s and 1740s. Most important is the Palazzo della Consulta, erected between 1732 and 1735.[18] The palace housed the papal congregation of the Consulta, as well as two small military bodies. The latter were assigned the ground floor, the mezzanine, and the attic, while the Consulta inhabited the main floor. Its complex function gives the building a correspondingly complex appearance, which Fuga tried to overcome by joining together the two lower floors. As a result, the proportions are somewhat undecided.[19] The plan, however, is well organized and represents a further development of seventeenth-century systematization. The symmetrically disposed staircase which opens onto the *cortile* is particularly convincing.[20] A still more spacious staircase is the outstanding feature of Fuga's Palazzo Corsini, built in 1736. The palace is placed at the foot of the Janiculum, and combines the characters of a city-palace and a *villa suburbana*. The plan shows a wide "U" which opens toward the gardens. It

304. *Turin, Palazzo Saluzzo-Paesana, atrium.*
305. *Turin, Palazzo Saluzzo-Paesana, vault of the atrium.*

306. *Turin, Palazzo Cavour, atrium.*
307. *Turin, Palazzo Cavour, detail of the atrium.*

is divided into two halves by the large skeletal staircase which is combined with a spacious vestibule. The solution is related to the great contemporary staircases in Central Europe, but in Rome it represents a unique achievement. The two courtyards created by the staircase are screened from the garden by means of elevated passages on arcaded pillars. In general, the disposition of the Palazzo Corsini is seen to be quite ingenious, but the expression is weakened by Fuga's dry detailing, which may be characterized as Late Baroque (lacking, however, its spontaneity and inner life). This lack also marks his Palazzo Cenci-Bolognetti of 1745. During the later part of his career Fuga was mostly active in Naples, where he built several palaces and villas, notably the immense Albergo dei Poveri (after 1750), which has a façade measuring 387 yards in length.

To find a flourishing Late Baroque palace architecture we must return to Piedmont, which also in this respect offers a most interesting balance between the Italian and the French styles. The city planning carried out in Turin during the seventeenth century emphasized the development of a systematized and uniform townscape. The palaces neither appear as individual blocks like many of the great Roman palazzi, nor do they have a French *cour d'honneur*.[21] Here more than anywhere else they "disappear" behind the continuous urban façades. Surface continuity, thus, determines the general character. Behind the walls, however, we encounter a rich Baroque world of courtyards, staircases, and interiors. As a transition we find the characteristic Turinese *androne*, which is usually shaped as a spacious centralized vestibule creating a feeling of festive openness between entrance and *cortile*. The type had already been introduced by Amedeo di Castellamonte and Guarini.

Toward the end of the seventeenth century plans were developed further and received a special Late Baroque interpretation. In the Palazzo Barolo in Turin by Gian Francesco Baroncelli (1692) we find a splendid symmetrical three-flight staircase in the axis of the vestibule, showing a rich plastic articulation. The most representative architect of the transitional period leading to the eighteenth century was Michelangelo Garove. In 1686 he started the construction of the attractive Palazzo Asinari, in which the star-shaped vault of the *androne* rests on twisted columns like the ones used by Bernini for the Baldacchino in St. Peter's. The complete lack of any horizontal entablature creates a feeling of lightness which prepares for the U-shaped *cortile*, connected with the *androne* by an open portico. The façade is basically Italian, but the smooth surface acts as a neutral background for the tall windows of almost French proportions. Their rhythmical distribution creates sophisticated tensions that give life to the simple composition, and the strongly emphasized tectonic keystones form a meaningful contrast to the playful vestibule behind. In Garove's University of Turin courtyard on Via Po (1713–20) we encounter

311. *Stupinigi, hunting lodge, plan.*

312. *Stupinigi, hunting lodge, aerial view.*
313. *Stupinigi, hunting lodge, façade overlooking the courtyard.* ▷

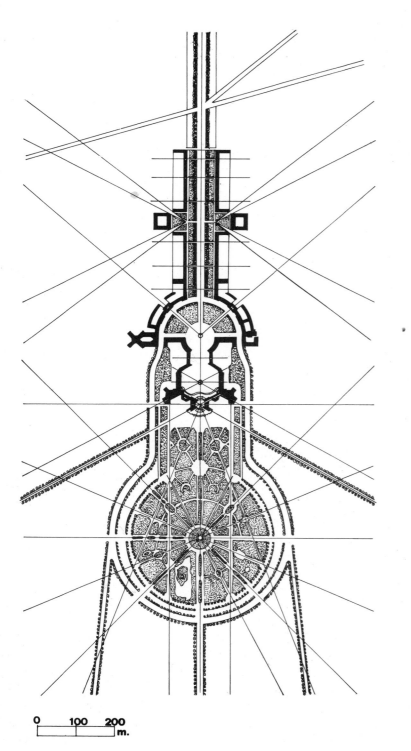

0   100   200
m.

314. *Stupinigi, hunting lodge, salon.*
315. *Diagrammatic drawing of the city of Vienna.*
316. *J.B. Fischer von Erlach: Engelhartstetten Castle, engraving.*
317. *J.B. Fischer von Erlach: Klesheim Palace, engraving.*

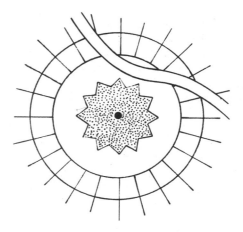

318. *J.B. Fischer von Erlach: sketch for a Lustgartengebäude for King Frederick I of Prussia.*
319. *J.L. von Hildebrandt: project for the Mansfeld-Fondi (Schwarzenberg) Palace.*
320. *J.L. von Hildebrandt: Mansfeld-Fondi Palace, project for a Gartenhaus, diagrammatic drawing.*

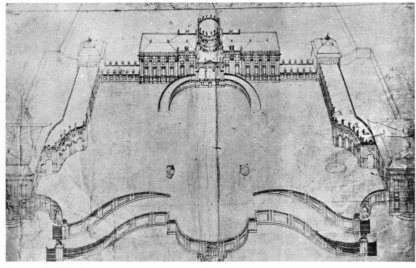

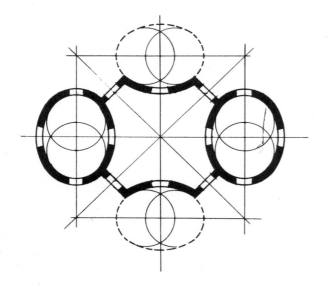

again a light and airy space which, despite some Manneristic details, well represents the environmental ideals of the eighteenth century.

The characteristic types described above found a prolific interpreter in Gian Giacomo Plantery, who is particularly well known for the vaults of his vestibules, the so-called *volte planteriane*. A beautiful example is offered by the Palazzo Cavour (1729), whose main vault is interpenetrated by six double-curved arches to create a complex and dynamic ensemble, which undoubtedly inspired solutions such as Vittone's S. Gaetano in Nizza. Plantery's main work is the large Palazzo Saluzzo-Paesana, built between 1715 and 1722 within the third city-extension of Turin. The somewhat conventional exterior is kept within the formal limits of Turinese urban architecture, but the *androne* and the *cortile* are splendid indeed. The vault of the *androne* is basically similar to that of the Palazzo Cavour. It is, as usual, connected with the courtyard by a portico. This tripartite portico is also repeated on the main floor and again on the other side of the *cortile*, whereas the lateral walls show a simpler articulation. A pronounced direction is thereby created, as well as a most expressive interplay of space and mass. The plastic modeling and the details are rich and varied, and contribute to the pleasing general character.

The basic characteristics of the Piedmontese palace are varied significantly in the Palazzo Ghilini (1730–33) in Alessandria by Benedetto Alfieri. The impressive façade shows superimposed orders, and appears more Baroque than the reserved exteriors of the Turinese palaces. The corner solution is particularly interesting: the elements are crowded together, creating an effect of powerful, muscular tensions. The *risalti*, however, are integrated into the façade by means of a regular succession of windows, and the continuity is also carried around the corners. The center of the façade is marked by a change in rhythm and by the double movement of a protruding balcony and an intruding niche. In the *androne*, however, the forms become calm. The plastic members of Garove and Plantery have become a system of simple Tuscan columns that carry an elegant vault. Together with the Palazzo Doria in Rome, the Palazzo Ghilini is possibly the most convincing city-palace in eighteenth-century Italy.

Among Italian architects of the eighteenth century, place of pride must be given to Filippo Juvarra. His city-palaces in Turin, however, do not rank among his most significant works. In the Palazzo Birago di Borgaro (1716–19) he obviously tries to define the character of the aristocratic palace as being basically different from the princely appearance of the Palazzo Madama, built shortly afterward. The result is a somewhat undecided juxtaposition of forms. More interesting is his contemporary Palazzo Martini di Cigala, whose façade has become a continuous surface on which the frames of the windows are drawn with delicate contours. The slightly projecting central *risalto* is also successfully inte-

323. *Vienna, Starhemberg-Schönburg Palace, plan.*

324. *Vienna, Starhemberg-Schönburg Palace, from an engraving by Salomon Kleiner.*

325. *Vienna, Belvedere Palace, plan.*

326. *Vienna, Upper Belvedere, façade.*

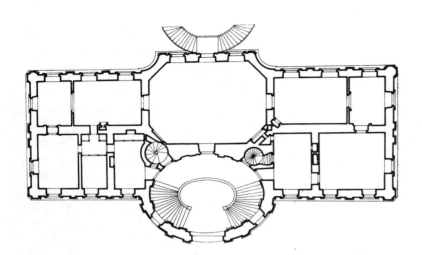

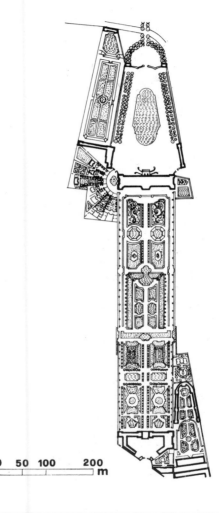

0 50 100   200
m

327. *Vienna, Upper Belvedere, detail of the façade.*

328. *Vienna, Upper Belvedere, detail of a pavilion.*
329. *Vienna, Upper Belvedere, façade.*
330. *Vienna, Upper Belvedere, detail of a window.*

233

331. *Vienna, Upper Belvedere, fountain in the gardens, from an engraving by Salomon Kleiner.*

332. *Vienna, Upper Belvedere.*

333. *Vienna, Upper Belvedere, façade overlooking the gardens, from an engraving by Salomon Kleiner.*

334. *Vienna, Upper Belvedere, façade overlooking the gardens.*

335. *Vienna, gardens of the Belvedere.*
336. *Vienna, Lower Belvedere, façade.*
337. *Vienna, Upper Belvedere, sala terrena.* ▷

338, 339, 340. *Vienna, Upper Belvedere, staircase.*

341. *Vienna, Palace of Prince Eugene, from an engraving by Salomon Kleiner.*

342. *Vienna, Palace of Prince Eugene, façade, from a contemporary engraving.*

343. *Vienna, Strattmann Palace, from an engraving by Salomon Kleiner.*

grated into the wall. The attractive vestibule shows an original system of interlacing arches instead of the usual vault. In general, the building may be characterized as a worthy eighteenth-century interpretation of the Turinese city-palace. The great talent of Juvarra, however, becomes manifest in the royal hunting lodge of Stupinigi, which he built for Vittorio Amedeo II between 1729 and 1731.[22] The original plan with diagonally disposed arms branching out from a central rotunda recalls Fischer von Erlach's palace for Count Althan and Boffrand's Château de Malgrange, but Juvarra himself had also been experimenting with the problems of diagonal organization since the very beginning of his career.[23] In Stupinigi, however, the rotunda and its arms constitute only the focus of a much larger layout. The straight road from Turin approaches the palace and forms a wide avenue flanked by service buildings. Before reaching the palace proper it opens into a large semicircle. The palace responds with a smaller semicircle that forms the first introduction to the deep, complex *cour d'honneur*. A smaller rectangle with contracted ends follows just before the main hexagonal court, which has truncated corners. All the spaces interpenetrate, creating a continuous pulsating effect. The building, which defines the complex spatial organism, consists of long wings spreading out in several directions with no fixed limits. Two of the four arms of the main palace thus continue to define the courtyard, whereas the other two are interrupted. They are echoed by other diagonally oriented arms added to the truncated corners of the hexagonal part of the court. The building therefore appears as an infinitely extended, open organism which interacts with exterior space. The extension, however, is not of the dominant, rhetorical kind found in Versailles. The complex movement, due to the diagonally disposed wings, is more intimate and expresses the new relationship to nature typical of the eighteenth century. The extensive layout is most efficiently centered on the large *salone*. Here Juvarra created one of his greatest spaces, and again demonstrated his ability to characterize different functions. The *salone delle feste* at Stupinigi has a festive character indeed. Its complex spatial delimitation and abundant decoration have an overwhelming effect. And it is still structurally clear and easily perceptible, because of the introduction of a dominant baldachin carried on four pillars. These pillars are connected with the outer wall by means of an undulating gallery that secures the horizontal integration of the space. The *Zweischaligkeit* and the vertical continuity of the space have a strong affinity with contemporary churches in Central Europe, to which the *salone* in Stupinigi forms the most splendid secular counterpoint.[24] Although Stupinigi does not show the sophisticated articulation of the Belvedere in Vienna or the equilibrated monumentality of the Residenz in Würzburg, it may be considered the most ingenious of all eighteenth-century palaces. If offers a new and valid interpretation of the Baroque concepts of centralization

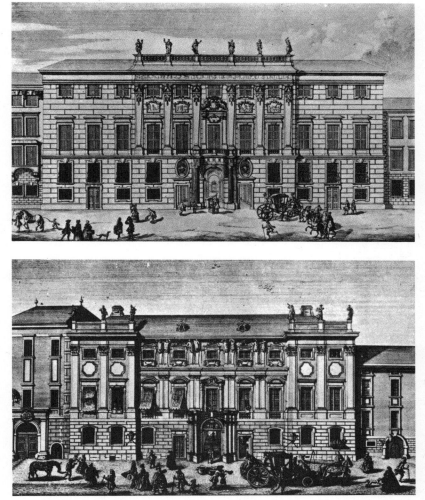

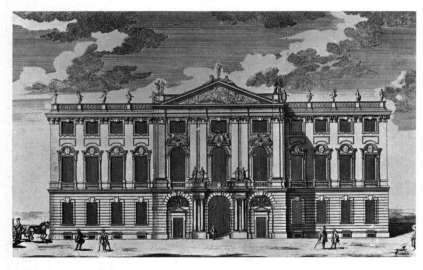

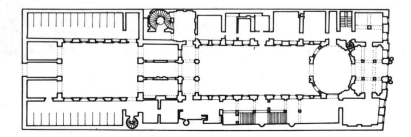

and extension, and, in spite of its scale, expresses the intimate and sensuous approach of that epoch.

Historical Synthesis and Formal Differentiation

The great Late Baroque palace architecture of Austria was born when the Turks were defeated outside Vienna in 1683.[25] The Austrian victory was a decisive turning point in the history of the country, which assumed the role of a leading power in Europe. Its artistic program had a clear political basis, and the principal aim was to outdo the art of its French rival, Louis XIV. We have already mentioned the fundamental contribution of Fischer von Erlach, who had just finished his studies in Italy and was ready to put his exceptional talent at the service of the Austrian emperor. We have mentioned in particular his project for the "Austrian Versailles"—Schönbrunn. Our analysis, however, demonstrated an approach which was quite different from the French *esprit de système.* The reasons are several: a stronger medieval tradition, a closer contact with Italy, and above all the late birth of the Austrian Baroque. It is, in fact, usually characterized as a *Spätstil,* and therefore was a synthesis rather than a particular axiomatic system.

The Austrian approach becomes evident when we look at the urban structure of Vienna. Medieval Vienna was an exceptionally concentrated city and it also had an exceptionally powerful focus: the tall tower of St. Stephen's Cathedral. After 1683 no attempt was made to transform this dense organism by means of geometrical planning. Many new buildings were erected but the Gothic street pattern was left intact. The Baroque additions to the city formed a ring around the old core, separated from the latter by a belt of open land in front of the fortifications. The structure may be compared to that of the planet Saturn.[26] This ring was composed of hundreds of garden-palaces, which in general were oriented toward the old focus. The solution, thus, may be understood as a variation on the Baroque themes of centralization and extension, but without the Cartesian geometrization found in Paris and Turin. Because of the rising land the outer ring allowed for a free view toward the city proper; all the garden-palaces were, so to speak, belvederes. The effect must have been splendid, as testified by Lady Montague, wife of the English ambassador to Turkey, who visited Vienna in 1716: "I must own I never saw a place so perfectly delightful as the faubourg of Vienna."[27] The choice of an elevated position goes back to the Middle Ages, and it was generally preferred in the great palaces and *Reichsstifte* of the Central European Late Baroque. The singular synthesis of sacred and secular architecture in the Austrian *Staatskunst* is also expressed in this way, because, in Sedlmayr's words, "the buildings of this kind are not profane. They are the residences of the terrestrial Gods, of the German Apollo, of Hercules, of the German Mars and their paladins; they constitute a sphere, sacred

in itself, which is equaled on the level of religious art, and which indeed surpasses the latter for a short time."[28]

The architectural concretization of the great theme is due mainly to Fischer von Erlach. His project for Schönbrunn, and his numerous designs for garden-palaces from the 1690s, initiated the rich development of the Austrian Baroque. Some of his buildings remained on paper, and others have since disappeared, such as the above-mentioned palace for Count Althan and the *Lustgartengebäude* for Count Strattmann and Count Schlick. Elsewhere, however, palaces have been preserved that illustrate his basic intentions. The castle of Engelhartstetten in Niederweiden (c.1694) is an interesting synthesis of French and Italian concepts. The oval rotunda with symmetrical wings evidently stems from Le Vau's Château du Raincy and Vaux-le-Vicomte, but the plastic articulation gives testimony to Fischer's Berninian background.[29] The design for the palace of Klesheim outside Salzburg (1700–9) is more original. Between two symmetrical wings containing the *appartements* we find a splendid skeletal vestibule with a monumental double-flight staircase attached behind the large arcaded windows of the garden wall. In spite of the Italianate articulation, a truly new kind of monumentality is created here which convincingly represents the Austrian ideals. Fischer's projects for garden-palaces culminated with his monumental design of such a structure for King Frederick I of Prussia (1704), which appears as an enlarged version of the central part of his first Schönbrunn project.[30]

It was, however, Fischer's rival, Johann Lucas von Hildebrandt, who was to design the most accomplished garden-palaces of the Austrian Baroque. Soon after his return from Italy, where he had spent his childhood and youth, Hildebrandt started the construction of a splendid palace for Count Mansfeld-Fondi (1697). The building is known today under the name of the Schwarzenberg Palace, after the family which took it over in 1716.[31] The almost freestanding *corps-de-logis* consists of a domed salon between two wings, following the well-known model by Le Vau. The articulation, however, shows a strong desire for integration and enrichment. A colossal order of pilasters gives coherence to a lively and sensitive plastic articulation that clearly shows the Italian background of the architect. Tall hipped roofs are put over the wings, but they do not serve to identify the single volumes in the French manner. Instead they integrate the wings proper with the recessed parts that flank the central rotunda. The two parts are also integrated by the above-mentioned pilasters, but they are simultaneously differentiated, for the pilasters on the central part of the building (which included the salon) are coupled. The coupled pilasters, however, appear on a smooth background, whereas the wall of the wings is rusticated. The wings have a more massive appearance, whereas the central part is simultaneously emphasized and opened up. An equally conscious and meaningful articulation is scarcely to be found in any

348. *Vienna, Daun-Kinsky Palace, detail of the façade.*
349. *Vienna, Daun-Kinsky Palace, interior.*

other work of the period, and testifies to Hildebrandt's exceptional abilities. His basic aim may be defined as simultaneous unification and differentiation, by means of a simple but obviously rich treatment of the wall. In this respect he proves to be the true follower of Borromini. Fischer von Erlach's different approach is illustrated by the modifications he carried out after Prince Schwarzenberg took over the palace. Fischer enlarged the windows of the central garden *risalto*, allowing them to penetrate through the architrave and frieze. The continuous wall of Hildebrandt is thereby transformed into a juxtaposition of volumes in the Berninian manner. In general, the Schwarzenberg Palace demonstrates how the Austrian architects tried to surpass their French counterparts by combining the more modern plans of the French with the richness of Italian articulation. The original masterpieces which resulted rank among the most accomplished achievements of Baroque palace architecture.[32] The Schwarzenberg Palace is also notable for its treatment of exterior space. The large *cour d'honneur* is approached by symmetrically disposed undulating ramps, which are echoed in the curved termination of the flanking service buildings. Again we see echoes of Hildebrandt's Italian background and remember the contemporaneous Borrominian revival in Rome, which was due to Specchi and De Sanctis. The service buildings, the garden walls, and the main *corps-de-logis* are joined together by a sophisticated use of surface continuity. On the garden side a similarly interesting layout of walls, stairs, and fountains was planned. It was also to have incorporated the ingenious garden-pavilion mentioned in Chapter One.

Between 1700 and 1706 Hildebrandt built the smaller Starhemberg-Schönburg Palace in Vienna. The beautifully integrated *corps-de-logis* of this garden-palace is organized around a diagonally disposed oval vestibule and an octagonal salon. The vestibule was originally open and created a transition between the building and the *cour d'honneur*. The salon was crowned by a skeletal belvedere perforated by large chasuble-shaped windows.[33] Both façades are integrated by a continuous order of colossal pilasters, which appear in a coupled version on the *ressaut* of the vestibule. The windows of the basement and the main floor are joined together by diagonally disposed Borrominian window frames, which seem to open up the wall. In general, the palace represents the most advanced achievement in any country around the turn of the century, already introducing the eighteenth-century concepts of an integrated, freestanding volume and a continuous enveloping wall.

Hildebrandt's career as a palace architect culminated with the great Belvedere, the Viennese palace built for Prince Eugene of Savoy, whose leading role in the military life of the Austrian Empire made him the Emperor's equal.[34] The extensive layout consists of two parts, the Lower Belvedere and the larger Upper Belvedere. By about 1700 Hildebrandt had worked out a plan for the gardens and incorporated a general

354. *Prague, Villa Portheim, façade overlooking the garden.*
355. *Prague, Villa Amerika, façade.*

356. *Prague, Villa Amerika, doorway.*

357. *Pommersfelden, Schloss, detail of the façade.*   358. *Pommersfelden, Schloss, façade.*

359. *Pommersfelden, Schloss, façade overlooking the garden.*

360. *Pommersfelden, Schloss, detail of the stables.*

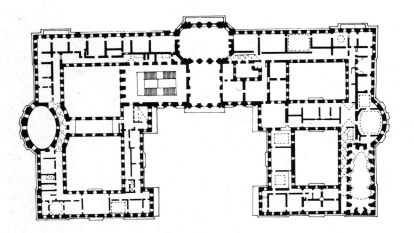

project for the lower palace, which was finally built between 1714 and 1716. The idea of adding the larger building at the top of the hill must stem from a later date; it was erected in 1721–22. The result is a very original organism, in which the infinite perspective of the Baroque garden has been transformed into an enclosed space. The elements of *parterre* and *bosquet* are still there, but they now form part of a more intimate and private world. At the same time, however, the upper palace dominates the surrounding space like a medieval castle—a convincing synthesis of local tradition, foreign importation, and the new eighteenth-century approach to space.[35] The Belvedere gardens are today perfectly restored and offer the most enchanting experience of a Late Baroque exterior space.

The lower palace is based on a relatively conventional *cour d'honneur* plan; because of its irregular site, it fans out from the narrow entrance. The gate is preceded by a half-oval space, an idea probably developed independently of Delamair's buildings in Paris.[36] The main rooms of the palace are contained within a relatively small *ressaut* which has a double-height salon in the middle and is integrated with the extended wings by means of an ingenious interpenetration of volumes. The flanking rooms of the *ressaut* have the same roof as the wings, but display the wall articulation of the central salon. A continuous entablature also helps to tie the different parts together, whereas the treatment of the wall shows sophisticated variations. Hardly anywhere else is Hildebrandt's mastery so convincingly evident.

In the upper palace the same characteristics appear splendidly enriched and varied. The building is preceded by a large *cour d'honneur* on the upper level. The beautiful entrance gate attests to Hildebrandt's original and inventive spirit.[37] From a distance the palace appears as a flat surface with a richly modeled silhouette. A large water basin blocks the longitudinal axis and forces the visitor to approach the building obliquely. As a result the rich interplay of large volumes is perceived: the transparent vestibule in the middle, the flanking three-story *appartements*, and the corner pavilions. The various volumes are unified by a continuous, albeit differentiated, wall. A similar treatment characterizes the garden façade. Because of the sloping land, what was a basement on the other side has become a ground floor, and the three-story wings are united by the upper part of the protruding salon to form a majestic front. The sloping land also allowed for an ingenious solution to the interior distribution of spaces. From the entrance a flight of stairs leads half a story down to the *sala terrena*, and another flight half a story up to the main salon. This split-level disposition gives a feeling of spatial continuity hardly found in any other Baroque palace. The character of the *sala terrena* is defined by powerful atlantes which carry the baldachin-shaped vault. The staircase is circumscribed by a skeletal structure of herm-pilasters be-

367. *Würzburg, Residenz, façade overlooking the courtyard.*
368. *Würzburg, Residenz, façade overlooking the garden.*

tween which the wall is perforated by doors, windows, and niches. The plastic articulation and the decoration are extremely rich. In the great Marmorsaal the infinite formal variations of the interior and exterior are synthesized in a system of coupled composite pilasters which have a simple majestic conviction. All in all, the Upper Belvedere may be considered the greatest single achievement of Late Baroque secular architecture, uniting all the basic intentions of the epoch into a highly original synthesis. The volumetric integration and the skin-like outer wall are related to contemporary French solutions, but Hildebrandt's articulation is different. It is characterized neither by French restraint nor by Italian plasticity, but is an entirely new invention: a vibrating, seemingly alive surface whose forms appear, disappear, and change like the characters in a fairy tale. And still the compositional logic is strict and convincing.

Although the most original Austrian contributions to Late Baroque architecture are found among the garden-palaces, we must also say a few words about the city-palaces. Very early in his career Fischer von Erlach was given several large commissions for such residences by members of the Austrian aristocracy. His first work, the Strattmann Palace (1692), was completely rebuilt later, but a print shows a richly elaborate building with *ressauts* articulated by colossal pilasters at both ends and five recessed bays in between. The main stories are put over a rusticated basement, like Bernini's Palazzo Chigi-Odescalchi in Rome. Prince Eugene's city-palace in the Himmelpfortgasse (1696), in which the whole façade shows a colossal order over a rusticated base, is more convincing. The long, relatively flat wall is enriched by strong plastic accents: an appropriately monumental work is the result. A still closer affinity to the Berninian model is shown by the Batthyány Palace (1699–1706) in Vienna. The projection of the central *ressaut* is very slight, and the building is best described as a single rusticated wall where the five central bays have become distinguished by the application of colossal herm-pilasters. The detailing is particularly sensitive and contributes to the general attractive character of the façade. The later Viennese palaces of Fischer represent more restrained variations on the same theme, so that they approach certain solutions of Palladio. In the Böhmische Hofkanzlei (1708–14) and the Trautson Palace (project 1709; construction begun 1710), for instance, the central *ressaut* is crowned by a triangular pediment and is in general more strongly differentiated from the rest of the façade.

The Daun-Kinsky Palace by Hildebrandt (1713–16) shows a characteristic difference of approach. Rather than stressing the particular character of the central *ressaut*, Hildebrandt makes it appear as a variation within a continuous wall. The façade is also unified horizontally and vertically by a sophisticated treatment of the windows: their frames are partly repeated all along the building, and partly differentiated in the central bays; the windows of the basement and the first floor are joined

372, 373. *Würzburg, Residenz, staircase.*
374. *Würzburg, Residenz, staircase.*▷
375. *Würzburg, Residenz, Kaisersaal.*▷

◁ 376. *Würzburg, Residenz, Gartensaal.*

377. *B. Neumann: "medium" project for the Hofburg in Vienna, plan.*
378. *B. Neumann: "medium" project for the Hofburg in Vienna, section.*
379. *B. Neumann: "large" project for the Hofburg in Vienna, plan.*

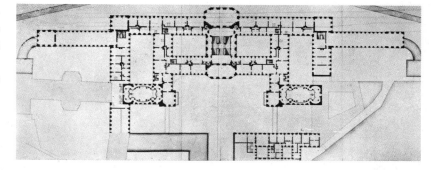

together by means of original detailing. The concave portal, whose broken segment gable embraces the richly decorated central window on the first floor, is particularly beautiful. The Daun-Kinsky Palace is marked by Hildebrandt's wish for simultaneous integration and differentiation, and it may be considered the most accomplished among the city-palaces of the Austrian Baroque.[38]

Expressive Articulation

Eighteenth-century Bohemia had a more peripheral relationship with Austria's *Staatskunst*. We find there an active Counter-Reformatory movement, and a correspondingly dominant ecclesiastical architecture. However, many beautiful city-palaces were built in Prague, and country seats in the provinces. As in Vienna, the secular architecture of the Late Baroque was introduced by Fischer von Erlach in the Clam-Gallas Palace in Prague (1713). The somewhat complex façade with three *ressauts* and a picturesque silhouette must have attracted the Bohemians, because it became a model for the major palaces of the local masters, Johann Santini Aichel and Kilian Ignaz Dientzenhofer.

Fischer's appearance, however, had been preceded by that of Giovanni Battista Alliprandi, who built the garden-palace at Liblice (1699) in imitation of Fischer's large *Lustgartengebäude* and the Lobkowitz Palace in Prague (1703), following Fischer's general idea of a rotunda between symmetrical wings.[39] The disposition of the Clam-Gallas Palace was varied by Santini Aichel in his Thun-Hohenstein Palace (1710–20; sculptural work after 1720), where the three *ressauts* are integrated with the rest of the wall by means of ingenious transitional bays. The articulation shows Santini Aichel's lack of true plasticity: thin profiles and surreal details are drawn on the surface. The general character is accentuated by its contrast with Matthias Braun's splendid dynamic eagles which flank the entrance. The same personal approach is found in Santini Aichel's castle of Karlová Koruna (Karlskrone), near Chlumec (1720–21). The plan shows a central rotunda interpenetrated by three diagonally disposed square blocks. H. G. Franz has shown that the unusual solution derives from a garden-pavilion project by Fischer von Erlach.[40]

The Clam-Gallas scheme was also varied in Kilian Ignaz Dientzenhofer's Sylva-Tarouca Palace in Prague (1743–51), where it is combined with a continuous giant order and Hildebrandtian details. The façade is a fine example of simultaneous integration and differentiation. The attractive building contains a splendid staircase. Among Dientzenhofer's works much attention has always been given to the garden-palace he built for Count Michna after his return from Vienna in 1717. Generally known as the Villa Amerika, its layout consists of three small pavilions which form an open *cour d'honneur*. The central one is an exceptionally

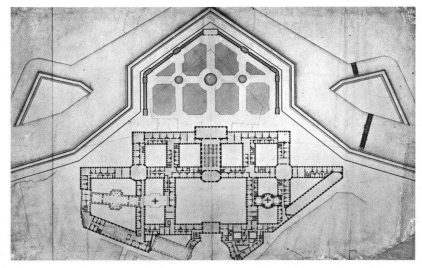

380. B. Neumann: *project for the Stuttgart Residenz, plan.*
381. B. Neumann: *project for the Stuttgart Residenz, elevation of the palace.*
382. B. Neumann: *project for the Stuttgart Residenz, section and plan of the palace.*

fine essay in Hildebrandtian articulation, combined with a characteristic Bohemian plasticity. The composition of the garden-palace Kilian Ignaz built for himself in Prague between 1725 and 1728, known as the Villa Portheim, is more personal. The rusticated ground floor is characterized by horizontal continuity, whereas the volumes become free in the vertical direction. They are, however, unified by a cornice over the main story, and the cornices of the towers which mark the corners of the building also continue to form the usual horizontal break in the Mansard roof—a new plastic interpretation of the Hildebrandtian concept of simultaneous integration and differentiation.[41] In general, the Bohemian palaces are based on Austrian models, but a characteristic preference for dynamic and strongly expressive solutions is evident.

Integration and Regional Variation

In spite of direct relationships and common aims, architecture in Germany was more complex than in Austria. The first Schönbrunn project certainly created a model for further development, but French and Italian influence was also very strong, and the large and divided country required different regional interpretations. A decisive step toward the creation of a German Late Baroque palace architecture is represented by the great Schloss Pommersfelden built (1711–18) by Johann Dientzenhofer for the Elector of Mainz and Bishop of Bamberg, Lothar Franz von Schönborn. The client was one of the great personalities of the Baroque Age, and had a typical passion for building. His large palace, however, was not luxurious in our sense of the word; rather it was a natural and necessary part of the Baroque way of life. Lothar Franz was a dilettante architect himself, and was very concerned that his building have the French *commodité*. He therefore asked Boffrand to visit Pommersfelden as a consultant, and through his nephew in Vienna, Friedrich Karl, he also received the help of Hildebrandt. The basic disposition shows a "U" with a *cour d'honneur* and pronounced corner pavilions. A most impressive novel feature, however, is the dominant central unit which incorporates a great symmetrical staircase, a *sala terrena*, and the Imperial Hall. The idea of making an unusually large and monumental staircase is supposed to have originated with Lothar Franz himself, but the truly splendid solution must be due to a trained architect. The documentation published by Bruno Grimschitz[42] shows that the interior of the staircase is mainly the work of Hildebrandt, whereas the other principal rooms and the exterior clearly represent the style of Johann Dientzenhofer.[43] The contributions of both, however, are equally important. The monumental staircase introduced an element that was to play a prime role in the palaces of Neumann; the same may be said of its powerful exterior.

The palace in Pommersfelden therefore forms a natural introduction to Neumann's work. In 1719, still at the very beginning of his career, he was commissioned to build the great Residenz in Würzburg for Prince-Bishop Johann Philipp Franz von Schönborn, a brother of Friedrich Karl, who became his successor in 1729. Whereas the bishops of Würzburg traditionally resided in the old Marienberg Castle, Johann Philipp Franz wanted to move into the city. In 1720 the foundation-stone for the new residence was laid and in 1723 the northwestern pavilion was completed. The history of the large enterprise is rather complex. In 1723 Neumann was sent to Paris to obtain advice from De Cotte and Boffrand, and in 1724 Boffrand himself visited Würzburg. The other members of the Schönborn family also brought their architects—Maximilian von Welsch from Mainz and Hildebrandt from Vienna. Moreover, Johann Dientzenhofer was employed from the beginning as a supervisor. In spite of many complications, Neumann succeeded in carrying out his original idea, which combines a *cour d'honneur* disposition with inner courtyards in both wings. It was thereby possible to give the large building a better distribution of spaces and shorter internal communications, for a general improvement of the *commodité*. A dominant central volume, as in Pommersfelden, was naturally incorporated. Originally Neumann planned two spacious staircases, symmetrically disposed on each side of the central vestibule. One of them was taken away because of the negative judgment of the French architects, and Boffrand even found the remaining one "rather large." Except for this change, the Frenchmen did not have much direct influence on the planning. Von Welsch, however, added the oval *ressauts* on the transverse axis, and Hildebrandt contributed considerably to the decoration of the main façades and the Hofkirche. In 1737 the staircase was built, followed in 1739 by the rest of the *corps-de-logis*; in 1744 the building itself was finished except for the interior decoration, which was still going on when Neumann died in 1753. Here Neumann had as collaborators the great Italian fresco painter Giambattista Tiepolo and the stuccoist Antonio Bossi. The result is one of the most extraordinary *Gesamtkunstwerke* in existence.[44]

The position of the Residenz at the periphery of the old town of Würzburg, its functional character, and the limited size of the building site together determined the solution, which may be called a synthesis of city-palace and garden-palace. In general, then, the building appears as a massive block, but it contains a *cour d'honneur* and a longitudinal axis which is actively related to the natural space beyond. As a consequence the problem of architectural articulation was basically different from the indeterminate extension we encounter in Versailles, the Grand Trianon, or Stupinigi. The Residenz in Würzburg is a finished, carefully balanced composition, but the unusual size made the achievement of such a result very difficult indeed. If we study other projects of the epoch, it is tempting to conclude that Neumann alone was capable of solving the task.[45] In doing this he exploited the Italian, French, and

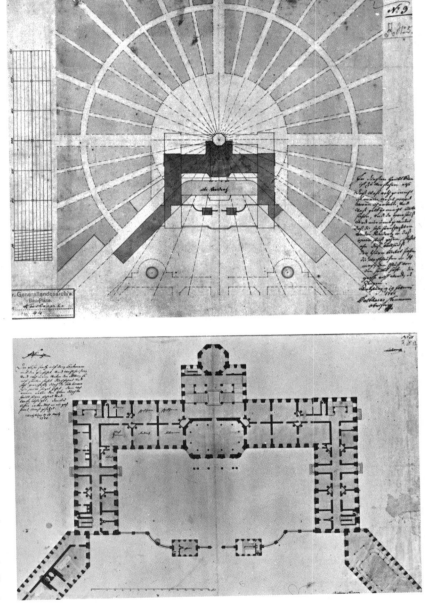

385. *B. Neumann: project for the Residenz at Karlsruhe, engraving.*

386. *B. Neumann: "small" project for the Residenz at Karlsruhe, relation of the palace to the park.*

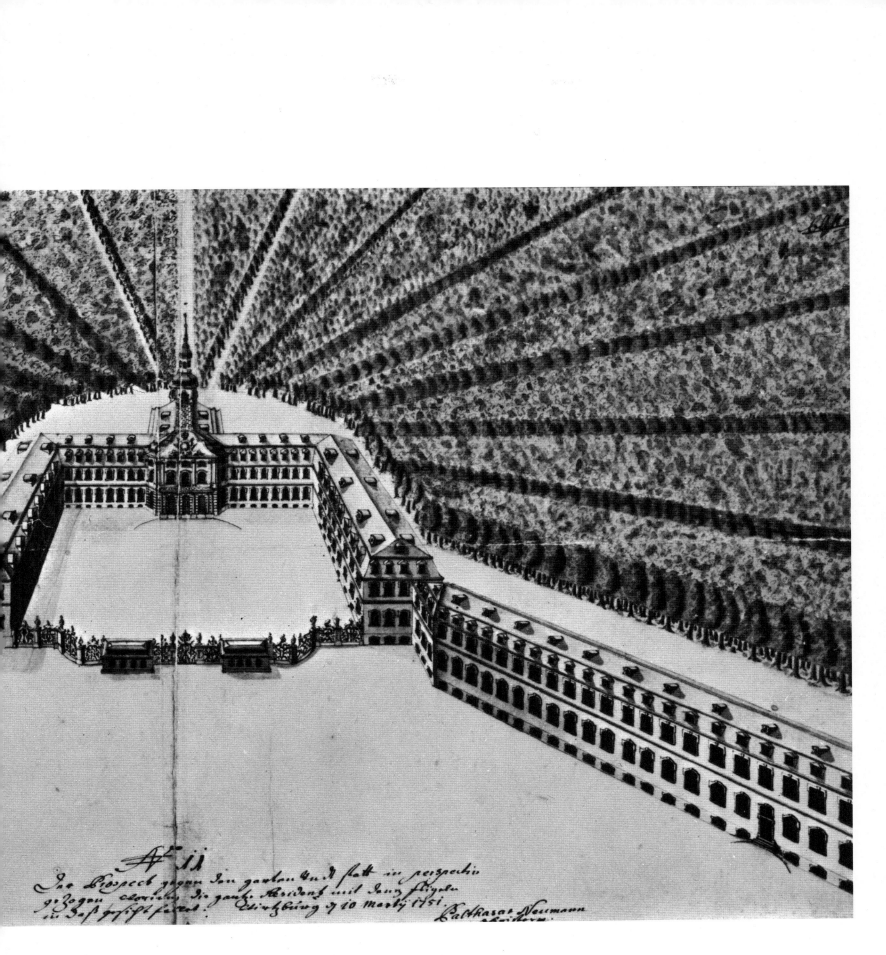

N.° 11

Der Prospect gegen den garten Und statt in perspectiv
gezogen ebenfalls, die gantze Residentz mit denen flügeln
in das geschick setzet. Würtzburg d 10 Martij 1751.
Balthasar Neumann

387. *Munich, Amalienburg, plan.*
388, 389. *Munich, Amalienburg, exterior.*

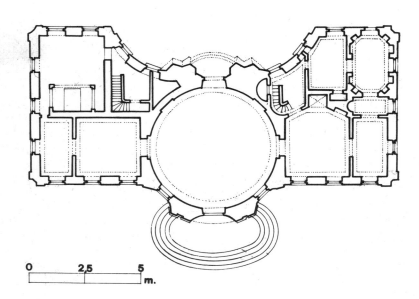

Austrian traditions. Thus we find the varied surface continuity of Hildebrandt, but also the plastic power of the Italian Baroque and the simple monumental relationships of French classicism. Continuity is secured by carrying the main cornices all around the building and by the employment of repeated, superimposed orders. The latter, however, are varied to express the basic organization and to characterize the different parts of the building. In the *cour d'honneur* the pilasters are replaced by columns, which are also used to integrate the central wall and the wings as Delamair had done in the Hôtel de Soubise. The plain Doric order of the ground floor gives emphasis to the splendid composite one of the *bel-étage*, which finds a festive conclusion in Hildebrandt's richly shaped gable. The garden *ressaut* shows a particularly strong Hildebrandtian influence and recalls the Upper Belvedere. The ingenious transitional bays on both sides of the *ressaut* proper also vary a typical idea of the Viennese master. The strong plasticity of the main front, however, constitutes an original German interpretation of the classical tradition.

The famous disposition of the interior also represents a new contribution, although it was prepared for in Pommersfelden.[46] Vestibule, Gartensaal, staircase, Weisser Saal, and Kaisersaal form a group of incomparable magnificence and beauty. The Gartensaal is a most charming interpretation of the traditional cave-like *sala terrena*, showing a large but relatively low vault resting on a ring of slender and elegant columns, so that a large baldachin is formed. The Rococo stuccoes of Antonio Bossi (1749) create the impression of the vault growing out of the columns like a large plant. The staircase may be the most grandiose ever built. When one mounts it, the side walls are not visible and the room appears infinitely extended under Tiepolo's glorious frescoes.[47] The Weisser Saal forms a necessary pause between the splendors of the staircase and the octagonal Kaisersaal, which constitutes a worthy focus for the whole palace. The relatively simple structure of this room consists of a succession of fluted, composite columns which carry a great vault, interpenetrated by large openings on the diagonals and the main axis. This monumental space is crowned by Tiepolo's airy frescoes.

Simultaneous with the construction of the palace in Würzburg, Neumann designed projects for other residences, none of which, however, was built.[48] During 1746 and 1747 he designed three different plans for the Hofburg in Vienna.[49] The basic disposition of the "small" project (which exists in three variations) is closely related to the original solution in Würzburg, that is, a combination of a three-wing *cour d'honneur* layout and block-like side buildings with inner courtyards. In addition, the *corps-de-logis* has been split by means of narrow courts to allow for a freer distribution of the rooms and a more systematic sequence of spaces along the main axis. One plan shows a great symmetrical staircase inside the garden *ressaut*. The ideas are monumentalized in the "me-dium" project, in which the *corps-de-logis* has two fully developed inner courtyards, shedding light on the most magnificent staircase Neumann ever designed. The "large" project, finally, presupposed a complete rebuilding of the area, leaving only Joseph Emanuel Fischer von Erlach's Hofbibliothek and Hofreitschule. And still the layout repeats the ideas of the smaller projects. The former *cour d'honneur*, however, has become a great enclosed court which is preceded by a new *cour d'honneur* with curved "embracing" lateral walls. In general, the design appears as a gigantic modernization of a royal city-palace such as the Louvre. Unfortunately, we do not have drawings that show how Neumann would have articulated the immense façades.

Between 1747 and 1749 Neumann devised a "small" and a "large" project for the Residenz in Stuttgart. As in Vienna, he wanted to give the building a clear urban definition. Therefore he planned a very wide *cour d'honneur* which seems to embrace the whole town. In the "small" project it consists of a series of curved and straight spaces which gradually concentrate the movement on the central axis of the palace.[50] In the "large" project the solution is simpler but basically analogous. On the other side of the building the axis continues into the garden. However, the three elements—town, palace, and garden—are related in a way that is quite different from the seventeenth-century solution at Versailles. Whereas Versailles is planned by means of a superior infinite geometrical system, which gives all the elements an indeterminate extension, Stuttgart shows an interaction of three clearly defined units: the compact medieval town, the extended but "finite" palace, and the garden whose axis is halted by a curved pavilion—a monumentalized version of the eighteenth-century approach found in some of the layouts of Hildebrandt. The palace in Stuttgart should have consisted of exceptionally long and narrow wings. It therefore put Neumann's skill in articulation to the test. His solution is masterly in its powerful simplicity: by joining together the two upper floors he could erect a colossal order over a rusticated base, thereby giving tectonic substance to the continuous wall.[51] Integration is also secured by large Mansard roofs. The danger of monotony is avoided by voluminous *ressauts*, which are united with the wall by means of transitional bays as in Würzburg, and by a continuous succession of windows. The most interesting feature of the interior is a monumental staircase which projects into the garden like a transparent glazed cage. The "small" project for Stuttgart shows Neumann at his best, and would have represented the culmination of eighteenth-century palace architecture. In spite of its great scale the "large" project is spatially and plastically less interesting.[52]

The third of Neumann's unexecuted projects for large residences is of a more special kind. In 1750 it was decided to rebuild the palace at Karlsruhe, and a competition among several architects was organized.

More than the others, Neumann tried to respect the symbolic city plan, dating from 1715, which was centered on an octagonal tower. Thirty-two roads radiate from this tower, symbolizing a centralized state. As the first "servant" of this state, the count had his palace erected within one quarter of the circle and joined to the tower by a narrow passage. Neumann retained this system, and above all did not want to pull the tower down, as suggested by some of the other participants in the competition. His project is preserved in three variations. The first and largest shows a characteristic combination of *cour d'honneur* and block-like building with two inner courtyards. The tower is directly incorporated into the garden front as a central *ressaut*. Because of its particular situation, the *cour d'honneur* widens at angles of 45° on both sides, embracing the whole town. A rectangular, more private court, however, has been added in front of the *corps-de-logis*. As usual, the interior spaces are planned around a large symmetrically disposed staircase. The second project is somewhat simplified: the inner courtyards have been omitted, and the building appears as a normal U-shaped organism with oblique wings added toward the town. The *corps-de-logis* is joined to the old tower by a truly monumental staircase. The exterior articulation is unusually simple, and indicates that Neumann here was planning for a Protestant ruler. In Karlsruhe Neumann also demonstrated his exceptional abilities in giving a simple and convincing form to a complex building type. All three residences, in fact, combine powerful simplicity with spatial and plastic richness.

Neumann's great achievement dominates German eighteenth-century architecture in such a way that the buildings of other architects appear less interesting than they actually are. We must at least mention two other talented architects who carried out works of considerable importance. François de Cuvilliés was born in France and studied with Jacques-François Blondel. He worked, however, in Bavaria, where he introduced the Rococo, which he developed into an exceptionally rich mode of expression. His early Piosasque de Non Palace in Munich (1726–32) had a very interesting plan showing a series of fluent, interdependent spaces which may be compared to certain contemporary designs of Kilian Ignaz Dientzenhofer.[53] The façade is typically French, having large windows with semicircular or segmental arches. The application of decorative detail, though, shows a German lack of restraint. In the Holnstein Palace (1733–37), Cuvilliés arrived at a certain synthesis of the French tradition and the monumental city-palace introduced by Fischer von Erlach. A colossal order is erected over a rusticated base, and the windows of the *bel-étage* have "Italian" frames. The masterpiece of Cuvilliés is his famous Amalienburg, a *Lusthaus* in the garden of Munich's Nymphenburg Palace (1734–40). Here the elements of the garden-palace are reduced to essentials. Within a simple rectangle, a central rotunda is pushed forward to form a shallow *cour d'honneur* on one side and a *ressaut* on the other. The court is part of a circle, whereas the *ressaut* has a more complex shape, creating a continuous transition with the wings. The articulation is extraordinarily sensitive and gives the building the appearance of a precious jewel box. And, in fact, it does contain a jewel: it is the circular salon which, together with Boffrand's salon in the Hôtel de Soubise, may be considered the most enchanting interior of the Rococo. Whereas Boffrand's room preserves a certain tectonic structure, Cuvilliés' salon dissolves in a play of ornaments, mirrors, and pastel colors.

In Westphalia, far up in northwestern Germany, we also find a certain regional style which was created by the talented architect Johann Conrad von Schlaun. Schlaun's work is very rich and includes everything from farms and mansions to churches and palaces.[54] Among the latter we may single out the ingenious Erbdrostenhof in Münster (1755–57). The triangular building site led to a most original variation on the semi-urban palace. Placing the building along one side of the triangle, Schlaun obtained one shorter façade which curves concavely to form a *cour d'honneur*. On the other side a convex façade expands into the garden, but a concave central *ressaut* indicates a counter-movement. The fluid handling of the façades is also reflected in the plans, which show rooms of an almost Gaudi-like irregularity. The articulation of the exterior, however, is simple and powerful. It is based on the well-known theme of a colossal order over a rusticated base. The central *ressauts* of both façades are integrated with the wings by means of transitional bays, a solution probably inspired by the works of Neumann. Toward the end of his career Schlaun also built the large bishop's residence—called simply the Schloss—in Münster (1767–73), which appears as a personal and quite successful variation on themes from Neumann's great projects. Above all Schlaun's forms are softer; his rounded corners and undulating *ressauts* show how Borromini's spirit remained alive until the final stages of Late Baroque architecture, although it is here combined with many other traditions. In any case, Schlaun's works represent a singular synthesis of local and cosmopolitan tendencies.

Picturesque Pompousness

The palaces of the Russian Late Baroque are also based on a symbiosis of local character and foreign importation. They are mainly the work of Bartolomeo Rastrelli, an Italian who had spent his childhood in France and settled in St. Petersburg at the age of sixteen.[55] He may therefore be considered a Russian architect, and indeed his works confirm this interpretation. Under the tsarinas Anna Ivanovna and Elizabeth he functioned as court architect and built the principal palaces in and outside the capital. This period in Russian history was characterized by the desire to make manifest the power of the state, a desire born of a generally

390. *Munich, Amalienburg, circular salon.*
391. *Munich, Amalienburg, circular salon, detail of the decorations.* ▷

394. *Münster, Erbdrostenhof, exterior.*
395. *Münster, Schloss, detail of the façade.*

healthy and optimistic national attitude. Whereas Western Europe had reached the end of an epoch, Russian civilization was still at its height, and its architecture was truly Baroque.

Rastrelli's first works, the Biron Palace in Jelgava (1736–40) and the Summer Palace in St. Petersburg (1740–44; demolished), still have an undecided character, and the somewhat complicated Voronzov Palace (1746–55) in St. Petersburg represents a transitional phase. In the Stroganov Palace (1750–54), however, he found his highly efficient and personal style. Whereas the former buildings had been garden-palaces with a *cour d'honneur*, the Stroganov Palace is a typical urban building, erected on a corner site of the Nevski Prospekt. The two façades show the usual theme of a colossal order over a rusticated base. The interpretation, however, is quite new and "Russian." The distinguishing feature consists of *ressauts* (which only approximately correspond to the plan behind) defined by strongly emphasized, applied columns. The *ressauts* terminate in segmental frontispieces which resemble the gables of the old Russian churches. All the other details have a pronouncedly picturesque character and contribute to a generally lively and somewhat pompous expression. We find, thus, neither the tectonic substance of Neumann nor the sophisticated articulation of Hildebrandt, but a kind of childlike (albeit positive) joy in presenting a splendid façade. Between 1747 and 1752 Rastrelli remodeled the garden-palace of Mon Plaisir at Peterhof, built by Le Blond in 1716–17. Its character resembles that of the Stroganov Palace, but the articulation is simpler and more restrained. The plastically shaped, swelling Mansard roofs are related to certain solutions of Hildebrandt and Neumann, and their common source is probably the Russian onion dome. In Rastrelli's great palace at Tsarskoe Selo (1752–56), the motifs from the Stroganov Palace are multiplied and repeated ad infinitum to create a festive but somewhat oppressive effect. The long narrow building consists of more massive *ressauts* alternating with skeletal stretches of wall, all tied together rhythmically by colossal columns. In the Winter Palace at St. Petersburg (1732–36; new project 1753; reconstruction 1754–62) the articulation is more convincing. The four façades of the large, approximately square block with an inner courtyard appear as variations on the same theme, again taken from the Stroganov Palace. The giant columns dominate toward the river Neva; the other elevations show an alternation of emphasized *ressauts* and more neutral parts. The general character introduced in the Stroganov Palace is enriched by the use of columns on the ground floor as well, but what is gained in abundance is lost in formal structure. Again the façades have only an approximate correspondence to the distribution of spaces behind. The classical members, hence, have been given a purely decorative function.

396. *St. Petersburg (Leningrad), Stroganov Palace, façade.*

Stylistic Pluralism

The Baroque architecture of England stems from the grand but somewhat arbitrary style of Wren. Early in the eighteenth century, however, a new creative originality became manifest in the works of John Vanbrugh and Nicholas Hawksmoor.[56] Their careers in general correspond to the reigns of Queen Anne and King George I, an epoch which saw the hegemony of the aristocracy and the wealthy bourgeoisie more firmly fixed. It was also the period when England's power reached its peak with the great victories of the Duke of Marlborough over Louis XIV. Thus, the social and political basis for a Baroque artistic development was present, but idiosyncratic English traditions interfered in various ways, and the result was a highly original national style. These traditions involve four factors crucial to English art: Gothicism, Protestantism, Palladianism, and Democracy. England therefore could not accept the rhetorical style of the Catholic Counter-Reformation, nor could it adopt the infinite axes and perspectives of French state architecture.

It is not easy to distinguish between the individual contributions of John Vanbrugh and Nicholas Hawksmoor, who usually worked in close collaboration. We may safely say that together they created the English Baroque. Whereas Vanbrugh was a colorful and internationally oriented architect equally active as a playwright, Hawksmoor was a true professional who concentrated on working with his drawing-pen. Their collaboration started in 1699 when Vanbrugh, apparently without any experience, was commissioned to design Castle Howard in Yorkshire for Charles Howard, Earl of Carlisle.[57] Hawksmoor became his assistant and draftsman, and the result was a truly splendid building. The great layout comprises a wealth of diverse elements and constitutes a piece of historical architecture even more comprehensive than Fischer von Erlach's first Schönbrunn project. The main entrance gate was designed as a medieval tower in classical disguise, surrounded by four Egyptian obelisks. The side entrances have the form of something between a Roman arch and a Turkish kiosk. The *cour d'honneur* (with lateral base courts) evidently has French origins, but appears dressed up in a heavy Doric style which may recall such Mannerist buildings as Giulio Romano's Palazzo del Tè in Mantua. The *corps-de-logis* is crowned by a Roman dome, while the lateral courts are flanked by tall medieval towers. The succession of giant pilasters toward the garden has a Palladian flavor, whereas the garden axis terminates in the portico of a classical temple. Among the garden "furniture" we find another temple resembling Palladio's Villa Rotonda, a pyramid, a crenellated medieval tower, a large obelisk, a wall with bastions, and a large mausoleum shaped like a Roman round temple (the latter by Hawksmoor, 1729–40).

It may seem incredible that so many varied elements can be unified into a whole. The general layout, however, is as ingenious as the details

are disparate. From the approximately square central block, straight wings branch out to form an extended, somewhat monotonous, garden front. Other wings, broken at right angles, define the spacious *cour d'honneur*, and curved arcades are added in the corners to create a more organic connection with the central block.[58] The base courts are integrated with the wings of the *cour d'honneur* by means of lateral axes of symmetry. The transverse axis of the *cour d'honneur* also continues through the base courts and their lateral entrances, flanked by the above-mentioned medieval towers—a very sophisticated layout which is hardly equaled by any French or Central European work from the same date. Within this systematic order, however, the individual parts have a different characterization. This is not done by means of classical principles such as superposition: the changes are more thoroughgoing and founded on sophisticated psychological principles. Perhaps "romantic" would be an appropriate descriptive term, but it is a romanticism that goes beyond the idyllic fairy tale. Castle Howard, in fact, is surreal, almost frightening in its expression. One also experiences this feeling in its interiors: the great hall has a *Zweischalig* structure, in which a central dome on corner pillars is surrounded by an outer zone containing symmetrically disposed stairs and a gallery. The expression, however, is basically different from the light and liberating spaces of, say, Vittone. Instead we are in a profoundly serious world which seems to exist outside human time and space.

In Blenheim Palace Vanbrugh and Hawksmoor carried their ideas further. The great house was offered by Crown and Parliament to the Duke of Marlborough after his great victory over Louis XIV in 1704. Queen Anne herself presented him with Woodstock Park near Oxford, and Vanbrugh tells us that "her Majesty was Graciously pleased to build the duke an house as a monument of his Glorious Actions." In June of 1705, Lord Treasurer Godolphin signed a warrant appointing Vanbrugh architect of the works. The design, however, had been made several months before, and ten days after the warrant had been issued, the foundation-stone was laid. In 1712 construction ceased because the Marlboroughs were exiled, but in 1716 work was resumed. Finally, in 1727, the large project was finished by Hawksmoor.

The general layout is a monumentalized version of Castle Howard. In Blenheim the *cour d'honneur* of the former house has become a truly "great court," whose transverse axis succeeds in integrating the base courts. The corners of the *corps-de-logis* are marked by vertically oriented pavilions that indicate a regular rectangular block. On this ancient fortress plan, however, is superimposed a modern palace whose *cour d'honneur* penetrates into the mass. This ingenious combination constitutes one of the most powerful palaces in the history of Baroque architecture. The disposition of the *corps-de-logis* has a certain affinity with Neumann's

398. *Castle Howard, general plan.*
399. *Castle Howard, plan of the central core.*
400. *Castle Howard, perspective view, from an engraving in Vitruvius Britannicus.* ▷

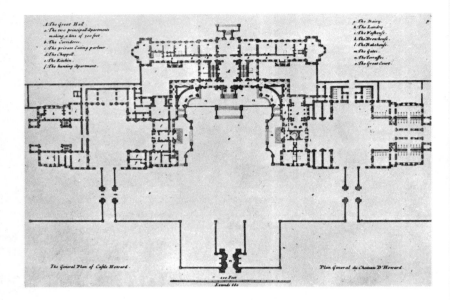

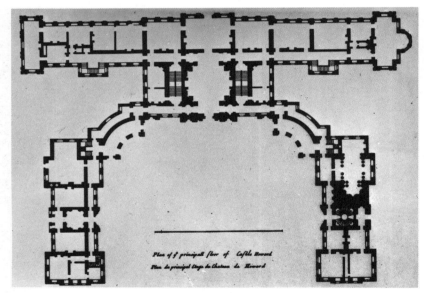

401. *Castle Howard, façade overlooking the garden.*
402. *Castle Howard, northwest façade.*

great projects made four decades later; it contains two inner courts and a great central hall flanked by symmetrical staircases. The hall has double spatial delimitation as in Castle Howard, but the dimensions are more monumental and the character less surreal. The colossal Corinthian columns in the corners, the triumphal arch on the main axis, and the majestic arcades on both sides create a space reminiscent of Roman grandeur. The exterior articulation also shows an integration of the heterogeneous elements found in Castle Howard. The great classical inheritance is still present, but its elements have been fused into a new synthetic language. The general character is powerful and masculine, but the heavy masses are crowned by delicately perforated turrets and attics of almost Borrominian invention. Toward the garden the serious expression is made slightly milder by the use of neutral wall surfaces and fluted orders, and the side elevations contain an almost idyllic note through the introduction of semicircular bays in the center. The desire for individual characterization found in Castle Howard is thus still present, but the means have become more sophisticated and the variations occur within one convincingly integrated form.

After Blenheim Vanbrugh and Hawksmoor planned several other houses, among which we may single out the original and fascinating Seaton Delaval in Northumberland (1720–21)—a sort of "abbreviation" of Blenheim. The main building is a square block with corner towers to which a great court with flanking base courts has been attached. The two elements, however, are added together rather than integrated, although the rusticated base creates a kind of continuity. In general, the medieval character is more pronounced than in the former works. The two main façades have different characterizations: colossal Tuscan-Doric columns flank the entrance toward the court, whereas the garden façade has a deep Ionic portico in the middle. Seaton Delaval is a singular synthesis of a medieval castle and a Renaissance villa, its massing and details having an almost frightening strength.[59]

Conclusion

Our discussion of the Late Baroque palace has shown many individual and regional approaches, but also some basic common trends. In general we may say that the longitudinal axis of the High Baroque tended to lose its dominant importance, even in the residences of the absolutist princes and monarchs. It no longer formed the core of an infinitely extended system; the range became more restricted and intimate. The love for intimate and comfortable living even led many French architects to block the axis entirely, a tendency usually found in conjunction with other Rococo characteristics, such as the abolition of the classical orders and the introduction of a continuous enveloping wall. In Central Europe, however, the longitudinal axis was maintained to give the palace the de-

405. *Blenheim Palace, plan.*
406. *Blenheim Palace, façade overlooking the courtyard.*

407. *Blenheim Palace, aerial view.*

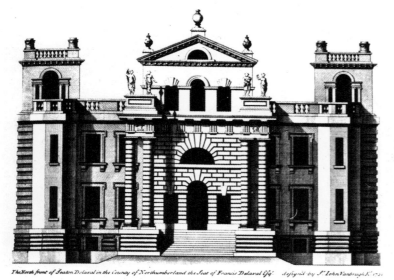

The North front of Seaton Delaval in the County of Northumberland the Seat of Francis Delaval Esq.   design'd by Sr. John Vanbrugh Kt. 1721

Elevation Septentrionale de Seaton Delaval dans le
Comte de Northumberland Maison de Delaval Esqr.

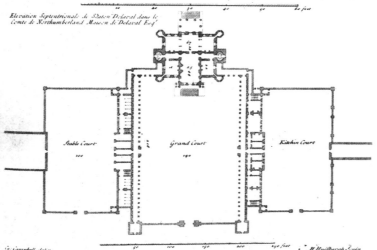

Stable Court

Grand Court

Kitchin Court

sired representative distribution of spaces. But the system to which it belongs no longer pretends to be universal and infinite. The great residences of Neumann, for instance, are not timeless solutions like Versailles, but have an empirical relationship to a concrete environment. Without trying to communicate actively with the surroundings, the palace turned inward, so to speak—a tendency which is also expressed by the growing interest in splendidly decorated salons. In these interiors a brilliant but transitory life took place; it is deeply significant that a transitional space such as the staircase became the focus of the great Central European residences. The weakening and gradual abolition of seventeenth-century dogmatism was also combined with a new pluralistic approach which aimed at a fuller understanding of all phenomena and an adequate characterization of the individual situation. We have found this approach in the works of Juvarra, and particularly in the historical architecture of Fischer von Erlach and Vanbrugh. In spite of their very personal character, the buildings of Vanbrugh therefore represent a general trend of this epoch. For a better understanding of this fact we may compare Blenheim with Le Vau's Vaux-le-Vicomte. In both palaces a modern plan with *cour d'honneur* is superimposed on a medieval castle with a tower in each corner.[60] But there is a basic difference: whereas Le Vau's building represents a departure from the ancient model, Vanbrugh intends his as a return. (Between them we find the systematic, truly seventeenth-century works of Hardouin-Mansart.) Vanbrugh's works therefore predict the imminent death of the classical palace. In 1717, in fact, he built himself a medieval castle in Greenwich, the first truly Romantic house of the eighteenth century.

Being a manifestation of a hierarchical and relatively static society, the Baroque palace could not survive the Enlightenment, social upheavals, and the Industrial Revolution. However, its forms have haunted architects until our own time, not only because of its pretensions, but because the new types of habitation inherited its basic problems of articulation. Ever since Roman times, in fact, when apartment buildings were put up in Ostia, architects have been concerned with the problem of giving identity and structure to extended multi-story buildings. Whereas the palace was a functionally differentiated organism which called for a correspondingly articulate form, the apartment house has a repetitive, uniform content. Already during the eighteenth century we see how architects attempted to endow such a building type with interest by using elements and principles borrowed from the palace. We find, for instance, that functionally equal stories appear as if they were a basement, a mezzanine, a *piano nobile*, and an attic. Such a division between form and content is already very pronounced in the Late Baroque palaces of St. Petersburg. Thus we see that the architects as usual were more sensitive and receptive to the changing times than were their clients.

409. *Seaton Delaval, façade overlooking the courtyard.*
410. *Seaton Delaval, detail of the Ionic portico.*

411. *Seaton Delaval, façade overlooking the garden.*

Introduction

The seventeenth century offered a certain degree of choice between different systems or ways of life, yet each system claimed to have absolute and comprehensive validity. The pluralism of the Baroque Age, therefore, represented a possibility rather than a reality. During the eighteenth century, however, Baroque pretensions faded away. Man realized that life can be lived in different ways and thus made pluralism operative. But of course he still needed a synthesis. Instead of a dogmatic synthesis by exclusion, the new synthesis became one of inclusion—that is, a result of experience and empirical research. This is the background for the new historical approach that distinguishes Late Baroque architecture. As experiences differed from place to place, so architecture also attained a more pronounced original color than before. Some architects, however, tried to create an all-inclusive synthesis, viewing their situation as being determined by the total inheritance from the past. We have seen that Fischer von Erlach was the great protagonist of this approach. Others tried to abstract universal and natural elements from history. Believing that the Greek temple was derived from the primitive hut, they arrived at Neoclassicism. Others again must have felt the death of the old systems as a tragic loss, or the new freedom as a state of uncertainty and conflict. As a result the architecture of the eighteenth century presents an extremely complex picture, not easily reduced to a few common denominators. Because of the slow change in society and the strong vestiges of an architectural tradition, we can, however, still point out the significant structural types, and we can study the varieties of their interpretation. In the preceding chapters we have discussed the church and the palace. Both were inherited from the seventeenth century, and both originally represented the chief Baroque systems: Counter-Reformatory Catholicism and absolutist monarchy. Although they were in a certain sense opposed to the ideas of the Enlightenment, these two systems had such a powerful momentum in their rich traditions that they could not merely wither away. Moreover, at any time in history man needs forms which define his position in an ordered universe—and, as we all know, new forms hardly come into being through revolutions. But the church and the palace had to adapt to the new psychic and social climate, and profound changes took place during the first decades of the eighteenth century. The churches of Christoph Dientzenhofer were still Baroque in their directed dynamic movement. But gradually the intentions changed, the movement lost its impetus, the center became more important than the path. And the center was no longer experienced as the origin of outwardly radiating forces. Instead the movement was turned inward, and infinity became a spiritual rather than a concrete geometrical phenomenon. The exterior correspondingly lost importance, and became primarily a "tower," whose relation to the environment was basically different from the active interaction sought in the High Baroque.[1] In secular architecture we find an analogous development. The longitudinal axis directed toward infinity is blocked, within or outside the building, and great halls and staircases become the primary elements. As the wall is where the transition between inside and outside takes place, its articulation undergoes a corresponding change. Continuity becomes essential, and enclosed volumes replace the openly extended skeletal organisms of Guarini and Hardouin-Mansart. All these formal innovations express a general cultural change, as outlined above. They may, however, develop in different ways, due to local and personal factors. Below we will take a closer look at these varieties of Late Baroque architecture.

France

When discussing the church in Chapter Two, it was not thought necessary to include any examples from France. Being primarily an architecture of the state, the French Baroque always favored the palace, so that the church played only a secondary role. Architects such as François Mansart and Jules Hardouin-Mansart, however, still built masterpieces which remain within the great Roman Catholic tradition, although the latter with his royal chapel in Versailles introduced a new approach which was to have a basic importance for subsequent developments. The use of a straight entablature on columns did away with Baroque complication and produced a new, self-evident clarity. In 1714 Louis-Gérard de Cordemoy wrote that the Val-de-Grâce "would have been infinitely more beautiful if in place of all these useless and heavy arcades, these pilasters and these broad pillars . . . columns had been used for carrying the rest of the building."[2] Cordemoy's main concern was to see the pillars of a church replaced by columns. The idea was taken over by Marc-Antoine Laugier, who found a source of inspiration in Gothic churches. He wrote: "I enter Notre-Dame. . . . At first glance my attention is captured, my imagination is struck by the size, the height and *the unobstructed view of the vast nave*. . . .[3] From there I go to St-Sulpice. . . . I see nothing but heaviness and clumsiness. There are heavy arches set between heavy pilasters. . . ."[4] As a consequence, Laugier wanted to design a church that combined a slender Gothic structure with the beauty of classical detail—an aim, however, which had already been satisfied by the Versailles chapel. In fact, we do not have to wait for the Neoclassical churches built after 1750 to find at least some of these new ideas realized. St-Sébastien in Nancy, built between 1720 and 1731 by Jean-Nicolas Jennesson, has Ionic columns carrying a barrel vault, whereas St-Jacques in Lunéville (1730–45), based on a plan by Boffrand, comes close to the spatial effect of a Gothic *Hallenkirche*. Elegant columns divide nave and aisles, carrying a series of "Bohemian caps" and a saucer dome over the crossing. The Ste-Madeleine in Besançon by Nicolas Nicole

(1746–66), where the columns of the nave are coupled, is very light and sophisticated. Around the crossing a pillar is substituted for one of each pair so that the space appears varied within a continuous system.

French eighteenth-century ecclesiastical architecture followed its own course and did not form part of general Late Baroque developments. Its great masterpiece was Ste-Geneviève (the Panthéon) in Paris by Jacques-Germain Soufflot (first project 1756; alterations 1764–90). In spite of its Neoclassical forms, Ste-Geneviève essentially represents the diaphanous centralized church of the eighteenth century, a convincing synthesis of European tradition and specifically French intentions.[5] An exception to the general trend is offered by Juste-Aurèle Meissonier's project for the façade of St-Sulpice (1726). The concave-convex movement and the use of plastic members is fully Baroque, although some details give the façade a Rococo look. Obviously, the project was in too strong a contrast with French taste, which generally concealed what it permitted of expressive forms behind an elegant though rational and reserved façade. After a competition held in 1731, St-Sulpice was given a two-story columnar portico by Jean-Nicolas Servandoni.

The French eighteenth-century palace has already been discussed in detail. We have seen how its reserved façades hide a differentiated organism that serves an elegant and sophisticated life. Its character is not enclosed; the many large openings create an airiness and a happy feeling of communication with the surroundings. Instead of Baroque extension, though, we may talk about an enjoyment of the qualities of light and color. Moreover, space remains intimate although it may dissolve in ornament, decoration, and transparency. For the most part, the buildings are relatively small, and have a private rather than official character. There are, however, some exceptions, such as Boffrand's projects for the Château de Malgrange and his Château de Lunéville for the Duke of Lorraine (1709–19). In general, Lunéville is characterized by the neutral walls of the period, yet a certain absolutist pretension is introduced by the application of a giant temple front on each side of the building where it is penetrated by the longitudinal axis.

The French eighteenth century had no truly great architects like those of the seventeenth. Instead we find a very high general quality, which represented the last refined stage of a continuous tradition. Pierre Lassurance and more especially Robert de Cotte gave Hardouin-Mansart's regular organisms a new and elegant interpretation which in general has remained as our notion of the eighteenth-century or Rococo house. Their approach was continued among the members of the next generation by such architects as Jean Courtonne and Jacques V Gabriel. A more individual attitude is found in the works of the talented Pierre-Alexis Delamair, whose masterpiece, the Hôtel de Soubise, sums up the tradition in an admirable way. We may compare his achievement to that of

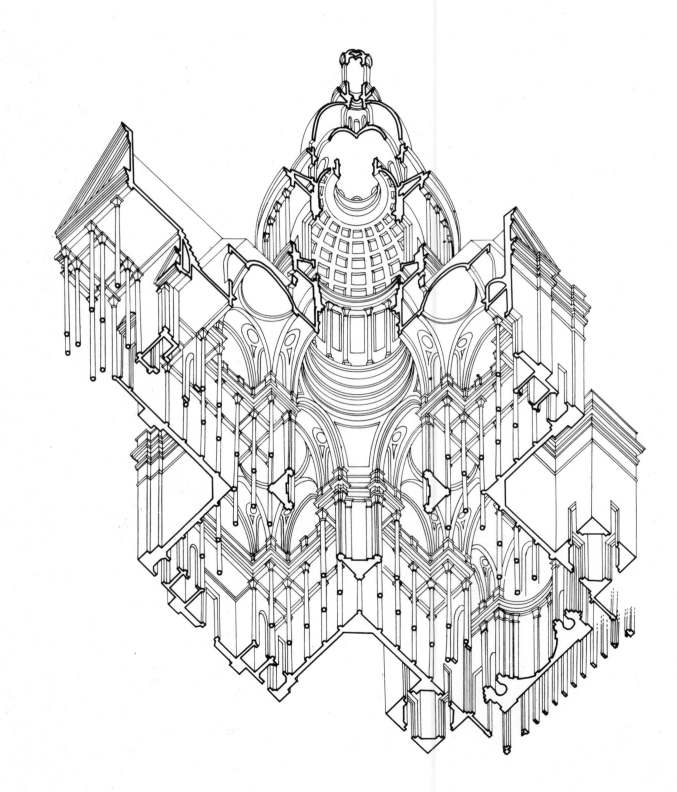

419. *Lunéville, the château, aerial view.*

420. *J.-A. Meissonier: drawing for a Rococo interior.*

421. *Marino, S. Maria del Rosario, axonometric section drawing of the interior.* ▷

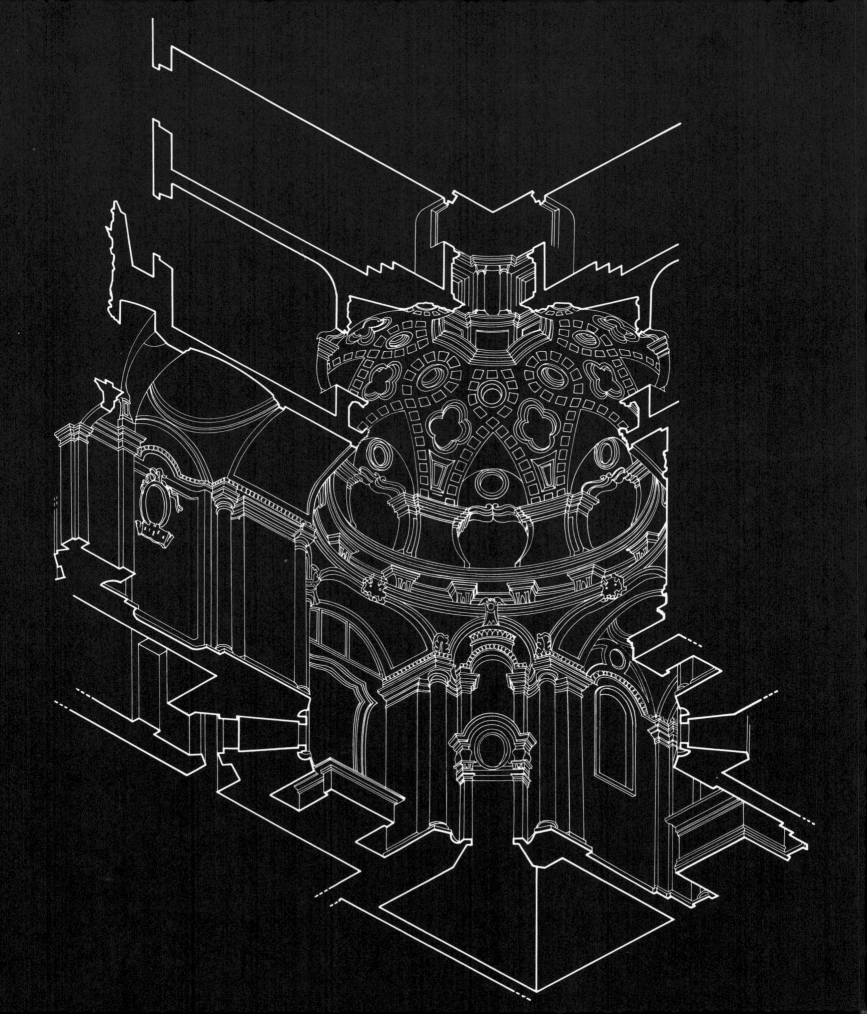

422. *Rome, S. Lorenzo in Lucina, baptistery, view of the lantern.*
423. *Rome, S. Maria Maggiore, façade.*

422. Rome, S. Lorenzo in Lucina, baptistery, view of the lantern.
423. Rome, S. Maria Maggiore, façade.

Neumann in Germany, but his promising career was cut short by his powerful enemies at its very inception. Boffrand, who succeeded Delamair, had an exceptionally long and prolific career. His works are distinguished by a certain Baroque power, but he could also create such Rococo masterpieces as the oval salon in the Hôtel de Soubise. In general he is the most versatile of eighteenth-century French architects and the only pronouncedly French representative of the new pluralism, a fact we have already pointed out in Chapter One when referring to the varied articulation of his Hôtel Amelot de Gournay.[6] The next generation, with Ange-Jacques Gabriel, already followed Neoclassicism, although the Place Louis XV (today the Place de la Concorde), with its synthesis of landscape and urban milieu, must be counted among the masterpieces of Late Baroque city planning. Gabriel's buildings evidently aimed at a revival of the *grand goût* of the seventeenth century.

In general, French Late Baroque and Rococo architecture finishes with the generation of architects born about 1670, while in Germany it culminates with the generation born around 1690. The only exception is Juste-Aurèle Meissonier, whose exceptionally fluid and dynamic Rococo creations transcend the normal limits of surface articulation. His transitory forms really represent the end of a development, a fact that is also confirmed by the limited number of his achievements.[7] "After all, for Meissonier decorativism was the only way in which he could realize his artistic ideas. As for the tradition to which these ideas belong, one must look to Italian Baroque illusionism, of which they are the last offspring. Rocaille, just like the fantastic stage settings of the Bibiena and Burnacini families, was an extreme attempt to create a work of illusion and idealize reality. The fact that this illusionism is only to be found in decoration proves that it was an *extreme* attempt."[8]

Italy

During the eighteenth century Roman architecture was reduced to a provincial status. Only on the urban level do we find works that reach wide importance, first of all those of Alessandro Specchi, who is the only notable representative in Rome of the generation born about 1670—the generation of Boffrand, Johann Dientzenhofer, Hildebrandt, and Vanbrugh. The fundamental contribution of Specchi was to revive the ideas of Borromini in a period dominated by the dry academicism of Carlo Fontana. The next generation, however, is quite well represented, although none of the architects in question had importance beyond the local scene. Filippo Raguzzini designed the ingenious Piazza S. Ignazio discussed earlier, as well as the Ospedale di S. Gallicano (1724–26), but is generally rather clumsy. Giuseppe Sardi evidently had considerable talent and built the original church of S. Maria del Rosario in Marino as early as 1710–13. The main space represents a somewhat crude anticipation of the rotunda theme of Kilian Ignaz Dientzenhofer and Johann Michael Fischer, and is covered by a dome that transforms the interlacing ribs of Guarini into an ornament. The diaphanous tendencies present, however, are confirmed in Sardi's later works, such as the very beautiful baptismal chapel in S. Lorenzo in Lucina (1721).[9] The talented Gabriele Valvassori, whose Palazzo Doria we have discussed, also belongs to the same generation. All were inspired by the Borrominian tradition, whereas those born in the 1690s became conscious of the crisis of Late Baroque architecture, a crisis which led to Valvassori's professional demise. However, Pietro Passalacqua and Domenico Gregorini created a truly Baroque work in the façade and vestibule for Rome's S. Croce in Gerusalemme (1743), whereas the works of Ferdinando Fuga are characterized by a rather ambivalent approach. His early buildings, such as the attractive Cellamare Chapel in Naples (1726–27), show a fluid articulation and interesting use of light. Later, though, he becomes increasingly dry and uninspired. An exception is his celebrated façade and portico for S. Maria Maggiore (1735–43) in Rome, whose rich play of light and dark is produced by a double system of superimposed columns. The inner order, together with arches and stretches of entablature, forms a continuous skeleton on which *aediculae* are applied. The articulate character becomes most evident when compared with the extremely infelicitous façade of S. Giovanni in Laterano (1733–36), built by Alessandro Galilei. More than any other structure in Rome, the latter confirms the death of a great tradition.

In the preceding chapters we have given much attention to the architecture of Piedmont, which is of exceptional quality in the eighteenth century. Only the Piedmontese succeeded in making an essential contribution to the development of Late Baroque architecture, ecclesiastical as well as secular. Foremost among them is Filippo Juvarra. He was active in several places, including his native Messina, but it was in Turin that he could develop his pluralistic approach, which demonstrates that a great work of architecture cannot exist in a vacuum: it needs a comprehensive milieu to become truly meaningful. Instead of concentrating on a particular theme, Juvarra treated every building type and space according to the circumstances. His work as a stage designer must have sharpened his powers of characterization. In fact, his buildings appear as "characters," or actors, on the stage of urban life. At the same time, however, his solutions are variations on general themes derived from the European tradition. His works therefore have a rare human range and represent one of the greatest achievements of Late Baroque architecture.[10] His singular combination of function and sentiment, great form and splendid detail is also truly Italian. The extraordinary talent of Juvarra is already evident in his first important work, and the only one he left behind in Rome, the splendid little Antamori Chapel

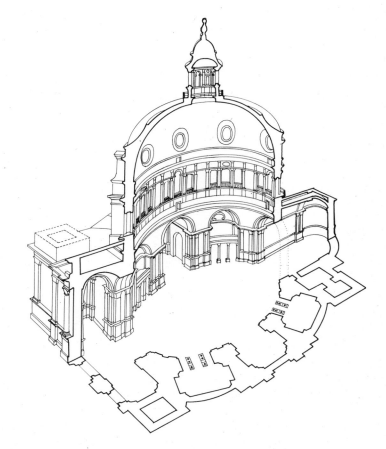

in S. Girolamo della Carità (1708). Here a simple rectangular space has been transformed into a miracle of Baroque expression by means of a baldachin vault, which creates an effect of centralization, and a large oval window behind the altar which introduces a longitudinal movement. The forces are concentrated on the head of S. Filippo Neri who appears with incredible persuasive power in front of the window.

When Juvarra went to Turin in 1714 several local architects of some standing were already active there and in the province. We have already mentioned Michelangelo Garove, who worked for Guarini and later tried to continue the dramatic and powerful style of his master. The generation of Juvarra is represented by Francesco Gallo and Gian Giacomo Plantery. Gallo, who lived in Mondovì, did a great deal of work in the province and built an extraordinary number of parish churches.[11] They show a general high quality, but remain within the limits of local construction ability. We ought, however, to mention the great dome he erected on Vittozzi's unfinished Santuario di Vicoforte, a pilgrimage church at Mondovì (1728–33). Plantery worked mostly as a palace architect in Turin, demonstrating a considerable talent for spatial and plastic articulation.

The Piedmontese Baroque was long-lived and even around 1700 several architects were born who carried on the tradition from Guarini and Juvarra. Costanzo Michela, who was active from about 1730, must have been born around the turn of the century. His little church of S. Marta in Agliè (1740–60) is a tour de force of plastic modeling. The elongated building appears as a continuous undulating shape, whose movement even includes the tall *campanile*. The interior consists of a succession of three centralized units—the first hexagonal, the second square with internally convex walls, and the third circular. The three are integrated by means of pulsating juxtaposition, and the walls appear as neutral surfaces alternating with wide wall-pillars. The surprisingly original and mature work reveals an exceptional talent, which somehow did not find the opportunity for further development.

Benedetto Alfieri became a royal architect in 1739 after starting his career as a lawyer. His varied production continues the pluralistic approach of Juvarra, ranging from Neoclassical forms to such bizarre creations as the semicircular S. Giovanni Battista in Carignano (1757–64). By far the most important representative of the last generation, however, is Bernardo Vittone, who, with his parish church at Borgo d'Ale (1770–78), created one of the very last masterpieces of Baroque architecture. Unlike Juvarra, Vittone concentrated on a few basic themes which he varied throughout his long and prolific career. We have already analyzed his diaphanous centralized space, which also appears in several smaller works, such as the splendid chapels in the Villa del Cardinale and the Villa Cipresso, both built about 1750 in the Turinese hills. Here again we find

the characteristic skeletal system of pillars, arches, and ribs forming an open baldachin of incomparable beauty. Vittone's secular works are overshadowed by his churches, but there too he proved to be an architect capable of functional and urbanistically valid solutions. Educated in Rome, assistant to Juvarra and editor of Guarini's architectural writings, Vittone had the best opportunity to pursue a great official career. Instead he chose to build churches for religious orders and small communities. "With courageous determination he went against the prevailing fashion of the day, denouncing the absurdity of wasting an artistic heritage such as that of the Baroque, which was far from having exhausted its potential and capable of receiving an extraordinary stimulus from the contact with the new scientific methodologies."[12]

Next to Piedmont, the most interesting Late Baroque architecture in Italy is found in the southern parts of the country. In Naples we encounter a colorful architectural milieu and a truly inventive personality in Ferdinando Sanfelice. Among his many and varied works his staircases have primary importance. The mild Neapolitan climate made it possible to insert this typical Late Baroque element as an open skeletal structure between the *cortile* and the garden. A beautiful example is offered by the Palazzo Sanfelice ·(1725–28), which belonged to the architect's family.[13] Earlier, in 1708, Sanfelice made a *scalinata* in front of the church of S. Giovanni a Carbonara, which in important respects prefigures the Spanish Stairs in Rome.

Neoclassical tendencies appear in the large Royal Palace at Caserta (1751–74) by Luigi Vanvitelli. The layout shows a somewhat paradoxical combination of an infinite Baroque axis and an enclosed rectangular building which should have resembled the Escorial with corner towers and a dome in the center.[14] The rectangular block is simply pierced by a longitudinal movement without any attempt at creating a more organic interaction between building and environment. Inside, however, the axis is related to the four courtyards in quite an interesting way, and the skeletal octagonal hall in the center, to which a grand staircase is added, has a magnificent effect. In general, Caserta represents an attempt at combining the Baroque concepts of center and extension with the Neoclassical desire for a finished, schematic form, with a certain rigidity as the result.

The most lively and colorful Late Baroque architecture in Italy is found in Sicily. After the earthquake in 1693, which devastated most of the towns in the eastern part of the island, a glorious period of reconstruction began. The architectural center was Catania, whose Late Baroque townscape is due mainly to the prolific Giovanni Battista Vaccarini. His works have a high quality, but do not represent any significant contribution to European developments. Among his many designs we may single out the façade of Catania Cathedral (1734–58), which is articulated

429. *Agliè, S. Marta, plan.*
430. *Carignano, S. Giovanni, plan.*
431. *Alessandria, Palazzo Ghilini, atrium.*

432. *Naples, Palazzo Sanfelice, interior view of the staircase.*
433. *Naples, Palazzo Sanfelice, exterior view of the staircase.*▷

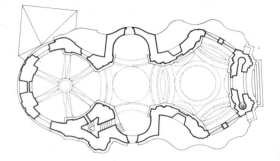

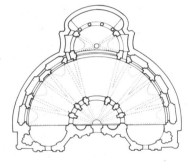

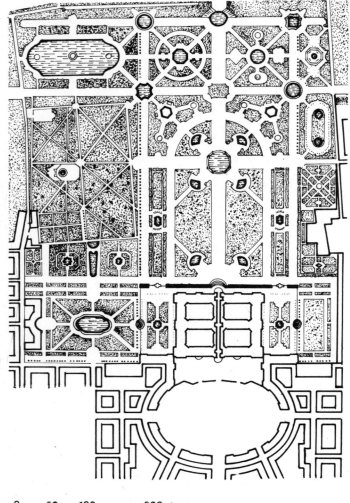

0 50 100 200
m.

by superimposed freestanding columns indicating an undulating horizontal movement, and his more original church of S. Agata (1735–67), whose façade shows a Borrominian interplay of convex and concave bays. The work of Vaccarini was continued by Stefano Ittar.[15]

The most significant works of the Sicilian Baroque, however, are found in the towns of the southeast. Some of them were entirely rebuilt on new sites, such as the picturesque Noto, which offers a singular example of a Baroque townscape. Its orthogonal layout is centered on a complex of richly articulated public buildings, mainly the creations of Rosario Gagliardi and Vincenzo Sinatra. The former is undoubtedly one of the most interesting architects of his generation, but so far his work has never been the subject of serious research.[16] His masterpiece is S. Giorgio in Ragusa Ibla (1746–66), whose front represents a convincing synthesis of façade and *campanile*. The solution consists simply of topping a two-story basilica façade with a third, narrower story which houses the bells. The vertical direction is emphasized by triads of superimposed freestanding columns, which also create a dynamic movement toward the center of the façade. The Northern motif of the tower-façade, which is most unusual in Italy, had a long tradition in Sicily. It culminated in the work of Gagliardi, whose solutions may be compared to contemporary works in Central Europe. In the church of S. Giorgio in Modica all three stories are united by superimposed columns. The façade, however, is plastically less powerful than that of S. Giorgio in Ragusa Ibla, and indicates the imminent end of a tradition. It may be the work of Gagliardi himself or of his follower Sinatra.

In western Sicily the most important manifestations of Baroque architecture are the numerous villas built for the aristocrats of Palermo outside their city. Here we find a surprising variety of original plans, based on complex geometrical patterns, which are also used to integrate the main buildings with their environments. The more interesting are those originating from the inventive genius of Tommaso Maria Napoli, Dominican priest and mathematician. His Villa Palagonia (1715) represents an original variation on the usual plan of the Baroque garden-palace. It has wings forming a shallow *cour d'honneur*, and an oval *salone* in the middle. The building, however, is bent in such a way that it fans out from the entrance toward the garden. Thus the embracing function of the court and the opening up of the garden loggia are simultaneously emphasized. The entrance is furthermore distinguished by a splendid staircase, and the building is surrounded by secondary wings which follow a pattern of intersecting circles. In his Villa Valguarnera (1721) the plan is more normal, but again we find an embracing forecourt and a splendid staircase in front of the entrance. The Sicilian Baroque is in general colorful and picturesque, although it never approaches the formal dissolution of Spanish architecture.

Spain and Portugal

The tendency in Spanish architecture of the seventeenth century was to transform the wall into a continuous surface ornament. This property is already present in Francisco Bautista's cathedral of Madrid (S. Isidro), dating from after 1629. During the eighteenth century it culminated with such works as the sacristy in the Cartuja (Charterhouse) of Granada, decorated by an unknown master after 1742. Here the quite normal structural system is completely absorbed by an exuberant ornamentation. The intention behind the fascinating space was evidently to arrive at a surreal interplay of light and decoration, which transcends the rational and anthropomorphous content of classical architecture. Baroque persuasion, thus, has been transformed into a play with the transitory and perishable, which may be compared to the Rococo. A decorative approach also distinguishes the works of the Churriguera brothers who were active during the first decades of the century. The illusionistic architecture thus formed found its most famous manifestation in the *Transparente* (1721–32) in Toledo Cathedral by Narciso Tomé.[17] The construction of the *Transparente* was undertaken to provide a showcase in which the Blessed Sacrament could be exposed and venerated from both the choir and the ambulatory of the church. To fulfill this function Tomé created a chapel without walls—that is, so to speak, constructed only of light. The architect removed the Gothic vault and instead added a Vittonian light-chamber. The decorative altar scenery is thereby illuminated from above and the space becomes irrationally open.

In a spatial sense, Spanish eighteenth-century architecture does not offer anything of importance for the rest of Europe. Its decorative approach was brought across the Atlantic Ocean to Mexico and to Central and South America, where we find some of the most exuberant examples of ornamental architecture.[18]

In Portugal we encounter a somewhat more restrained style. The leading architect was a German, Johann Friedrich Ludwig, who under the name of João Federico Ludovice built the great palace-convent at Mafra (1717–30). The most original and charming works of the Portuguese Baroque, however, are found in Brazil, and are mainly the creations of the talented mulatto sculptor and architect António Francisco Lisboa, called Aleijadinho. In his works decoration again serves to emphasize the formal articulation of expansive volumes. A major example of his style is offered by S. Francisco in Ouro Preto (1766–94).

Austria

The great works of the Austrian Baroque play a leading role in the general development of the style, which explains why most of them have already been discussed above. Our comments have shown that the main aim was the development of a *Staatskunst* which could compete with the

440. Noto, *ducal palace (present-day town hall), façade.*

441. Noto, *monastery of the Salvatore and church of the Immacolata.*
442. Noto, *cathedral, façade.*
443. Ragusa Ibla, *basilica of S. Giorgio, façade.* ▷

◁ 444. Modica, S. Giorgio.

445. Bagheria (Palermo), Villa Palagonia, plan.
446. Bagheria (Palermo), Villa Palagonia, exterior.
447. Bagheria (Palermo), Villa Valguarnera.

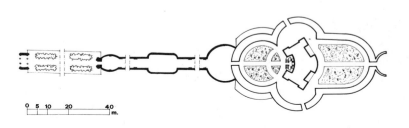

great style of Louis XIV. Palace architecture, hence, was of primary importance, whereas churches receded somewhat into the background. Many architects contributed to the variety and splendor of the Austrian Baroque, but it was chiefly the creation of Johann Bernhard Fischer von Erlach. Born in 1656, Fischer belonged to the first generation of Late Baroque architects, and when the reconstruction of Vienna started after 1683 he was practically alone on stage.[19] Fischer's historical approach gave his works a wide range and rich variation, but common to all of them is a truly Roman monumentality. One of his main themes was the domed oval, a Baroque motif *par excellence* because of its evident synthesis of centralization and extension. As a clear statement of aim it appears in his first important work, the palace at Frain (Vranov) in Moravia, built for Count Althan between 1688 and 1695. Even its position is extraordinary: like a medieval castle, the building hovers on a rock high above the dark valley of the Thaya. The main structure, the Ahnensaal, emerges as a powerful volume reminiscent of the large rotundas of Roman palaces and *thermae*. The interior has the character of a pantheon for the Althan family: in ten niches between the windows we find statues of the most prominent ancestors of Fischer's client, while the frescoes that cover the great dome depict the virtues of the house of Althan.[20] The architectural articulation is very simple: the wall is divided into a regular succession of windows and niches, flanked by flat pilasters. The vault, however, is perforated by large oval *oculi* which more than anything else determine the powerful character of the space.

An oval space was used over and over again by Fischer, and it also forms the focus of his late masterpieces, the Karlskirche (1715–37) and the Hofbibliothek (project 1716), both in Vienna.[21] The Karlskirche represents the culmination of Fischer's historical architecture, and is one of the greatest monuments of the entire epoch. A competition in 1715, in which Hildebrandt and Ferdinando Galli-Bibiena participated, was won by Fischer and the foundation-stone was laid in February of 1716. Most visitors find it difficult to form a coherent image of its heterogeneous elements. The church proper consists of a longitudinal oval crowned by a tall dome. It is preceded, however, by a wide front which has a temple portico in the middle, flanked by two Roman triumphal columns and low Baroque towers. Help toward an adequate perception of its structure is offered by Sedlmayr, who talks about an "architectural counterpoint," and gives a fascinating analysis of the complex symbolism behind Fischer's invention.[22] The most natural way of looking at it is to see the Baroque towers, the dome, and the connecting wall between them as a body with "embracing" arms like St. Peter's in Rome or François Mansart's church of the Minimes in Paris. In front of this modern organism we find three historical elements. Obviously, Fischer was inspired here by the description of Solomon's temple in the Bible. The

ancient motif, however, has been Christianized, for the reliefs on the columns and the central pediment depict the deeds and the apotheosis of S. Carlo Borromeo, to whom the church is dedicated. The composition is dominated by the crowning drum.[23] The Karlskirche, thus, really represents a synthesis of the eras of Solomon, Augustus, and Christ as well. Nowhere in the history of Baroque architecture do we find a more grandiose conception. The interior may be characterized as a Baroque cathedral. Looking forward, the space appears longitudinally directed; upon raising one's head the interior is seen to be unified into a powerful oval. The Karlskirche, however, is not part of the general development described in Chapter Two. It remains a unique work, intentionally as well as architecturally.

In the Hofbibliothek the interior is the real protagonist of the solution, whereas the exterior appears as a skin wrapped around the large volumes.[24] Again the focus is a domed oval with *oculi*, as at Frain. Two longitudinal spaces are added to show frescoes of the sciences of peace and war. And between them, in the dome, the fresco is one in glorification of the Emperor. The articulation of the exterior is based on three *ressauts* which appear as variations on the same theme. The lateral ones are crowned by the *globus terrestris* and the *globus coelestis*, accompanied by figures representing the earthly and the heavenly sciences. In the middle Pallas Athena throws Envy and Ignorance to the ground. In general the program unifies the concepts of enlightenment and monarchical absolutism and may be due to Leibniz, who demonstrated an active interest in the planned building.[25] "In the attempt to build a temple of science, Fischer's art surpassed itself."[26]

Whereas Fischer concretized the imperial aspects of Austrian state art, the works of Johann Lucas von Hildebrandt are more intimate and human. Hildebrandt already belongs to the generation of architects of the Régence and Rococo, and his work shows the sensibility and sophistication typical of the time. But it is also based on the anonymous vernacular architecture of his country, and therefore appears as particularly "real." Hildebrandt, so to speak, brought Austrian state architecture down to earth and gave it roots in its own soil. Rather than juxtaposing the present with a great past, he offers a synthesis of a more introspective, psychological nature, by means of gradual transitions between large and small, closed and open, plain and rich.

We have already cited the developmental importance of Hildebrandt's early churches and we have discussed his most important palaces in detail. A few more works, however, deserve to be mentioned. One of Hildebrandt's most splendid projects is the great plan of 1719 for the reconstruction of Stift Göttweig (the monastery had been destroyed by fire the year before). The design shows a fortified heavenly castle high on a hill overlooking the surrounding landscape. The approximately

449. *Toledo, cathedral, the Transparente.*

450. *Toledo, cathedral, the Transparente, detail of the vault.*

◁ 451. *Braga, the via crucis and church of Bom Jesus.*
452. *Ouro Preto, S. Francisco, façade.*

square monastery has strongly pronounced octagonal towers in the corners. The long wings are articulated by voluminous *ressauts* within a continuous but varied wall. The center is marked by the dome of the reconstructed Gothic church and two tall bell-towers. The gate pavilion on the bastion toward the west is a masterpiece of plastic modeling. About three-quarters of the great design was built, leaving the western front unfinished as well as the church, where the towers lack steeples and the dome is missing entirely. Nevertheless, Göttweig is one of the greatest of Baroque monasteries because of its beautiful position and the architectural quality of its finished parts. Hardly anywhere else has the concept of the *Civitas Dei* on earth been given a more magnificent interpretation. From the later years of Hildebrandt's career we may single out the project for the tower-façade of Würzburg Cathedral (1731). The solution has a certain resemblance to Gagliardi's above-mentioned façades, but Hildebrandt's design is more convincingly integrated as well as differentiated, and offers a splendid interpretation of this important theme of Late Baroque architecture.

In comparison with Fischer von Erlach and Hildebrandt, the other architects of the Austrian Baroque had a more provincial character. Some of them possessed a considerable talent and created works of originality and beauty. A particular feeling for plastic articulation distinguishes the buildings of Matthias Steinl, who created his masterpiece, the tower-façade of the abbey church at Zwettl, toward the end of his long life (1722). The extremely convincing structure consists basically of three elements: a neutral undulating surface, "positive" and "negative" figures applied to this surface, and a few elongated vertical members which tie the whole composition together. A similarly successful tower distinguishes the church of the convent in Dürnstein, initiated by Steinl in 1721 and completed in 1733 by Joseph Munggenast, who had also worked at Zwettl.[27] In the church and library of Altenburg (1731) Munggenast finally created an independent work of high quality.

A particularly rich and varied production was left behind by Johann Michael Prunner, who was active in Linz and Upper Austria. His works are clearly influenced by Hildebrandt and show a preference for continuous undulating surfaces and nervous details. Thus he often approaches a full dissolution of such classical elements as architraves and frontispieces. The latter are usually transformed into bent and broken lines which run like restless living beings across the walls. His most convincing creation is the Trinitätskirche (1714–24) in Paura near Lambach, which has a circular plan with three apses, forming thus a symbolic triangle whose corners are emphasized by towers. The building is distinguished by a successful plastic differentiation and integration, and is numbered among the most fascinating Late Baroque shrines scattered throughout Central Europe.

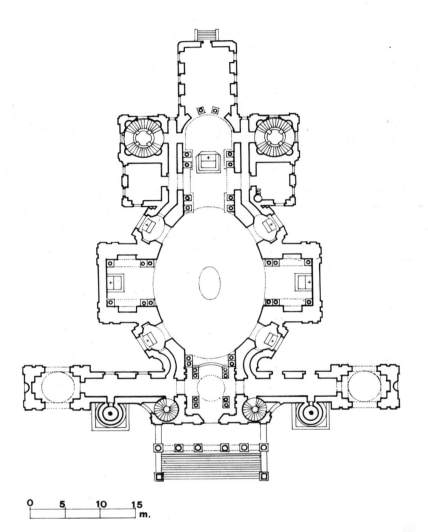

Jacob Prandtauer, however, the creator of the great monastery at Melk, was more important than any of the architects mentioned above. Still more than Hildebrandt, Prandtauer gave Austrian Baroque architecture a foundation in local crafts and building traditions. An immigrant from the Tyrol, he aided in the reconstruction of Lower Austria after the Turkish invasion, progressing from simple mason to creative architect. Among his numerous works, the monastery of St. Florian occupies one of the foremost places. It was initiated in 1686 by Carlo Antonio Carlone; Prandtauer took over its construction in 1708 and built the splendid Marmorsaal as well as the great staircase (which had been left unfinished by Carlone), one of the most beautiful in the history of Baroque architecture.

Bohemia

The architecture of Bohemia has a very specific character. From the Middle Ages it has been distinguished by a singular combination of exalted expression and logical order. As most of the architects working in Bohemia came from abroad, the Bohemian style appears to be determined by a particular *genius loci*. The brothers Christoph and Johann Dientzenhofer, for example, worked with the same themes and spatial principles, but the interpretations were different—the former being Bohemian-oriented, the latter Franconian. Perhaps the Bohemian character may be explained as a result of the joining of Slavic and German elements; at any rate, it is most evident during the Baroque period, when its immanent expressionism was exploited and strengthened by the Counter-Reformatory need for persuasion and participation.

We have already discussed in detail the significant contributions of Christoph Dientzenhofer and his son Kilian Ignaz Dientzenhofer to the development of the Late Baroque church. In fact, the two carried the spatial *ars combinatoria* of Guarini to its ultimate conclusion, realizing thereby a last great achievement in the history of European ecclesiastical architecture. Both are eminently Bohemian in their mode of expression and represent the most truly dynamic current in Late Baroque architecture. This is clearly shown by Kilian Ignaz's courtyard in the monastery of Broumov (project 1726; construction 1728-38). Here the central part of each wall protrudes into the space as if pushed forward by mighty forces. In the middle the wall bursts open, whereas the corners seem almost nonexistent. The convex central parts actually correspond to oval spaces behind, thus illustrating Kilian Ignaz's complementary treatment of mass and space. In beautifully condensed form his principles appear in the chapel of the Imperial Hospital on the Hradčany in Prague (1732-34). An octagon with internally convex sides forms the usual point of departure. Only one secondary oval, however, is added to house the altar, indicating the open character of the organism. The exterior is

455. *Vienna, Karlskirche, exterior.*
456. *Vienna, Karlskirche, detail of the exterior.*
457. *Vienna, Karlskirche, interior of the dome.* ▷

a wonderful study in plastic articulation, based on ingenious simplifica-
tions and transformations of classical motifs. We may notice how the entablature is interrupted on the main axis to give place to a large
chasuble-shaped window. A keystone indicates the weight of the small
tower above. Undoubtedly, the systematic trend in Baroque architecture,
as well as plastic dynamism, culminated with Kilian Ignaz Dientzenhofer. Toward the end of his life, however, his expression became more
calm, as in the pure and charming little church in Paštiky (1747–
51), upon which he bestowed much attention despite his poor health.

The most important of the secondary architects of Bohemia have been
mentioned above, including the elegant Giovanni Battista Alliprandi, the
extremely colorful and nervous Ottaviano Broggio, and the inventive Jakob Augustoni.[28] More detailed attention, however, must be given to
the extraordinary genius Johann Santini Aichel (Giovanni Santini).[29]
From the very beginning of his career he built in the Gothic as well
as Baroque style. His Gothic buildings arose out of a conscious demand
for the Gothic manner by his clients. This general desire, however, was
satisfied in a less direct way by other architects, and we have reason to
believe that Santini Aichel himself must have felt deeply attracted by the
Gothic forms. Our analysis of his abbeys in Sedlec and Kladruby has
shown that Santini Aichel's Gothic has a basically decorative character:
the ribs have no tectonic function, and in reality the buildings consist
of continuous surfaces onto which lines are "drawn." Another typical example is offered by his shrine of St. John Nepomuk on the Green Mountain near Ž'dár (Saar) in Moravia (1719–22). Its plan is derived from
the five-pointed star, which according to legend appeared around the
head of the saint. The exterior lacks plasticity in spite of the dominant
use of concave forms. In fact, the most surprising thing about the building is the complete absence of the dynamism that seems to be indicated
by its plan. The volumes are juxtaposed without continuity, and the
structure appears static and lifeless. The interior has an analogous character, being enclosed by an immaterial surface decorated with interlacing
ribs. We may also point out the interruption between the lower part and
the dome. In general, the space of St. John Nepomuk exhibits the same
surreal character found in Sedlec and Kladruby.

In spite of their apparent differences, the Baroque works of Santini Aichel do share the same basic properties.[30] The large Premonstratensian
pilgrimage church (1713–35) at Křtiny in Moravia has a plan based
on a Greek cross. The exterior does not show any differentiation between
primary and secondary parts, as in the buildings of the Dientzenhofers,
but indicates a monolithic volume on which the classical members are
applied. Moreover, the interior lacks true plasticity. The walls and the
vault form a continuous surface, defined horizontally by an unbroken entablature (like that on the exterior), and again we find the characteristic

458. *Vienna, Hofbibliothek, plan of the upper story.*
459. *Vienna, Hofbibliothek, exterior.*

460. *Vienna, Hofbibliothek, hall.* ▷

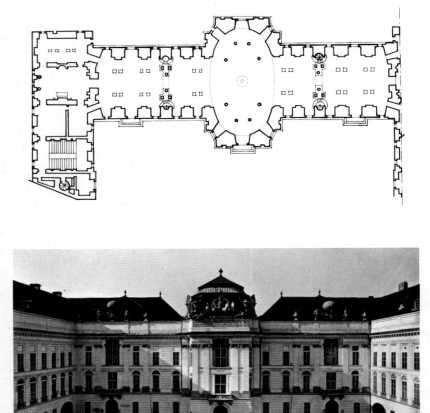

applied pilasters which end blindly. In all, the space is completely static. In Santini Aichel's last work, the large church of the convent in Rajhrad, near Brno (1722), the same principles are employed in connection with a longitudinal organism. The plan consists of a succession of three centralized cells which are defined as independent units surrounded by a monolithic wall. A general horizontal coherence, however, is created by a continuous entablature. Again we find the applied members that are suddenly cut off.

The works of Santini Aichel, thus, are full of contradictions.[31] His buildings may be longitudinal, but express no real movement in depth, or they may be centralized, yet without indicating centrifugal or centripetal forces. The applied members are cut off as if to tell the viewer that heaven always remains distant and inaccessible. The main constituent element is a continuous wall which makes the spaces appear closed and inescapable. The architecture of Santini Aichel is therefore deeply tragic. Earlier than any of his fellow architects, he must have felt the contradictions inherent in the eighteenth century—the new dichotomy between thought and feeling—as well as the disintegration of the great European anthropomorphic tradition. This is why he preferred Gothic forms, although even then he selected the most abstract properties of the medieval tradition, such as its interplay of irrational lines which seem to have no beginning and no end. His methods and aims can surely be related to other currents of the eighteenth century, such as the Rococo, but his sinister expression remains truly Bohemian.

Germany

All the aspects of Baroque architecture and all the varied artistic currents of Europe are summarized in one last great synthesis in German architecture. Its original contribution is the wall-pillar system of the Vorarlberg builders.[32] We have seen how the wall-pillar system made the open and dynamic spatial compositions of the Dientzenhofers possible. Although the development of this system must have been known to some of the Vorarlbergers, they continued to build their simple and straightforward wall-pillar halls. At a certain point, however, the desire for introducing centralization appears. A master such as Franz Beer was satisfied with a simple bi-axial layout in the church of Pielenhofen (1719). The talented Kaspar Moosbrugger, however, introduced new ideas into his projects for the great church of the monastery at Einsiedeln. By about 1703 he had designed a plan showing a large rotunda which precedes a conventional longitudinal organism with a domed crossing.[33] In his final project (1719) the elements form a most original succession: a large octagonal rotunda with the pilgrimage chapel in the middle is succeeded by a smaller nave covered by a "Bohemian cap" and a narrow crossing with a high dome. The space, thus, becomes taller

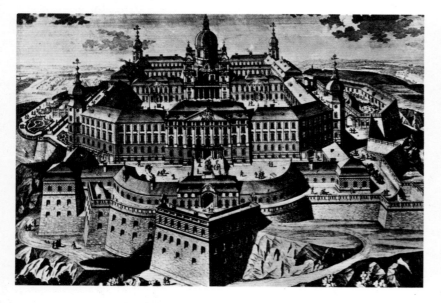

463. *Zwettl, parish church, façade.*

464. *Dürnstein, tower of the convent church.*

465. *Monastery of St. Florian, exterior view of the staircase.*
466. *Broumov, courtyard of the monastery.* ▷

467. *Prague, chapel of the Imperial Hospital, exterior.*

468. *Ž'dár, shrine of St. John Nepomuk, plan of the church and diagram of the perimetric walls.*

469. *Ž'dár, shrine of St. John Nepomuk, axonometric drawing.*

470. *Ž'dár, shrine of St. John Nepomuk, exterior.* ▷

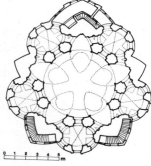

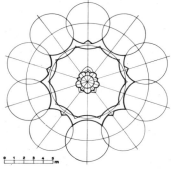

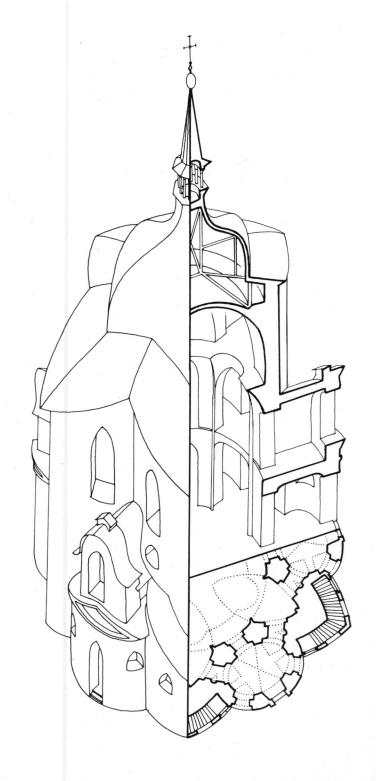

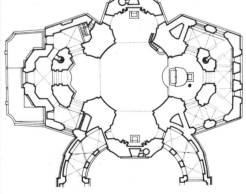

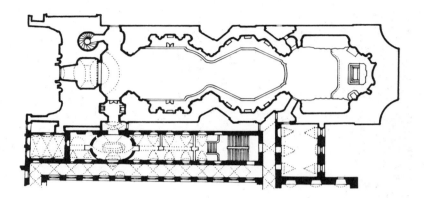

as it narrows down, and a very expressive movement in depth results. The wall-pillars are perforated everywhere, creating a general effect of openness and *Zweischaligkeit*. The façade has a convex center between flanking towers, as in Fischer von Erlach's Kollegienkirche, permitting a view of the expansive rotunda behind. A similar façade is found in the large monastery church at Weingarten (foundation-stone 1716; completed 1724), which was planned by Moosbrugger in collaboration with Donato Giuseppe Frisoni and Franz Beer.[34] The activity of the Vorarlberg builders culminated with the great church of the monastery at St. Gall in Switzerland, planned by Peter Thumb in 1749 and built from 1755 to 1766.[35] Here the Baroque architecture of Central Europe returns to its origin. The simple wall-pillar system again proves to offer the most elementary and powerful interpretation of the theme of the sacred path. But the church in St. Gall also contains a monumental rotunda at the very center of its longitudinal axis. It is as if God's people on their way carry with them their common center of meaning.

Through Johann Dientzenhofer, the Bohemian interpretation of Guarini's *ars combinatoria* became a constituent element in the development of the German Late Baroque. Equally active in ecclesiastical and secular building, Dientzenhofer paved the way for the achievements of Balthasar Neumann. Whereas at St. Gall primary importance is still given to the path, the buildings of Neumann are basically centralized organisms. We have recognized his fundamental theme in the dominant rotunda and the great staircase. Through such forms he managed to offer a last fundamental interpretation both to the church and to the palace—an achievement which is rare. By contrast, most other architects of the epoch were primarily either church builders or palace architects. In his solutions Neumann also exploited all the experiences offered by the various national traditions. This does not mean that he adopted the pluralistic approach of Juvarra; his style is more uniform, but has a formal language so rich that it may concretize any content. We should in this connection recall the succession of major spaces in the Würzburg Residenz. In general, his expression may be characterized as rich and simple, powerful and at the same time relaxed. It really represents a golden mean between the possible extremes of the epoch. The quality of his works is simply never questioned; he seems to convince everybody. This extraordinary achievement is based on an ideal combination of organizational power and sensibility to plastic and spatial form. A statement by Neumann is always clear and straightforward, but also richly articulate and carefully detailed.

To illustrate our general opinion we may mention two more interpretations of his basic theme—the centralized place where we "belong," without being isolated either physically or spiritually from the environment. The pilgrimage church of Käppele in Würzburg (begun 1748) is

478. *Einsiedeln, monastery church, plan.*
479. *Einsiedeln, monastery church, exterior.*
480. *Einsiedeln, monastery church, interior.* ▷

an elongated Greek cross with a dominant central rotunda and apse-shaped arms. The rotunda is defined as a large baldachin by means of breaks in the vault surface and the entablature, and rests on coupled columns at each corner. At the same time, however, the entire space is united by a horizontal succession of classical members carrying a straight entablature. The columns of the baldachin form part of this succession. Thus, two interpenetrating spatial definitions, which when taken alone are extremely simple, become a fathomless work of art when joined together. In 1731 Neumann finished the staircase in the palace at Bruchsal, begun by Anselm Franz Freiherr von Ritter zu Grünstein. Basically the space is a rotunda with an elevated platform in the middle which gives access to the rooms on the *bel-étage*. Between the platform and the wall two symmetrically disposed, curved flights of stairs rise from the ground floor. Hardly anywhere else has movement in space been more masterfully exploited. Walking up from the relatively dark vestibule into the splendid rotunda is an unforgettable experience.

Some of the other important architects of eighteenth-century Germany have already been discussed in detail: we have analyzed the great diaphanous octagons of Johann Michael Fischer and the centralized wall-pillar halls of Dominikus Zimmermann. Both are representative of the craftsmen-architects of the epoch who, through direct participation, created works of an incomparably concrete and personal character. The qualities of Fischer appear in condensed form in the beautiful Anastasia Chapel in Benediktbeuern (1750–58). Although the building is quite large, the function of the chapel is emphasized by its oval plan. The space is covered by a large baldachin resting on eight supports which are united in pairs to form wide wall-pillars on the diagonal axes. On the main axes the wall is treated as a secondary surface. All intervals are perforated by large openings which create the feeling of luminous extension.

Among the works of Zimmermann we ought to mention the parish church in Günzburg (1736–41). The building represents a simplified version of the churches in Steinhausen and Wies. Originally Zimmermann wanted freestanding columns, but in order to save money they were replaced by a succession of wall-columns which carry a large oval vault.[36] The entablature is interrupted on the main axes and all the walls are perforated by numerous freely shaped windows. The general effect is of a large baldachin immersed in a luminous continuum. The Anastasia Chapel and the church in Günzburg thus have a basic affinity, but the personal signature is very different, Zimmermann being more elaborate and decorative, Fischer rational and tectonic.

The "handmade" churches of the craftsmen-architects find their culmination in the works of the Asam brothers. Cosmas Damian was primarily a painter, whereas Egid Quirin worked as a sculptor and architect. Sev-

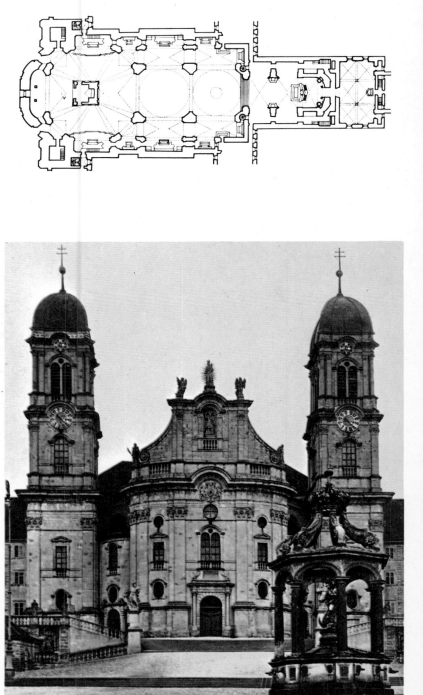

481. St. Gall, cathedral, plan.
482. St. Gall, cathedral, interior.

483. Würzburg, Käppele, plan.
484. Würzburg, Käppele, interior.
485. Bruchsal, staircase of the palace. ▷

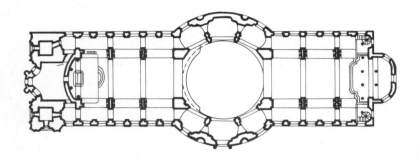

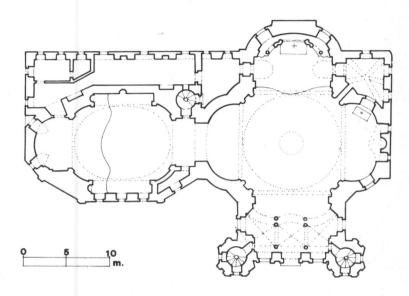

0   5   10
m.

486. *Benediktbeuern, Anastasia Chapel, interior.*
487. *Günzburg, parish church, detail of the interior.* ▷

eral times they decorated buildings by other architects (Osterhofen, Wahlstatt, Einsiedeln, Weingarten), but in some cases the brothers alone created dazzling *Gesamtkunstwerke*. In 1733 Egid Quirin even functioned as his own client when building the church of St. John Nepomuk (also known as the Asamkirche) in Munich at his own expense. Both brothers had studied in Rome (1712–14) and brought home a thorough knowledge of Bernini's *theatrum sacrum*. Already in the Benedictine abbey of Weltenburg (1716–18) they demonstrate a complete mastery, and appear as the foremost eighteenth-century representatives of the Baroque art of persuasion through realistic illusion. At hardly any previous time, however, had the entire space been so totally transformed into a tableau in which the visitor could fully participate. In Weltenburg the tectonic structure is still easily perceptible; the illusory effect is created mainly by the indirectly lit truncated dome and the main altar which appears on a luminous background, against which Egid Quirin's sculpture of *St. George and the Dragon* takes on an incredible presence. In St. John Nepomuk in Munich, instead, the whole space has become an integrated illusional representation. The high and narrow room is basically a simple bi-axial organism, but the decoration makes it appear like the stage of a magic heavenly drama. The façade is equally dramatic, but it also demonstrates Egid Quirin's ability in creating a simple, powerful form when needed. With the small Ursuline church in Straubing (1736–41) the art of the Asams approaches the lightness of the contemporary Rococo. The centralized plan also has an affinity with the unified rotundas of Fischer and Neumann. The Baroque heritage of the Asam brothers is, however, still strongly felt in the violent dynamism of their altars.[37]

The Baroque *theatrum sacrum* also had its secular counterpart. The interior of the Residenztheater in Munich (1750–53) by François de Cuvilliés, who did so much to introduce the Rococo into Germany, is particularly splendid. Above all, however, we ought to mention the outdoor theater of the Zwinger in Dresden (1709–32) by Mathaes Daniel Pöppelmann. Pöppelmann belonged to the first generation of native Baroque architects in Central Europe, and put his considerable talent at the service of Augustus the Strong of Saxony, who wanted to transform Dresden into a true capital city. A trip to Vienna and Rome in 1710 put Pöppelmann into contact with Hildebrandt and Carlo Fontana, and in 1715 he visited Paris and Versailles. The Zwinger was intended as a large enclosed courtyard for tournaments and similar performances. Pöppelmann himself called it a "Roman theater." The Zwinger should have formed part of a large palace, for which several plans have been preserved. The executed part consists of an approximately square court with U-shaped extensions on the transverse axis. The main axis should have united the Zwinger with a large garden toward the Elbe, but this side of the project was left unfinished. The main axis ends in a splendid gate-tower which

led to the open land beyond the city fortifications, while the transverse axis is terminated by voluminous transparent pavilions. The corners are defined by larger but less elaborate pavilions, and the whole complex is united by long skeletal galleries.[38] The general character of continuous extension is probably inspired by the Grand Trianon in Versailles, whereas the pavilions show a most original synthesis of plastic, skeletal structure and Hildebrandtian articulation.[39] The effect is very rich, but the plastic (and spatial) accents are wonderfully integrated into the space boundary by means of continuous horizontals. In general, the Zwinger is one of the most convincing and happy creations of the Baroque Age. Space does not permit us to discuss the other Baroque buildings of Dresden. The subject cannot be dropped, however, without mentioning the splendid tower-façade of the Katholische Hofkirche (1739–53) by Gaetano Chiaveri.

In northern Germany there are two centers of Late Baroque architecture: Münster and Berlin-Potsdam. We have already discussed the sophisticated *Backsteinbarock* of Johann Conrad von Schlaun, which is nowhere more charmingly evident than in the Rüschhaus (1745–48) near Münster. Its small layout is a wonderful synthesis of a local farmhouse and a Baroque hôtel, articulated with an extraordinary sense of proportion and detail. In Berlin and Potsdam the architecture of Frederick the Great appears as a highly official Neoclassicism. However, his Rococo *maison de plaisance*, Sanssouci (1745), has a certain dilettantish charm. It was designed by the King himself and his architect, Georg Wenzeslaus von Knobelsdorff.

Russia

The prime manifestations of the rich building activity under Peter the Great and the Tsarina Elizabeth have already been mentioned. During the early period the leading architect was the Swiss-Italian Domenico Trezzini, whose main work, the Cathedral of St. Peter and St. Paul in St. Petersburg (1712–23), is distinguished by an extremely tall spire which contrasts with the infinite horizontal extension of the city. Whereas the architecture of Peter the Great's age is characterized by a certain rational restraint, the period of Elizabeth is playful and exuberant. We have criticized the approach of its leading master, Bartolomeo Rastrelli, for its purely decorative use of the classical orders. In the church of the Smolny Convent, however, Rastrelli created a true masterpiece (1744–57). The centralized structure with a high dome and four flanking towers represents a convincing synthesis of the traditional Russian church and the intentions of the Baroque Age. A tall freestanding bell-tower was never built but would have been the crowning achievement of Russian and European tower building. The influence of Rastrelli was very great, and a multitude of picturesque palaces and churches were

489. *Munich, St. John Nepomuk (Asamkirche), exterior.* ▷
490. *Munich, St. John Nepomuk (Asamkirche), interior.* ▷
491. *Munich, Residenztheater, interior.* ▷

built in his manner until about 1760, when the vogue for Neoclassicism made its appearance. As a consequence, Rastrelli was dismissed as court architect in 1763.

Scandinavia

Sweden reached its peak of political power under Charles XI and Charles XII, and found a worthy architectural interpreter in Nicodemus Tessin the Younger, whose works have been treated in this author's *Baroque Architecture*. After the death of Charles XII in 1718, the absolutist monarchy was abolished and as a consequence we do not find any important Late Baroque architecture in Sweden. Denmark, however, experienced a new flowering under Christian VI (1730–46), which culminated under his son Frederik V. The two leading Danish architects were Laurids de Thurah and Niels Eigtved. De Thurah built the charming Eremitage in Copenhagen (1734–36), combining a sense of volume and Viennese articulation. His spiral tower for the church of Our Savior in Copenhagen (1750), inspired by Borromini's S. Ivo, is especially picturesque. De Thurah also published *Den Danske Vitruvius* (1746–49). The talented Eigtved worked for several years with Pöppelmann in Dresden and came home a full-fledged architect. His masterpiece was the Amalienborg Square with its surrounding palaces, but he also designed several other houses of quality.[40]

England

Among the different national varieties of Late Baroque architecture, that of the English is the most puzzling. The qualities which typically characterize a Baroque building are rarely found in England. Plastic modeling, "infinite" spaces, and rich, sensuous details are lacking. Instead the English buildings from the beginning of the eighteenth century appear rigid, finite, and strangely cold. It may be that Blenheim Palace symbolized a kind of absolutist power, and that its layout has properties in common with other Baroque palaces; nevertheless, its character seems quite different. The term English Baroque, therefore, has been introduced rather hesitatingly,[41] and has not become generally accepted. England represented a powerful system of its own kind. Instead of concretizing a particular choice among the existing sets of dogmas, the English system reflected a truly pluralistic society, including the clergy and aristocracy, as well as the burgher, the merchant, and the freethinker.

With this background it is not surprising that Vanbrugh and Hawksmoor arrived at the stylistic pluralism described above. We could also say that England skipped the single-minded phase of the High Baroque and arrived directly at a Late Baroque synthesis.[42] A similar thing happened in Austria, but the components there were quite different. In Aus-

tria the aim was mainly to create a synthesis of absolutist monarchy and dogmatic religion, and the corresponding art therefore became more normally Baroque, in spite of the comprehensive perspective introduced by Fischer von Erlach. The aim of Vanbrugh, instead, must have been to achieve a "democratic" architecture wherein every building is given a character appropriate to its use. In his "Proposals" for the "Fifty New Churches" of 1711 he indicated how they should be built, saying: ". . .which Grace shou'd generally be express'd in a plain, but Just and Noble Stile, without running into those many Divisions and Breaks which other buildings for Variety of uses may require; or such Gayety of Ornaments as may be proper to a Luxurious palace."[43] The idea of conformity between the architectural vocabulary chosen and the building's function may be traced back to Alberti, who gives numerous indications as to the character of various buildings.[44] In Quattrocento Florence, Alberti's ideas were related to a certain kind of democracy, as was their revival in Late Baroque England. England, in fact, was considered the new land of liberty. Whereas a man like the Earl of Shaftesbury therefore wanted a return to the way of the Greeks, Vanbrugh preferred the basically more advanced idea of pluralism. As we have seen, he did not only create various buildings in different styles, but he also gave a different characterization to their individual parts. We have also encountered this approach in the contemporary works of Juvarra. Perhaps it is not a mere coincidence that two men who were also active in the theater should show this heightened sense of psychological differentiation.

Vanbrugh's conception of the church, as it results from his "Proposals," was expressed only in an indirect way; in fact, he never appears as a church builder. We have reason to believe, however, that he strongly influenced the concept of the three churches begun by Hawksmoor in 1714: St. George-in-the-East (1714-29), St. Anne's, Limehouse (1714-30), and Christ Church, Spitalfields (1714-29).[45] All three show a stylistic pluralism not found in Hawksmoor's independent works, which were either "Classic" or "Gothick." What distinguishes these extraordinary buildings is not so much their simple rectangular plans and interior spaces[46] as their very special exterior character. All three are elongated organisms with powerful tower-façades. St. George-in-the-East is the more apparently "Gothick," having a crowning turret of octagonal form with a ring of buttresses, as well as four related staircase turrets flanking the nave. The entrance wall, however, is pronouncedly "Classic," and is preceded by freestanding Baroque stairs. The transition from these elements to the main turret is accomplished by way of an extraordinary bare and crystalline tower into which openings are cut as if with a razor blade. The side elevations have a similar character, but immense keystones are added to define the "basement" character of the ground floor. The openings of the entrances to the staircase towers are signifi-

492. Dresden, Zwinger, plan.
493. Dresden, Zwinger, the Langgalerie.
494. Dresden, Zwinger, the Kronentor. ▷

495. *Dresden, Zwinger, pavilion.*

496. *Dresden, Zwinger, courtyard.*
497. *Dresden, Zwinger, pavilion of mathematics and physics.*

windows above, however, are repeated all around the building, ~~~~~ a most successful horizontal integration. In general, St. George-in-the-East is a strongly expressive building of an almost surreal character. St. Anne's is closely related to St. George; here also we find a tall, somewhat bare tower crowned by a "Gothick" lantern. The forms, however, have become richer, so that the "Classic" as well as the latent "Gothick" aspects are strengthened. The continuity of the tower is emphasized by slender vertical members, but the entrance appears unusually Baroque, thanks to a protruding circular vestibule and a fan-shaped flight of stairs. Undoubtedly, St. Anne's is the most powerful of Hawksmoor's churches. Christ Church, however, is the most sophisticated. About 1723–24 Hawksmoor replaced the original idea of a flat front crowned by a little octagonal lantern with a splendid Palladian portico and a tall "Gothick" steeple.[47] The motif of the portico is varied in the tower as well as at the foot of the steeple, creating a most original vertical succession of related forms. The vertical continuity is further stressed by ingenious concave recesses along the sides of the tower—an almost Borrominian idea. The exterior of the nave is extremely simple and represents an unsurpassed masterpiece of controlled surface articulation. It prefigures certain works of Claude-Nicolas Ledoux.[48]

Hawksmoor's last and most accomplished church is St. Mary Woolnoth, built from 1717 to 1727, probably without the aid of Vanbrugh. Here, in fact, the formal vocabulary is classical and represents an interesting and original interpretation of known motifs. The plan is completely centralized, consisting of a square defined by a straight entablature carried by three columns in each corner and surrounded by an ambulatory. The central space is lit from above by four large semicircular windows. In general, it represents a most convincing "English" interpretation of the Late Baroque rotunda with double spatial delimitation. The main façade is somewhat related to the churches mentioned above, but the instrumentation is different. Over a tall rusticated ground floor a classical colonnade is erected which carries two small towers—a very ingenious transformation of an English medieval screen-wall by means of classical elements. The north wall shows concave Borrominian *aediculae* within rusticated niches which are tied together by a continuous base. In general, St. Mary Woolnoth may be considered the most consummate masterpiece of the English Baroque, a building which is simultaneously strictly organized and significantly free in its use of architectural forms and motifs.

Conclusion

The seventeenth century is characterized by great dogmatic systems. Its syntheses were always those of exclusion, that is, an expression of the *esprit de système*. Seen from within, however, the systems appeared

comprehensive and potentially without spatial limits. Therefore they had a persuasive power and aimed at expansion.

In the eighteenth century the situation became much more complex. All the same, we may speak of a Late Baroque period, which continued some of the basic trends of the previous century. What, then, characterizes the Late Baroque? The dogmatic systems still exist, but consciously or unconsciously they tend to give up their absolutist pretensions, and to a certain extent they also begin to form more or less inclusive syntheses. Existence, thus, becomes psychologically differentiated and individualized, and man's ideas correspondingly relativized. We may quote Jacques-François Blondel here: "All peoples have a character of their own, a way of feeling which is proper to them. . . ."[49] In this book we have used the word pluralism to denote this new state of affairs.

The architectural forms, therefore, also tend toward more pronounced individual characterization. Centralization, which symbolizes man's belonging to a place, becomes still more important, whereas the longitudinal movement loses its strength. The forces represented by the center, thus, are turned inward and no longer form part of an infinitely extended system. In other words, the buildings become more intimate and functional. This process naturally happened in different ways in different countries; we can, however, point out a general development which corresponds quite well to generations of architects.[50]

The first generation produced the great pioneers of architectural synthesis, who wanted to unify different traditions and create an inclusive architecture. These were born in the 1650s, and their foremost representatives are Fischer von Erlach and Christoph Dientzenhofer. In a certain sense Vanbrugh also belongs to this generation, but at the same time he forms a link with the succeeding one, which is marked by the desire for pluralistic characterization and corresponding formal differentiation, that is, a new *esprit systématique*. Born about 1670, the architects of this generation are numerous and show many varieties of approach. Their foremost representatives are Boffrand, Hildebrandt, Juvarra, and Santini Aichel. The third generation could perhaps be characterized as integrators. Their aim was to unify the different possibilities into a new kind of thematic whole, and their approach is characterized by a combination of the *esprit de système* and the *esprit systématique*. Of those born about 1690, the main representatives are Neumann, Kilian Ignaz Dientzenhofer, and Johann Michael Fischer. In a certain sense Vittone also belongs to this generation, but he is marked as well by the desire for "archetypal simplicity" so dear to the Neoclassical generation born about 1700.

In France the second and fourth generations were important: thus we find a differentiated and sophisticated Rococo which leads directly to Neoclassicism. In Austria the first and second generations were decisive

502. *London, St. George-in-the-East, exterior.*
503. *London, St. George-in-the-East, detail of the exterior.*

504. *London, St. George-in-the-East, façade.*

and created a wonderfully articulate historical synthesis. In Germany the third generation accomplished a singular integration which represents the culmination of Late Baroque architecture.

The complex aims, attitudes, and local circumstances make it futile to classify the different manifestations of the epoch by means of stylistic categories. To talk about German Rococo would be to grasp only one of the components of the comprehensive works created by German eighteenth-century architects. In any case, stylistic categories are approximations. The whole Baroque epoch is, in fact, characterized by many diverse currents which during a shorter or longer period had some basic aspects in common. The psychological and formal differentiation of the Late Baroque, thus, is already apparent in the works of Borromini. In general, it may be considered the most important aspect of the development. But we understand that it may be concretized in various ways, from the sensuousness of the Rococo to the frightening alienation of Santini Aichel.

The true aim of the Enlightenment was to free man from the systems, to allow him a better understanding and deeper feelings. The danger, of course, was of a split between thought and feeling, a danger which later became a tragic reality. In the Late Baroque, however, thought and feeling were still united, perhaps more fully than in any other epoch.

507. *London, Christ Church, Spitalfields, façade.*

508. *London, Christ Church, Spitalfields, detail of the steeple.*

509. *London, Christ Church, Spitalfields, detail of the exterior.*

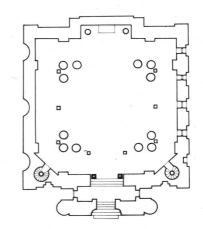

510. *London, St. Mary Woolnoth, plan.*
511. *London, St. Mary Woolnoth, exterior.*

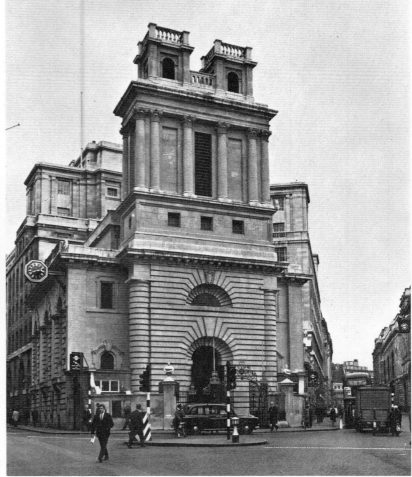

512, 513. London, St. Mary Woolnoth, details of the exterior.

514. *London, St. Mary Woolnoth, interior, from an engraving by J. Le Keux.*

NOTES

CHAPTER ONE

[1]D'Alembert, "Discours préliminaire" to the French *Encyclopédie* (1751).

[2]Voltaire, *Traité de Métaphysique*, quoted in E. Cassirer, *The Philosophy of the Enlightenment* (1932), Boston, 1955, p. 12.

[3]Locke, *An Essay Concerning Human Understanding*, 1690.

[4]Cassirer, *op. cit.*, p. 99.

[5]Newton, *Opticks*, London, 1730, Query 28.

[6]There were, of course, others—such as Holbach and Diderot—who rejected any form of religious faith.

[7]Cassirer, *op. cit.*, p. 251.

[8]The Jesuits were expelled from Portugal in 1759, from France in 1764, from Spain in 1767, and from Austria in 1773.

[9]Quoted in W. Braunfels, *Abendländische Klosterbaukunst*, Cologne, 1969, p. 265.

[10]Rousseau, *Social Contract*, quoted in Cassirer, *op. cit.*, p. 261.

[11]Berkeley, *Essay Towards a New Theory of Vision*, LXV.

[12]See W. Herrmann, *Laugier and 18th-Century French Theory*, London, 1962, p. 50.

[13]In 1770 the Elector of Bavaria ordered that all churches be built in "classical" style.

[14]The best general introduction to the Rococo is the article by Hans Sedlmayr and Hermann Bauer in the *Enciclopedia Universale dell'Arte*, Vol. XI, Venice-Rome, 1963.

[15]See Leibniz, *Monadologie*, Hamburg, 1958.

[16]The term stems from A. Dorner, *The Way Beyond Art*, New York, 1949.

[17]This fact was acknowledged by S. Giedion in *Space, Time and Architecture*, Cambridge, Mass., 1941.

[18]E. Guidoni, "Modelli Guariniani," in *Guarino Guarini e l'internazionalità del barocco* (ed. V. Viale), Turin, 1970.

[19]The result is well shown by a map of Paris and environs dating from 1740, reproduced in Norberg-Schulz, *Baroque Architecture*, New York, 1972, p. 10.

[20]Fischer von Erlach in a fragmentary letter preserved in the city archive of Prague, published by Georg Kunoth, *Die historische Architektur Fischers von Erlach*, Düsseldorf, 1956, pp. 120 ff.

[21]The project is known from Plate 2 in the fourth book of Fischer's *Entwurff einer historischen Architektur in Abbildung unterschiedener berühmter Gebäude des Altertums und fremder Völker* (Vienna, 1721), engraved by J.A. Delsenbach (see the letter fragment mentioned in note 20).

[22]A rather fantastic reconstruction of the palace in Persepolis appears as Plate XVI in the manuscript for the first book of Fischer's *Entwurff einer historischen Architektur*. . . . In the printed edition another plate was substituted for it. See Kunoth, *op. cit.*, fig. 102.

[23]See Kunoth, *op. cit.*, pp. 223 ff.

[24]Kunoth, *op. cit.*, p. 121.

[25]The disposition obviously goes back to the use of freestanding pavilions in certain French *maisons de plaisance*, above all at Marly.

[26]M. Heidegger, *Bauen Wohnen Denken. Vorträge und Aufsätze*, II, Pfullingen, 1967, p. 26.

[27]The number of stations varied after the *via crucis* was introduced during the fifteenth century. The choice of fourteen was proposed by Antonius Daza in his *Exercitii Spirituali* of 1626, but was confirmed by the Church only in 1731. See E. Kramer, *Kreuzweg und Kalvarienberg*, Kehl-Strasbourg, 1957.

[28]"Käppele" is the popular name for the pilgrimage church of Mariä Heimsuchung auf dem Nikolausberg. It consists of a sanctuary (1683) to which Neumann added a larger centralized church (1748–52). The construction of the *via crucis* was started in 1761.

[29]See Braunfels, *op. cit.*, pp. 230 ff.

[30]To see how Melk looked before its Baroque reconstruction, one may consult the print by Matthaeus Merian in *Topographia Provinciarum Austriacarum*, Frankfurt am Main, 1649, p. 26. For a short history of the convent, see P. Reginald, *Stift Melk*, Munich, 1957.

[31]R. Wittkower, *Art and Architecture in Italy 1600–1750*, Harmondsworth, 1958, p. 255.

[32]During the reigns of Queen Anne and George I a Baroque approach still dominated English architecture, culminating with Vanbrugh's construction of Blenheim Palace for the Duke of Marlborough. Thus, architecture still served the "hero who makes noise in the world."

[33]For a discussion of the landscape garden, see F. Hallbaum, *Der Landschaftsgarten*, Munich, 1927.

[34]Rousseau's description of the "Élysée" in *La Nouvelle Héloïse*, 1762, may be mentioned in this context.

[35]See H. Sedlmayr, *Verlust der Mitte*, Salzburg, 1948, pp. 94 ff.

[36]For a discussion of the Baroque city, see C. Norberg-Schulz, *op. cit.*, pp. 27-102.

[37]A.E. Brinckmann, *Stadtbaukunst*, Potsdam, 1925, pp. 63 ff. For the origin of the trident or *patte d'oie*, see C. Norberg-Schulz, *op. cit.*

[38]See A.W. Bunin, *Geschichte des russischen Städtebaues bis zum 19. Jahrhundert*, Berlin, 1961, pp. 129 ff.

[39]Portoghesi compares the port of the Ripetta with the undulating façade of Borromini's S. Carlino, where a street and a building interact in a similar way. See P. Portoghesi, *Roma barocca*, Rome, 1966, p. 339.

[40]De Sanctis was conscious of this fact: "Before deciding on the idea of the steps, I thought of conceiving something extremely simple, and very convenient. . . . And keeping constantly in mind that these steps should be enjoyed, traversed, and trod upon, so to speak, at any hour of a summer's day, it was considered highly appropriate to plant a row of trees, placed at suitable intervals, on each side of the steps. . . ." Quoted in Portoghesi, *op. cit.*, p. 342.

[41]See Guidoni, *op. cit.*

[42]See M. Rotili, *Filippo Raguzzini e il rococò romano*, Rome, 1951.

[43]Wittkower, *op. cit.*, p. 292. See also C. D'Onofrio, *Le fontane di Roma*, Rome, 1957, pp. 223 ff. After Salvi's death in 1751, the fountain was completed by Giuseppe Pannini.

[44]For the more important facts, see P. Lavedan, *Les villes françaises*, Paris, 1960, pp. 134 ff. See also P. Zucker, *Town and Square*, New York, 1959, pp. 183 ff.

[45]Quoted in S. Giedion, *Space, Time and Architecture*, 5th ed., Cambridge, Mass., 1967, p. 148.

[46]The idea is obviously inspired by the Piazza S. Pietro in Rome.

[47]See A. Cavallari-Murat, *Forma urbana ed architettura nella Torino barocca*, Turin, 1968, Vol. II, pp. 124 ff.

[48]The splendid church designed by Eigtved in 1752 was never built. It was to have had a very tall dome flanked by two *campanili*. See T. Faber, *Dansk arkitektur*, Copenhagen, 1963, p. 86. As a substitute a smaller domed structure was erected toward the end of the nineteenth century.

[49]For the history of the bridge, see K. Novotný and E. Poche, *The Charles Bridge of Prague*, Prague, 1947.

[50]Even the ancient Ponte Milvio in Rome has a statue of St. John Nepomuk. The general idea of a sculpturally embellished bridge may be traced back to Bernini's Ponte S. Angelo, also in the Eternal City.

[51]Several of the statues were replaced in the nineteenth century with works by Emanuel and Josef Max.

[52]See C. Norberg-Schulz, *Kilian Ignaz Dientzenhofer e il barocco boemo*, Rome, 1968, pp. 133 ff.

[53]Quoted in Giedion, *op. cit.*, p. 147. For a complete history of the new Bath, see W. Ison, *The Georgian Buildings of Bath*, London, 1948.

[54]John Summerson, *Architecture in Britain 1530–1830*, Harmondsworth, 1953, p. 224.

[55]See H. Sedlmayr, *Verlust der Mitte*, pp. 15 ff.

[56]For examples, see C. Norberg-Schulz, *Baroque Architecture*.

[57]See C. Norberg-Schulz, "Lo spazio nell'architettura post-guariniana," in *Guarino Guarini e l'internazionalità del barocco* (ed. V. Viale), Turin, 1970.

[58]The towers were originally much lower than they appear today and were crowned by lanterns of Guarinian derivation. They were made higher in 1757 and received their present form after a fire in 1818; the tall towers deprive the dome of most of its importance as the major plastic element of the ensemble. See H. Sedlmayr, *Johann Bernhard Fischer von Erlach*, Vienna-Munich, 1956, p. 176.

[59]The façade, however, was imitated: we may mention the churches in Weingarten, Einsiedeln, and Ottobeuren. For an analysis of the church, see F. Hagen-Dempf, *Die Kollegienkirche in Salzburg*, Vienna, 1949.

[60]Splendid examples are furnished by the Franciscan church in Salzburg (1408–52) and the church in Most (Brüx) in northern Bohemia (1517–48).

[61]A complete survey of the works of the Vorarlberg school is given in N. Lieb and F. Dieth, *Die Vorarlberger Barockbaumeister*, Munich-Zurich, 1960.

[62]The goal of Dientzenhofer's voyage was Marseilles. See H.G. Franz, *Die Kirchenbauten des Christoph Dientzenhofer*, Brno-Munich-Vienna, 1942, p. 14.

[63]See B. Grimschitz, *Johann Lucas von Hildebrandt*, Munich-Vienna, 1959.

[64]See note 57.

[65]This distinction has its origin in the Italian use of the palazzo as a winter dwelling and the *villa suburbana* for the summer. See Chapter Four ("The Palace") in C. Norberg-Schulz, *Baroque Architecture*, pp. 239-302.

[66]See Norberg-Schulz, *op. cit.*

[67]H. Sedlmayr and H. Bauer say that the Rococo wall has the character of "a definite structure, stratified in thin layers, from which the weight has been lifted by means of a number of large apertures.... The old orders of columns are usually absent.... The plastic and spatial dynamism of the Baroque gives way to a rapid movement of lines and vibrant surfaces." See their article on the "Rococo," in *Enciclopedia Universale del-l'Arte*, Vol. XI, Venice-Rome, 1963, p. 628.

[68]The building was demolished in 1869.

[69]Sedlmayr traces the idea back to a project for a villa in S. Serlio, *Sette libri dell'Architettura*, Book VII, Frankfurt, 1575. (See Sedlmayr, *Johann Bernhard Fischer von Erlach*, p. 92.) Whereas Serlio's design is a typical Renaissance exercise in abstract geometry, Fischer's solution obviously stems from a desire to create a more dynamic relationship between the building and its environment.

[70]A simplified version of the project was built by Alliprandi in Liblice in Bohemia (1699).

[71]See Grimschitz, *op. cit.*, Plates 7 and 9.

[72]The best available survey of Juvarra's works is the catalogue entitled *Mostra di Filippo Juvarra* (ed. V. Viale), Messina, 1966.

[73]See H. Bauer, *Rocaille*, Berlin, 1962, p. 47.

[74]See C. Norberg-Schulz, *Kilian Ignaz Dientzenhofer e il barocco boemo*, pp. 42 ff.

CHAPTER TWO

[1]The achievements of Kilian Ignaz Dientzenhofer, Balthasar Neumann, and Johann Michael Fischer are all in some way based on the pioneer creations of Christoph Dientzenhofer.

[2]Documentary evidence is scarce, but after the researches of H.G. Franz, there can hardly exist any doubt as to the authorship of Christoph Dientzenhofer.

[3]The solution is found in S. Maria dei Sette Dolori.

[4]See C. Norberg-Schulz, "Lo spazio nell'architettura post-guariniana," in *Guarino Guarini e l'internazionalità del barocco* (ed. V. Viale), Turin, 1970. The principle—based on a vertically directed pulsation—is prefigured in the central space cells of Guarini's projects for S. Filippo Neri in Casale and S. Gaetano in Vicenza, where the lower part contracts and the upper expands.

[5]See, for instance, the review by Vaclav Richer of H.G. Franz, *Bauten und Baumeister*, in *Uměni*, 1964, N. 3 (Prague).

[6]A comprehensive study of the works of Johann Dientzenhofer is still lacking. A provisional survey is given in R. Kömstedt, *Von Bauten und Baumeistern des fränkischen Barocks*, Berlin, 1963.

[7]The church was built in 1728–30 by Balthasar Neumann, who made a new centralized plan after Dientzenhofer's death in 1726.

[8]A comprehensive survey of his works is given in C. Norberg-Schulz, *Kilian Ignaz Dientzenhofer e il barocco boemo*, Rome, 1968.

[9]A more complex variation is found in Hildebrandt's façade for the Peterskirche in Vienna (1702).

[10]The plan which is usually reproduced is inaccurate. The correct projection of the arches which define the hexagon is a circular arc. A revised plan is published in Norberg-Schulz, *op. cit.*, p. 75.

[11]See Norberg-Schulz, *op. cit.*, for a description of St. Bartholomew (1726) and of the chapel in the Imperial Hospital (1733), both in Prague. See also H.G. Franz, *Studien zur Barockarchitektur in Böhmen und Mähren*, Brno-Munich-Vienna, 1943.

[12]A similar vault was used by Christoph Dientzenhofer in Smiřice.

[13] The plans of the early churches in the Broumov district (c. 1720) are ovals or elongated octagons, whereas the late works in Chválenice (1747) and Paštiky (1748) are composed as bi-axial successions of baldachins. From his middle years we have the rotunda with added narthex and the presbytery in Dobrá Voda (1733).

[14] A general survey is offered in H.-R. Hitchcock, *Rococo Architecture in Southern Germany*, London, 1968. See also J. Bourke, *Baroque Churches in Central Europe*, London, 1958.

[15] A monograph on Fischer is still lacking. The best surveys are found in F. Hagen-Dempf, *Der Zentralbaugedanke bei Johann Michael Fischer*, Munich, 1954, and N. Lieb, *Barockkirchen zwischen Donau und Alpen*, Munich, 1953. Hitchcock, *op. cit.*, does not offer any satisfactory analysis of Fischer's work and makes a futile attempt at defining its stylistic identity when he asks: "Was Fischer's work Baroque, or was it, at least more consistently, Rococo?" He also remarks that the term "Barococo" is hardly satisfactory.

[16] The plan of St. Anna is closely related to Kilian Ignaz Dientzenhofer's parish church in Vižnov, built in 1725–27, although the vertical articulation is different. See Norberg-Schulz, *op. cit.*, p. 69.

[17] Rinchnach may also be compared to Kilian Ignaz Dientzenhofer's church in Šonov, built in 1727–30, although the latter has only one pair of wide wall-pillars directly on the transverse axis. See Norberg-Schulz, *op cit.*, p. 72.

[18] In the parish church of Sandizell (1735–39) Fischer once more repeated the simple solution of Unering. Shallow transepts add to the potential *Zweischaligkeit*. It is doubtful whether the church was designed by J.B. Gunetzhainer.

[19] Fischer's original project shows a fully developed *Zweischaligkeit*. During the first year of construction (1737–38) the works were directed by P.J. Köglsperger, who altered the plans. It is not clear how Fischer had to integrate those parts built by Köglsperger when he was reinstated in 1739. The church was consecrated in 1751. See Lieb, *op. cit.*, pp. 67 ff., p. 150.

[20] We may recall the related solution by Kilian Ignaz Dientzenhofer in St. Nicholas in the Altstadt in Prague (1732–37).

[21] The church was bombed during World War II.

[22] The analogy to Kilian Ignaz Dientzenhofer's and Balthasar Neumann's mature solutions in Kutná Hora and Neresheim is evident.

[23] A comprehensive study on Zimmermann is still lacking. See, however, H.-R. Hitchcock, *German Rococo: The Zimmermann Brothers*, London, 1968; also the excellent chapter on Steinhausen and Wies in Lieb, *op. cit.*; and for Steinhausen in particular, A. Kasper and W. Strache, *Steinhausen*, Stuttgart, 1957.

[24] The ambulatory is usually conceived as an independent building surrounding the church (Ž'dár). In some cases it is attached to the outer wall of the church (Kappel), and in others it is incorporated into the church itself (Vierzehnheiligen). At Steinhausen it has become integrated into the basic spatial structure.

[25] The project was ready in 1744, but construction began two years later. Zimmermann settled in Wies during the years of construction, and remained there until his death in 1766. See Lieb, *op. cit.*; also C. Lamb, *Die Wies*, Munich, 1964.

[26] Factual information concerning Neumann's churches is found in H. Reuther, *Die Kirchenbauten Balthasar Neumanns*, Berlin, 1960.

[27] The church was consecrated in 1743 and secularized in 1803. It was torn down after 1821.

[28] Looking at the plan superficially, it might seem that the principle employed is pulsating juxtaposition. Since the walls and the vaults offer different spatial definitions, it is correct to talk about syncopated interpenetration. Pulsating juxtaposition is based on unambiguous spatial cells.

[29] For the planning of Vierzehnheiligen, see R. Teufel, *Vierzehnheiligen*, Lichtenfels, 1957.

[30] *Ibid.*, figs. 32, 38, 39.

[31] The solution is already suggested in one of Johann Dientzenhofer's projects for Holzkirchen.

[32] The church was planned in 1747–49. The foundation-stone was laid in 1750, but the consecration took place as late as 1792, almost forty years after Neumann's death in 1753. See Reuther, *op. cit.*; also G. Neumann, *Neresheim*, Munich, 1947.

[33] A similar indecision also distinguishes the projects for his last ecclesiastical building, the pilgrimage church of Maria-Limbach (1751–53). One alternative shows a disposition quite similar to Christoph Dientzenhofer's church in Cheb, while the executed building is a simple wall-pillar hall.

[34] An interesting transitional stage is represented by a design in which the rotunda and the arms of the cross plan are integrated in a way similar to that at Gaibach and in the Jesuit church at Mainz. See Neumann, *op. cit.*, fig. 30.

[35] See the chapters on Gothic and church architecture in Herrmann, *Laugier and 18th-Century French Theory*, London, 1962.

[36] It is worth pointing out that Vittone edited the first complete publication of Guarini's *Architettura Civile* (1737).

[37] The idea goes back to Bernini and Borromini, who used indirect sources of illumination, or the so-called *camere di luce*, to use Paolo Portoghesi's term.

[38] For detailed information on Vittone, see P. Portoghesi, *Bernardo Vittone*, Rome, 1966. See also the catalogue entitled *Bernardo Vittone architetto* (ed. N. Carboneri and V. Viale), Vercelli, 1967.

[39] B. Vittone, *Istruzioni diverse concernenti l'officio dell'Architettura civile*, Lugano, 1766.

[40] The later date (1760) suggested by some critics is hardly plausible. See Portoghesi, *op. cit.*, p. 221; also F. Gamarino et al., *S. Luigi Gonzaga di Corteranzo*, Turin, 1970. The solution of Corteranzo was proposed again (c. 1740) on a larger scale for the church of S. Chiara in Alessandria, which was never built.

[41] S. Gaetano was built between 1744 and 1749. Today it is called the church of the Misericordia.

[42] The solution is related to that by Kilian Ignaz Dientzenhofer at Wahlstatt.

[43] Recently restored, the church offers a very convincing introduction to the works of Vittone. See A. Corio, "Santa Chiara; storia e restauro," in the catalogue *Bernardo Vittone architetto* (note 38 above). The building of the church was initiated in 1754 and completed in 1756.

[44] A preliminary project shows a hexagonal disposition like that of the church in Vercelli, but the vertical development is different. Both alternatives are supposed to stem from 1742, although the executed version seems surprisingly mature for that early date.

[45] This sort of vertical movement was introduced by Michelangelo in the project for S. Giovanni dei Fiorentini.

[46] The date usually given is 1751, but the project may stem from an earlier date.

[47] Similar pendentives appear in the Ospizio di Carità at Carignano (1749), in SS. Pietro e Paolo at Mondovì Breo (1755), and in other projects.

[48] An accurate plan of Borgo d'Ale has never been published.

[49]We mean here the works done between 1720 and 1730, including St. John Nepomuk on the Hradčany.

[50]The church was destroyed during World War II. See H.G. Franz, *Die Frauenkirche zu Dresden*, Berlin, 1950.

CHAPTER THREE

[1]Compare, for instance, the wall articulation of the Place Vendôme (1698) with that of the Place des Victoires (1685), which is still Berninian in character; or Meudon with his earlier palaces.

[2]See E. Langenskiöld, *Pierre Bullet, the Royal Architect*, Stockholm, 1959.

[3]See Langenskiöld, *op. cit.*, figs. 13, 14, 15.

[4]The Hôtel Desmarets was demolished in 1800.

[5]An upper floor was added to the latter at a later period.

[6]Lassurance's and Giardini's project was carried out by Jean Aubert. The palace was extended by Soufflot and again completely rebuilt in the nineteenth century.

[7]A monograph on this interesting architect is still lacking. The Thurn und Taxis Palace in Frankfurt was destroyed in 1944.

[8]The addition of a third floor has changed the appearance of the building.

[9]The motif is repeated in A.-J. Gabriel's École Militaire in Paris, which was begun only ten years after the Palais de Rohan was completed.

[10]Delamair, however, did not belong to the dominant clique of Jules Hardouin-Mansart, and was severely criticized for not having obeyed the "basic rules of architecture." When his client, the Prince de Soubise, died in 1712, Delamair was replaced by Boffrand, who later added his famous oval salon. Whereas the two hôtels originally had a common garden, they are today separated by a nineteenth-century building.

[11]Spatially it has a certain kinship with Bernini's S. Andrea al Quirinale.

[12]The hôtel was begun by Gabriel in 1728 for the financier Peyrenc de Moras, and finished by Jean Aubert. It was later bought by the Duke of Biron, and today houses the Musée Rodin.

[13]A monograph is still lacking, however.

[14]Except for the diagonal disposition, the project is also closely related to Antoine Le Pautre's famous project (c. 1650) for a château.

[15]A comprehensive presentation of the French eighteenth century is still lacking. The best general survey is found in L. Hautecoeur, *L'architecture classique en France*, Vol. III, Paris, 1950, which contains a useful text but very inadequate illustrations. Interesting practical information is found in the supplement to Daviler's *Cours d'architecture* (1720 edition) as well as in J.-F. Blondel's books.

[16]For a more detailed analysis, see P. Portoghesi, *Roma barocca*, Rome, 1966, pp. 353 ff.

[17]Galilei's Neoclassical façades for S. Giovanni in Laterano and S. Giovanni dei Fiorentini stem from 1733–36.

[18]A survey of Fuga's works is given in R. Pane, *Ferdinando Fuga*, Naples, 1956.

[19]The original project shows a more convincing articulation based on a clear contrast between the two horizontal layers and a dominant central *risalto* (see Pane, *op. cit.*, fig. 20).

[20]It is probably inspired by Sanfelice's splendid staircases in Naples. See the last chapter in this book.

[21]The *cour d'honneur* is found in some Turinese palaces, but is due to their original function as freestanding *ville suburbane*.

[22]The interior decoration went on until Juvarra's departure for Spain in 1735.

[23]See his "Regio palazzo in villa per tre personaggi" (1705), and his project for a palace for the Count of Hesse-Kassel (1707), as well as numerous diagonally disposed theater designs. (V. Viale, *Mostra di Filippo Juvarra*, Messina, 1966.)

[24]Juvarra himself also made a centralized wall-pillar project for the cathedral in Turin in 1729, that is, the same year he started the construction of Stupinigi.

[25]See B. Grimschitz, *Wiener Barockpaläste*, Vienna, 1947.

[26]See H. Sedlmayr, "Das Werden des Wiener Stadtbildes," in *Epochen und Werke*, II, Vienna, 1960, pp. 257 ff.

[27]Sedlmayr, *op. cit.*, pp. 260–61.

[28]H. Sedlmayr, "Die politische Bedeutung des deutschen Barock," in *Epochen und Werke*, II, pp. 140 ff.

[29]The theme of Engelhartstetten was monumentalized in the project for a large *Lustgartengebäude* (mentioned in the first chapter), in which the Berninian character is still more evident. Engelhartstetten was considerably altered in 1760.

[30]The project was never built.

[31]For complete documentation, see the fundamental study by B. Grimschitz, *Johann Lucas von Hildebrandt*, Vienna, 1959.

[32]It would, however, be wrong to consider the buildings of Fischer and Hildebrandt as mere syntheses of French and Italian ideas. Above all, they are original inventions which by far surpass the solutions of their contemporaries.

[33]Together with Hildebrandt's contemporary Ráckeve Palace on the island of Czepel in the Danube (built for Prince Eugene after 1702), the Starhemberg-Schönburg Palace shows the first meaningful employment of the Guarinian chasuble-shaped window. It later became a standard motif of Hildebrandt's pupil Kilian Ignaz Dientzenhofer. The belvedere of the Starhemberg-Schönburg Palace has since been closed in and has received "normal" windows. The original Mansard roofs over the wings have been transformed into a somewhat peculiar attic.

[34]Having accompanied Prince Eugene on his campaigns in northern Italy (1695–96) as a military engineer, Hildebrandt later became the chosen architect of the prince, even taking over the construction of his city-palace in Vienna, which had been begun by Fischer von Erlach in 1696.

[35]Our interpretation is confirmed by Hildebrandt's Schönborn Palace in Göllersdorf, whose main garden is enclosed between the palace proper and a large orangerie (1710–13).

[36]The Starhemberg-Schönburg Palace, in fact, shows a similar solution on a larger scale.

[37]Together with Michelangelo, Borromini, and perhaps Pietro da Cortona, he is certainly the most important innovator within the formal language of "classical" architecture.

[38]The palace also contains a beautiful oval vestibule on the ground floor and a splendid staircase.

[39]Related solutions are often seen in the country seats of Bohemia. We may mention Veltrusy and Karlův Dvur (Karlshof), which are based on Fischer's Althan scheme, and the many palaces by Jakob Augustoni in which an oval salon is inserted between symmet-

rical wings. A particularly rich and sensitive solution is represented by Ploskovice Palace outside Litoměřice (probably by Ottaviano Broggio, c. 1720). Here the Berninian approach has been replaced by a vibrating and undulating surface articulation of Borrominian and Hildebrandtian derivation. See H.G. Franz, *Bauten und Baumeister der Barockzeit in Böhmen*, Leipzig, 1962.

[40]See H.G. Franz, *Studien zur Barockarchitektur in Böhmen und Mähren*, Brno-Munich-Vienna, 1943, pp. 96 ff.

[41]More detailed analyses are found in C. Norberg-Schulz, *Kilian Ignaz Dientzenhofer e il barocco boemo*, Rome, 1968.

[42]Grimschitz, *op. cit.*, pp. 78 ff.

[43]In the *sala terrena*, double curved arches are used in a way which prefigures Neumann's Hofkirche in Würzburg, while the Kaisersaal shows a Dientzenhoferian interruption of the entablature.

[44]For a good introduction to the history of the Residenz, see E. Bachmann, *Residenz Würzburg und Hofgarten*, Munich, 1970.

[45]Even Hildebrandt failed when he tried to tackle the immense dimensions of the Hofburg in Vienna. His ingenious surface articulation suddenly seems weak and petty. We may also recall again Antonio da Sangallo's project for St. Peter's in Rome, where the splendid members from the Palazzo Farnese *cortile* become rather ridiculous and incapable of structuring the large building.

[46]In general it must have been invented before the Upper Belvedere in Vienna.

[47]It is the largest ever painted, measuring 98 x 59 feet.

[48]Neumann added, however, a series of splendid staircases to palaces planned by other architects, and also built the large palace of Werneck as a summer house for Friedrich Karl von Schönborn (1733–45). Again Hildebrandt appeared as a somewhat interfering "consultant."

[49]Neumann's projects for Vienna, Stuttgart, and Karlsruhe are thoroughly discussed in the excellent study by Liselotte Andersen, *Studien zu Profanbauformen Balthasar Neumanns*, Munich, 1966.

[50]The palace executed by Retti is turned ninety degrees to the right, and therefore does not interact in the same meaningful way with the town.

[51]The order only appears as such (column or pilaster) on the *ressauts*; elsewhere the wall is articulated by tall panels and tied together by a continuous "undulating architrave," that is, by an architrave united with the segmental arches of the upper windows.

[52]It contains a great enclosed courtyard, like the "large" Vienna project.

[53]The circular vestibule is evidently derived from Le Pautre's Hôtel de Beauvais. For François de Cuvilliés, see F. Wolf, *François de Cuvilliés*, Munich, 1967.

[54]So far the only study on Schlaun is that of T. Rensing, *Johann Conrad Schlaun*, Munich-Berlin, 1954.

[55]Rastrelli, however, had some predecessors, such as the Italian Trezzini, the Frenchman Le Blond, and the German Schädel, the last of whom built a splendid castle for Prince Menšikov at Oranienbaum, Russia (1713–25).

[56]See H. Avray Tipping and C. Hussey, *English Homes: the Work of Sir John Vanbrugh and His School, 1699–1736*, London, 1928. Also K. Downes, *Hawksmoor*, London, 1959, and *English Baroque Architecture*, London, 1966.

[57]The house was still unfinished when Vanbrugh died in 1726.

[58]The arcades were only built in the left corner. The general motif stems from François Mansart.

[59]Seaton Delaval was apparently designed by Vanbrugh alone. Other late works by Vanbrugh, such as Eastbury (1718) and Grimsthorpe (1722), basically show a related approach. Hawksmoor, on the other hand, had already designed Easton Neston along similar lines about 1695.

[60]The motif of the corner "towers" is also found in other works of the eighteenth century, such as Johann Dientzenhofer's Pommersfelden, Hildebrandt's Upper Belvedere, and Kilian Ignaz Dientzenhofer's Villa Portheim.

CHAPTER FOUR

[1]We may in this connection recall the large façades of the Early Baroque, the volumetric interaction of Bernini, the undulating walls of Borromini, and the "complementarity" of Guarini which was further developed by the Dientzenhofers. In the eighteenth century all these solutions still appear in different combinations, but the typically new contribution is a relatively neutral outer wall which is "wrapped" around the interior. To give such an "introspective" organism identity in a wider context, the tower became essential.

[2]L.G. de Cordemoy, *Nouveau Traité de toute l'Architecture*, Paris, 1714. Quoted in W. Herrmann, *Laugier and 18th-Century French Theory*, London, 1962, p. 106.

[3]Italics mine.

[4]The Baroque system of St-Sulpice was designed about 1660 by Daniel Gittard and Le Vau. M.A. Laugier, *Essai sur l'Architecture*, Paris, 1753, quoted in Herrmann, *op. cit.*, pp. 69 ff. For the French, Gothic was purely intellectual, whereas for the builders of Central Europe it represented a living technical and artistic tradition.

[5]The general effect was considerably reduced when Quatremère de Quincy closed the forty-two lateral windows after the Revolution, transforming the diaphanous church into a lifeless mausoleum.

[6]L. Hautecoeur says: "His talent, culture, character, longevity, as well as the trust demonstrated in him by several princes, assured Boffrand of a place of prime importance among the architects of the first half of the eighteenth century." (*Histoire de l'architecture classique en France*, Vol. III, Paris, 1950, p. 124.)

[7]Meissonier published his *Livre d'Ornaments et Dessins* in 1734. See H. Bauer, *Rocaille*, Berlin, 1962.

[8]Bauer, *op. cit.*, p. 70.

[9]According to Nina A. Mallory, Sardi is not the author of the façades of the Maddalena and S. Maria della Neve, which Portoghesi attributes to him. See N.A. Mallory, "The Architecture of Giuseppe Sardi," *Journal of the Society of Architectural Historians*, Vol. XXVI, no. 2, May 1967.

[10]A comprehensive monograph on Juvarra is perhaps the most urgently needed work in the literature on Late Baroque architecture.

[11]See N. Carboneri, *L'architetto Francesco Gallo*, Turin, 1954.

[12]P. Portoghesi, *Bernardo Vittone*, Rome, 1966, p. 29.

[13]See M. Capobianco, "Scale settecentesche a Napoli," *L'architettura*, Vol. VIII, pp. 407 ff.

[14]The towers and the dome were never built, so that the monotony of the building has become rather oppressive. The original project is reproduced in F. Fichera, *Luigi Vanvitelli*, Rome, 1937.

[15]Stefano Ittar arrived in Catania in 1765 and died at Malta in 1790. See S. Boscarino, *Studi e rilievi di architettura Siciliana*, Messina, 1961, pp. 83 ff.

[16]An introduction is offered by F. Minissi, *Aspetti dell'architettura religiosa del settecento in Sicilia*, Rome, 1958. The churches of Gagliardi are found in Noto (S. Domenico, 1732–36; Chiesa del Collegio, 1736–46), Caltagirone (S. Chiara, 1749; S. Giuseppe, 1751), Niscemi (Madonna Addolorata; perhaps also the Madonna del Bosco), and Ragusa Ibla (S. Giuseppe; project for S. Giorgio, 1744). For the Baroque architecture of Sicily, also see A. Blunt, *Sicilian Baroque*, London, 1968, and M. de Simone, *Ville Palermitane*, Genoa, 1968.

[17]See N.A. Mallory, "Narciso Tomé's *Transparente* in the Cathedral of Toledo," *Journal of the Society of Architectural Historians*, Vol. XXIX, no. 1, March 1970.

[18]The works in general are only of local importance and do not have to be included in this survey. See G. Kubler and M. Soria, *Art and Architecture in Spain and Portugal and Their American Dominions 1500 to 1800*, Harmondsworth, 1959.

[19]Fischer returned to Vienna in 1686, whereas Martinelli arrived in 1690 and Hildebrandt in 1696. Fischer died in 1723.

[20]See H. Sedlmayr, *Johann Bernhard Fischer von Erlach*, Munich-Vienna, 1956, p. 91. Originally the exterior of the Ahnensaal was terminated by an attic with a ring of large vases, like a crown. The Mansard roof was built later by Fischer's son Joseph Emanuel.

[21]Both buildings were finished by Joseph Emanuel Fischer von Erlach. Fischer's original project for the church is known from four plates in the *Entwurff einer historischen Architektur*. . . .

[22]Sedlmayr, *op. cit.*, pp. 123 ff.

[23]In the execution by Joseph Emanuel Fischer von Erlach, the dome was made higher and the articulation of the drum more complex, whereby the intended effect of a crown was considerably reduced.

[24]The effect of the volumes was reduced when the wings were made to correspond with the height of the library proper (by Nikolaus Pacassi, 1763–69).

[25]Leibniz had been the director of the famous library in Wolfenbüttel, which was built (1706–10) by Hermann Korb as an oval space. See Sedlmayr, *op. cit.*, pp. 140 ff.

[26]Sedlmayr, *op. cit.*, p. 144.

[27]Steinl is probably also the author of the extraordinary undulating galleries in the church at Dürnstein. See E. Mungenast, *Joseph Munggenast*, Vienna, 1963, p. 50.

[28]See H.G. Franz, *Bauten und Baumeister der Barockzeit in Böhmen*, Leipzig, 1962. The churches of Broggio in and around Litoměřice are of a high quality, above all the chapel of S. Wenceslas, 1714–16, and the church in Osek, 1716.

[29]Santini Aichel's year of birth is usually given as 1667. Recent research by Kotrba has proved that the correct year is 1677. The theory that Santini Aichel can be the architect of the churches built by Christoph Dientzenhofer is thereby invalidated. Unfortunately, this change of date also means that he cannot have designed the beautiful chapel in Lomec, begun in 1694.

[30]In addition to his major works, we should mention the chapel of Panenské Břežany (Jungfernbřežan, 1705-7) and the shrine of Mariánske Týnice (Maria Teinitz, 1711-18). See H. G. Franz, "Gotik und Barock im Werk des Johann Santini Aichel," *Wiener Jahrbuch für Kunstgeschichte*, Vol. 14, 1950.

[31]A typical example is offered by the monastery in Zbraslav (Königsaal, 1716–32). Here the axis of the *cour d'honneur* ends blindly in a wall which has a pair of pilasters where the main entrance should have been.

[32]Although the Vorarlberg builders came from an Austrian region, they were active in Germany and Switzerland. Ironically, in the province of Vorarlberg itself we do not find a single Vorarlberg church.

[33]See N. Lieb and F. Dieth, *Die Vorarlberger Barockbaumeister*, Munich-Zurich, 1960, Plates 158 and 159.

[34]The relatively conventional disposition of the plan is due to the fact that the basic design of Moosbrugger was incorporated by Frisoni in the famous ideal plan (1723) for the whole convent. See H. Schnell, *Weingarten*, Munich, 1950.

[35]The elaborate eastern twin-tower façade was added in 1761–69 by Johann Michael Beer.

[36]See J. Schöttl, *Die Kirche zu unser Lieben Frau in Günzburg*, Munich, 1957.

[37]See the excellent study by E. Haufstaengel, *Die Brüder Cosmas Damian und Egid Quirin Asam*, Munich-Berlin, 1955.

[38]Originally, less than half of the present layout was planned as an orangerie. Transitory projects show extended gardens with fountains and pavilions. In 1718 it was decided to make a symmetrical replica of the first U-shaped wings. The original corner pavilions date from 1712, the large gate-tower (*Kronentor*) from 1714, and the central *Wallpavillion* from 1716–17. In the nineteenth century the fourth side, toward the Elbe, was closed off by Gottfried Semper's picture gallery. See H.G. Franz, *Der Zwinger zu Dresden*, Berlin, 1946. See also E. Hempel, *Der Zwinger zu Dresden*, Berlin, 1961.

[39]The plastic modeling of the *Wallpavillion* shows an undulating movement and corresponding details which are most probably derived from Christoph Dientzenhofer's St. Nicholas in Prague, which Pöppelmann must have seen on his way between Dresden and Vienna.

[40]See H. Lund and K. Millech, *Danmarks Bygningskunst*, Copenhagen, 1963.

[41]See K. Downes, *English Baroque Architecture*, London, 1966.

[42]Inigo Jones and Sir Christopher Wren in certain respects approach High Baroque systematism, and in others they foreshadow Late Baroque pluralism. As has been pointed out by John Summerson, Wren used entirely different vocabularies in building his small city churches and St. Paul's Cathedral.

[43]Quoted in S. Lang, "Vanbrugh's Theory and Hawksmoor's Buildings," *Journal of the Society of Architectural Historians*, Vol. XXIV, no. 2, May 1965.

[44]See Lang, *op. cit.* See also C. Norberg-Schulz, *Intentions in Architecture*, Oslo-London, 1963.

[45]See Lang, *op. cit.*, p. 148. Christ Church and St. George were consecrated in 1729, St. Anne in 1730. For detailed information, see K. Downes, *Hawksmoor*, London, 1959 (new edition, London, 1969).

[46]St. Anne and St. George show a centralizing tendency due to freestanding columns in front of each corner and a centralized ceiling, creating a Greek cross within the outer rectangle—a solution probably indebted to Byzantine ("Greek") models. The interior of St. George was destroyed during World War II.

[47]See K. Downes, *Hawksmoor*, London, 1969, p. 141. The steeple was rebuilt in simplified form in the nineteenth century.

[48]A possible connection of aims remains to be investigated.

[49]J.-F. Blondel, *Cours d'architecture*, Vol. III, Paris, 1771–77.

[50]For the problem of "generations" in the history of art, see W. Pinder, *Das Problem der Generation in der Kunstgeschichte*, Leipzig, 1928.

Between the Baroque of the seventeenth century and the Neoclassicism of the Enlightenment, we find a Late Baroque architecture which to a certain extent unified the esprit de système of the former and the esprit systématique of the latter. It inherited the building types and the forms of the Baroque, but mostly gave up its absolutist pretensions. Representing the end of a tradition, it was nostalgic rather than rhetorical, and substituted for Baroque persuasion a wish for individual characterization.

The period comprises a multitude of different and partly contradictory currents. Hence it is impossible to offer a precise stylistic definition. The attempt at distinguishing between Late Baroque and Rococo, for instance, always fails, as it would presuppose a rather arbitrary emphasis on certain aspects of a more complex totality. In this book, therefore, Late Baroque simply means a period which starts about 1690 and ends about 1760. Its basic properties, which in our opinion supersede the usual stylistic categories, have been discussed in the preceding chapters.

In spite of the relatively short span of time, the Late Baroque produced a great number of original and artistically important buildings. We have, therefore, found it necessary to discuss many examples, but hope that the main themes of the period are still recognizable. The method employed concentrates attention on the analysis of spatial structures, understanding space as one of man's basic existential dimensions. The exposition forms a natural sequel to the preceding volume in this history.

The author wants to thank those who have offered him inspiration and help through their writings or in direct discussion, in particular Prof. Hans Sedlmayr, Prof. Paolo Portoghesi, Prof. Werner Hager, Prof. Rudolf Wittkower, Prof. Heinrich Gerhard Franz, Prof. Erich Bachmann, and Prof. Ferdinand Schuster. He also wants to thank Dr. Carlo Pirovano, who has been in charge of the production of this volume. Special thanks are due to Mrs. Marcia Berg for correcting and typing the manuscript.

Oslo, November 1970

SYNOPTIC TABLES / BIOGRAPHIES / SELECTED BIBLIOGRAPHY /
INDEX / LIST OF PLATES / LIST OF PHOTOGRAPHIC CREDITS

ITALY	GERMANY	AUSTRIA	BOHEMIA	FRANCE AND OTHER EUROPEAN CENTERS
				1681–82 Tom Tower at Christ Church (Oxford) C. WREN
	1682–95 Pilgrimage Church (Schönenberg, near Ellwangen) M. THUMB, C. THUMB, F. BEER			
	1684 Pilgrimage Church begun (Kappel, near Waldsassen) G. DIENTZENHOFER			
1686 Palazzo Asinari (Turin) begun M. GAROVE	1686–92 Abbey Church (Obermarchtal) M. THUMB, C. THUMB, F. BEER	1686–1714 St. Florian Convent C.A. CARLONE, J. PRANDTAUER		
		1688 Project for the *Lustgarten-gebäude* of Count Althan (in the Rossau, near Vienna) J.B. FISCHER VON ERLACH	1688–95 Althan Palace (Frain, Moravia) J.B. FISCHER VON ERLACH	
		1690 (after) First project for Schönbrunn Palace (Vienna) J.B. FISCHER VON ERLACH		
1692 Palazzo Barolo (Turin) G.F. BARONCELLI		1692 Strattmann Palace (Vienna) J.B. FISCHER VON ERLACH		
		c. 1694 Engelhartstetten Castle (Niederweiden) J.B. FISCHER VON ERLACH		
		1694 Projects for the Dreifaltigkeitskirche and Kollegienkirche (Salzburg) J.B. FISCHER VON ERLACH		
		1696 City-Palace of Prince Eugene (Vienna) J.B. FISCHER VON ERLACH		
		1696–1707 Kollegienkirche (Salzburg) J.B. FISCHER VON ERLACH		
		1697 Project for a *Gartenhaus* for the Mansfeld-Fondi (Schwarzenberg) Palace (Vienna) J.L. VON HILDEBRANDT		

ITALY	GERMANY	AUSTRIA	BOHEMIA	FRANCE AND OTHER EUROPEAN CENTERS
		1698 Project for a *Lustgarten-gebäude* (Vienna) J.B. FISCHER VON ERLACH		
		1699–1706 Batthyány Palace (Vienna) J.B. FISCHER VON ERLACH	1699 St. Lawrence (Gabel) begun J.L. VON HILDEBRANDT	1699 Projects for Castle Howard (Yorkshire) J. VANBRUGH, N. HAWKSMOOR
			1699 Garden-Palace (Liblice) G.B. ALLIPRANDI	
			1699–c. 1712 Convent Church (Obořiště) C. DIENTZENHOFER	c. 1700 Château de Champs-sur-Marne (France) P. BULLET
		1700-1706 Starhemberg-Schönburg Palace (Vienna) J.L. VON HILDEBRANDT	c. 1700-1713 Chapel of the Castle (Smiřice) C. DIENTZENHOFER	c. 1700 Hôtel Rothelin d'Argenson (Paris) P. LASSURANCE
		1700-1709 Klesheim Castle (near Salzburg) J.B. FISCHER VON ERLACH		1700–1702 Hôtel Crozat (Paris) P. BULLET
		1702–27 Benedictine Monastery (Melk) J. PRANDTAUER	1703 Lobkowitz Palace (Prague) G.B. ALLIPRANDI	1702 Château de Montmorency (France) J.-S. CARTAUD
			1703 Rebuilding of Cistercian Abbey Church (Sedlec, near Kutná Hora) J. SANTINI AICHEL	
1703–5 Port of the Ripetta (Rome) A. SPECCHI			1703–11 St. Nicholas on the Kleinseite (Prague) C. DIENTZENHOFER	c. 1703–19 Projects for the Monastery Church (Einsiedeln) K. MOOSBRUGGER
				1704 Hôtel Desmarets (Paris) P. LASSURANCE
	1704–12 Cathedral (Fulda) J. DIENTZENHOFER			1704–9 Hôtel de Soubise (Paris) P.-A. DELAMAIR
				1705–8 Hôtel de Rohan (Paris) P.-A. DELAMAIR
				1705–27 Blenheim Palace (Oxfordshire) J. VANBRUGH, N. HAWKSMOOR

ITALY	GERMANY	AUSTRIA	BOHEMIA	FRANCE AND OTHER EUROPEAN CENTERS
			1707 Church of St. Clare (Cheb) C. DIENTZENHOFER	1707 Hôtel d'Evreux (Paris) P. BULLET
1708 Antamori Chapel in S. Girolamo della Carità (Rome) F. JUVARRA		1708–14 Böhmische Hofkanzlei (Vienna) J.B. FISCHER VON ERLACH		
1708 Staircase of S. Giovanni a Carbonara (Naples) F. SANFELICE				
	1709–32 Zwinger (Dresden) M.D. PÖPPELMANN	1709–12 (or 1716?) Trautson Palace (Vienna) J.B. FISCHER VON ERLACH	1709–15 Church of St. Margaret (Břevnov, near Prague) C. DIENTZENHOFER	1709–19 Château de Lunéville (France) G. BOFFRAND
1710 Palazzo Pichini (Rome) A. SPECCHI				1710 Hôtel de Ludes (Paris) R. DE COTTE
1710–13 S. Maria del Rosario (Marino) G. SARDI	1710–13 Benedictine Abbey Church (Banz) J. DIENTZENHOFER		1710–20 Thun-Hohenstein Palace (Prague) J. SANTINI AICHEL	1710–13 Hôtel Amelot de Gournay (Paris) G. BOFFRAND
	1711–18 Schloss Pommersfelden (near Bamberg) J. DIENTZENHOFER			
			1712 Reconstruction of Benedictine Abbey (Kladruby) J. SANTINI AICHEL	1712 Projects for the Château de Malgrange (near Nancy) G. BOFFRAND
				1712–23 Cathedral of St. Peter and St. Paul (St. Petersburg) D. TREZZINI
			1713 Clam-Gallas Palace (Prague) J.B. FISCHER VON ERLACH	1713 Hôtel d'Estrées (Paris) R. DE COTTE
1713–20 Courtyard of the University (Turin) M. GAROVE		1713–16 Daun-Kinsky Palace (Vienna) J.L. VON HILDEBRANDT	1713–35 Premonstratensian Pilgrimage Church (Křtiny) J. SANTINI AICHEL	1713–19 Rebuilding of the Hôtel de la Vrillière (Paris) R. DE COTTE
		1714–16 Lower Belvedere (Vienna) J.L. VON HILDEBRANDT		1714 St. George-in-the-East, St. Anne's, Limehouse, and Christ Church, Spitalfields (all in London) begun N. HAWKSMOOR

ITALY	GERMANY	AUSTRIA	BOHEMIA	FRANCE AND OTHER EUROPEAN CENTERS
		1714–24 Trinitätskirche (Paura, near Lambach) J.M. PRUNNER		1714 Hôtel de Torcy (Paris) G. BOFFRAND
1715 Basilica of La Superga (near Turin) F. JUVARRA				1715 Projects for the Nevski Prospekt (St. Petersburg)
1715 Villa Palagonia (Bagheria, near Palermo) T.M. NAPOLI				1715 Delimitation of one side of the Place de la Carrière (Nancy) G. BOFFRAND
1715–22 Palazzo Saluzzo-Paesana (Turin) G.G. PLANTERY		1715–37 Karlskirche (Vienna) J.B. FISCHER VON ERLACH		
1716 Palazzo Martini di Cigala (Turin) F. JUVARRA				
1716 Palazzo Birago di Borgaro (Turin) F. JUVARRA		1716 Project for the Hofbibliothek (Vienna) J.B. FISCHER VON ERLACH		1716-17 Mon Plaisir (Peterhof) A.-J.-B. LE BLOND
1716–28 Quartieri Militari (Turin) F. JUVARRA	1716–18 Benedictine Abbey Church (Weltenburg) C.D. ASAM, E.Q. ASAM			1716–35 All Souls' College (Oxford) N. HAWKSMOOR
	1716–24 Monastery Church (Weingarten) K. MOOSBRUGGER, D.G. FRISONI, F. BEER		1717–20 Villa Amerika (Prague) K.I. DIENTZENHOFER	1717–30 Palace-Convent (Mafra) J.F. LUDOVICE
			1717–23 Church of Our Lady of Loreto on the Hradčany (Prague) C. DIENTZENHOFER	1717–27 St. Mary Woolnoth (London) N. HAWKSMOOR
1718–21 Façade and staircase of Palazzo Madama (Turin) F. JUVARRA	1719 Church (Pielenhofen) F. BEER	1719 Project for the reconstruction of Stift Göttweig (near Rossatz) J.L. VON HILDEBRANDT		1718 Hôtel Seignelay (Paris) G. BOFFRAND
	1719–44 Residenz (Würzburg) B. NEUMANN		1719–22 Shrine of St. John Nepomuk on the Green Mountain (near Žʼdár) J. SANTINI AICHEL	

ITALY	GERMANY	AUSTRIA	BOHEMIA	FRANCE AND OTHER EUROPEAN CENTERS
			1720–21 Castle (Karlová Koruna, near Chlumec) J. SANTINI AICHEL	1720 Hôtel de Noirmoutier (Paris) J. COURTONNE
			1720–28 Pilgrimage Church (Nicov) K.I. DIENTZENHOFER	1720–21 Seaton Delaval (Northumberland) J. VANBRUGH, N. HAWKSMOOR
			1720–29 Church of St. John Nepomuk on the Hradčany (Prague) K.I. DIENTZENHOFER	1720–22 Palais de Bourbon (Paris) P. LASSURANCE
				1720–31 St-Sébastien (Nancy) J.-N. JENNESSON
1721 Baptistery of S. Lorenzo in Lucina (Rome) G. SARDI	1721 Schönborn Chapel begun (Würzburg) B. NEUMANN	1721–22 Upper Belvedere (Vienna) J.L. VON HILDEBRANDT		1721 Hôtel de Matignon (Paris) J. COURTONNE
1721 Villa Valguarnera (Bagheria, near Palermo) T.M. NAPOLI		1721–33 Tower of Convent Church (Dürnstein) M. STEINL, J. MUNGGENAST		1721–32 Transparente of the Cathedral (Toledo) N. TOMÉ
		1722 Tower-façade of Abbey Church (Zwettl) M. STEINL	1722 Convent Church (Rajhrad, near Brno) J. SANTINI AICHEL	1722 Hôtel de Roquelaure (Paris) begun P. LASSURANCE
1723–26 Spanish Stairs (Rome) F. DE SANCTIS			1723–31 Monastery Church of St. Edwige (Wahlstatt) K.I. DIENTZENHOFER	1722 Hôtel de Lassay (Paris) P. LASSURANCE
1724–26 Ospedale di S. Gallicano (Rome) F. RAGUZZINI	c. 1724 Projects for the Abbey Church (Holzkirchen) J. DIENTZENHOFER		1724–26 Church of St. Adalbert (Počaply) K.I. DIENTZENHOFER	
1725–28 Staircase of the Palazzo Sanfelice (Naples) F. SANFELICE			1725–28 Villa Portheim (Prague) K.I. DIENTZENHOFER	1725 Project for the enlargement of the old town (Bath) J. WOOD THE ELDER
	1726 Frauenkirche (Dresden) G. BÄHR			1726 Project for the façade of St-Sulpice (Paris) J.-A. MEISSONIER

ITALY	GERMANY	AUSTRIA	BOHEMIA	FRANCE AND OTHER EUROPEAN CENTERS
1726–27 Cappella Cellamare (Naples) F. FUGA	1726–29 Premonstratensian Abbey Church (Osterhofen) J.M. FISCHER		1726–38 Monastery (Broumov) K.I. DIENTZENHOFER	
	1726–32 Piosasque de Non Palace (Munich) F. DE CUVILLIÉS			
	1727 Thurn und Taxis Palace (Frankfurt) R. DE COTTE			
	1727 Reconstruction of Benedictine Church (Rinchnach) begun J.M. FISCHER			
	1727 Benedictine Church (Münsterschwarzach, near Kitzingen) begun B. NEUMANN			
1727–28 Piazza S. Ignazio (Rome) F. RAGUZZINI	1727–32 Parish Church (Wiesentheid) B. NEUMANN			
	1727–33 Pilgrimage Church (Steinhausen) D. ZIMMERMANN			
	1727–33 St. Anna-am-Lehel (Munich) J.M. FISCHER			
1728–33 Dome of the Santuario di Vicoforte (Mondovì) F. GALLO				1728–31 Hôtel Peyrenc de Moras-Biron (Paris) J. GABRIEL
1729 Porta Palazzo (Turin) F. JUVARRA				1728–34 Queen Square (Bath) J. WOOD THE ELDER
1729 Palazzo Cavour (Turin) G.G. PLANTERY				1728–42 Palais de Rohan (Strasbourg) R. DE COTTE
1729–31 Hunting Lodge of Stupinigi (near Turin) F. JUVARRA	1729–39 Pilgrimage Church (Gössweinstein) B. NEUMANN		1729–39 St. John on the Rock (Prague) K.I. DIENTZENHOFER	

ITALY	GERMANY	AUSTRIA	BOHEMIA	FRANCE AND OTHER EUROPEAN CENTERS
1730–33 Palazzo Ghilini (Alessandria) B. ALFIERI	1730–32 Parish Church (Unering) J.M. FISCHER			1730–40 Projects for the gardens of Chiswick, Stowe, and Rousham (England) W. KENT
				1730–45 St-Jacques (Lunéville) G. BOFFRAND
1731–33 Palazzo Doria (Rome) G. VALVASSORI	1731 Staircase of the Palace (Bruchsal) completed A.F.F. VON RITTER ZU GRÜNSTEIN, B. NEUMANN	1731 Church and Library (Altenburg) J. MUNGGENAST		
1732–35 Palazzo della Consulta (Rome) F. FUGA	1731 Project for the tower-façade of the Cathedral (Würzburg) J.L. VON HILDEBRANDT			
1732–36 Chiesa del Carmine (Turin) F. JUVARRA	1731–32 Plan for the Hofkirche (Würzburg) B. NEUMANN			
1732–62 Trevi Fountain (Rome) N. SALVI, G. PANNINI	1731–39 Kollegienkirche (Diessen) J.M. FISCHER		1732–34 Chapel of the Imperial Hospital on the Hradčany (Prague) K.I. DIENTZENHOFER	
	1733 Church of St. John Nepomuk, or Asamkirche (Munich) E.Q. ASAM		1732–35 Church of St. Francis Xavier (Opařany) K.I. DIENTZENHOFER	
1733–36 Façade of S. Giovanni in Laterano (Rome) A. GALILEI	1733–37 Holnstein Palace (Munich) F. DE CUVILLIÉS		1732–36 St. Mary Magdalen (Karlovy Vary) K.I. DIENTZENHOFER	
1734 Façade of the Cathedral (Catania) G.B. VACCARINI	1734–40 Amalienburg in the gardens of Nymphenburg Palace (Munich) F. DE CUVILLIÉS		1732–37 St. Nicholas in the Altstadt (Prague) K.I. DIENTZENHOFER	1734–36 Eremitage (Copenhagen) L. DE THURAH
	1735–39 Church of St. Mary (Ingolstadt) J.M. FISCHER		1733–43 Parish Church of St. Clement (Odolená Voda) K.I. DIENTZENHOFER	1734–45 Towers of Westminster Abbey (London) N. HAWKSMOOR, J. JAMES
1735–43 Façade and portico of S. Maria Maggiore (Rome) F. FUGA	1735–44 Church of St. Michael (Berg-am-Laim, near Munich) J.M. FISCHER		1734–35 Projects for the Ursuline Convent (Kutná Hora) K.I. DIENTZENHOFER	1735 Oval Salon of the Hôtel de Soubise (Paris) G. BOFFRAND

ITALY	GERMANY	AUSTRIA	BOHEMIA	FRANCE AND OTHER EUROPEAN CENTERS
1735–67 S. Agata (Catania) G.B. VACCARINI	1735–51 Pilgrimage Church of Maria Schnee (Aufhausen, near Regensburg) J.M. FISCHER			
1736 Palazzo Corsini (Rome) F. FUGA	1736–41 Parish Church (Günzburg) D. ZIMMERMANN			1736–40 Biron Palace (Jelgava) B. RASTRELLI
	1736–41 Ursuline Church (Straubing) C.D. ASAM, E.Q. ASAM			
	1736–50 Clemenswerth hunting lodge (near Sögel, Westphalia) J.C. VON SCHLAUN			
1738–39 Pilgrimage Chapel of the Visitation (Vallinotto, near Carignano) B. VITTONE			1737–53 Dome and bell-tower of St. Nicholas on the Kleinseite (Prague) K.I. DIENTZENHOFER	
	1739–53 Tower-façade of the Katholische Hofkirche (Dresden) G. CHIAVERI			
	1739–56 Parish Church (Heusenstamm) B. NEUMANN			
c. 1740 S. Luigi Gonzaga (Corteranzo) B. VITTONE	1740–45 Parish Church (Etwashausen) B. NEUMANN			1740–44 Summer Palace (St. Petersburg) B. RASTRELLI
1740–60 S. Marta (Agliè) C. MICHELA	1740–45 Parish Church (Gaibach) B. NEUMANN			
	1741–52 Benedictine Abbey Church (Zwiefalten) J.M. FISCHER			
1742 S. Chiara (Brà) B. VITTONE	1742 Projects for Jesuit churches (Mainz and Würzburg) B. NEUMANN			1742 (after) Decoration for the Sacristy of the Cartuja (Granada) ANONYMOUS

ITALY	GERMANY	AUSTRIA	BOHEMIA	FRANCE AND OTHER EUROPEAN CENTERS
	1742 Project for the Monastery Church (Langheim) B. NEUMANN			
1743 Façade and vestibule of S. Croce in Gerusalemme (Rome) P. PASSALACQUA, D. GREGORINI	1743–63 Pilgrimage Church of Vierzehnheiligen (on the Main, near Staffelstein) B. NEUMANN		1743–51 Sylva-Tarouca Palace (Prague) K.I. DIENTZENHOFER	
	1744–54 Pilgrimage Church (Wies, near Steingaden) D. ZIMMERMANN			1744–57 Church of Smolny Convent (St. Petersburg) B. RASTRELLI
	1744–63 High altar for the Pilgrimage Church of Vierzehnheiligen (on the Main, near Staffelstein) J.J.M. KÜCHEL			
c. 1745 S. Gaetano (Nizza) B. VITTONE	1745 Sanssouci (Potsdam) G.W. VON KNOBELSDORFF			
c. 1745 S. Chiara (Turin) B. VITTONE				
1745 Palazzo Cenci-Bolognetti (Rome) F. FUGA	1745–48 Rüschhaus (near Münster) J.C. VON SCHLAUN			
1746–66 S. Giorgio (Ragusa Ibla) R. GAGLIARDI		1746 Project for the Hofkirche (Vienna) B. NEUMANN		1746–55 Voronzov Palace (St. Petersburg) B. RASTRELLI
		1746–47 Projects for the Hofburg (Vienna) B. NEUMANN		1746–66 Ste-Madeleine (Besançon) N. NICOLE
	1747 Benedictine Church (Neresheim) commissioned B. NEUMANN			
	1747–49 Projects for the Residenz (Stuttgart) B. NEUMANN		1747–51 Church of St. John the Baptist (Paštiky) K.I. DIENTZENHOFER	1747–52 Mon Plaisir by Le Blond remodeled (Peterhof) B. RASTRELLI
	1748 Pilgrimage Church of Käppele (Würzburg) begun B. NEUMANN			
	1748–66 Benedictine Abbey Church (Ottobeuren) J.M. FISCHER			1749–66 Monastery Church (St. Gall) P. THUMB

ITALY	GERMANY	AUSTRIA	BOHEMIA	FRANCE AND OTHER EUROPEAN CENTERS
c. 1750 Chapel in the Villa del Cardinale (near Turin) B. VITTONE	1750 Projects for the Residenz (Karlsruhe) B. NEUMANN			1750 Spiral tower for the Church of Our Savior (Copenhagen) L. DE THURAH
c. 1750 Chapel in the Villa Cipresso (near Turin) B. VITTONE	1750–53 Interior of the Residenztheater (Munich) F. DE CUVILLIÉS			1750–54 Palaces on the Amalienborg Square (Copenhagen) N. EIGTVED
1750 Parish Church (Grignasco) begun B. VITTONE	1750–58 Anastasia Chapel (Benediktbeuern) J.M. FISCHER			1750–54 Stroganov Palace (St. Petersburg) B. RASTRELLI
1750 (after) Albergo dei Poveri (Naples) F. FUGA				1752 Project for Place Stanislas (Nancy) E. HÉRÉ DE CORNY
1750–56 S. Chiara (Vercelli) B. VITTONE				
1750–c. 1760 S. Maria di Piazza (Turin) B. VITTONE				1752 Project for Frederiks Kirke (Copenhagen) N. EIGTVED
1751–74 Royal Palace (Caserta) L. VANVITELLI				1752–56 Palace (Tsarskoe Selo) B. RASTRELLI
				1753–62 Rebuilding of the Winter Palace (St. Petersburg) B. RASTRELLI
				1754–58 King's Circus (Bath) J. WOOD THE ELDER, J. WOOD THE YOUNGER
1755 S. Croce (Villanova di Mondovì B. VITTONE	1755–57 Erbdrostenhof (Münster) J.C. VON SCHLAUN			1755–63 Place Louis XV, today the Place de la Concorde (Paris) A.-J. GABRIEL
1756 Piazza Palazzo di Città (Turin) B. ALFIERI				
1757–64 S. Giovanni (Carignano) B. ALFIERI				1757–75 Gardes Meubles, Place de la Concorde (Paris) A.-J. GABRIEL

ITALY	GERMANY	AUSTRIA	BOHEMIA	FRANCE AND OTHER EUROPEAN CENTERS
1758 S. Michele (Rivarolo Canavese) B. VITTONE				
	1759–66 Church of St. Marinus and St. Arianus (Rott am Inn, near Wasserburg) J.M. FISCHER			
	1763–66 Church of the Brigittines (Altomünster) J.M. FISCHER			1764–90 Ste-Geneviève, today the Panthéon (Paris) J.-G. SOUFFLOT
				1765 Brock Street (Bath) J. WOOD THE YOUNGER
	1767–73 Schloss (Münster) J.C. VON SCHLAUN			1767–74 Royal Crescent (Bath) J. WOOD THE YOUNGER
1770 Parish Church (Borgo d'Ale) begun B. VITTONE				
				1789–93 Lansdown Crescent and Somerset Place (Bath) J. PALMER, J. EVELEIGH

ACERO Y ACEBO, VICENTE

Dates and places of birth and death are unknown. However, Acero is known to have been active between 1714 and 1738. He devoted himself chiefly to the design and construction of cathedrals. His designs were often radically altered, not only because their construction took too long, but also because his taste came to be regarded as no longer modern. The first period of his career (1714–20) was spent in designing and building Guadix Cathedral. Between 1720 and 1729 he designed Cádiz Cathedral, whose construction actually began in 1722. He continued the building of the tobacco factory in Seville and also designed the façade of Málaga Cathedral.

ALFIERI, BENEDETTO

Born 1700 in Rome; died 1767 in Turin. Alfieri started on a legal career in Asti, but turned to architecture. In 1730 he was working on the reconstruction of the Palazzo Mazzetti di Frinco in Asti and drawing up plans for the Palazzo Ghilini in Alessandria, which was built between 1730 and 1733. He was then summoned to Turin, where he directed work on the Teatro Regio and later the conversion of the Palazzo Chiablese (1736–40).

In 1739 he accepted the appointment as first Royal Architect. He succeeded Juvarra in a number of important buildings: the Royal Palace, the Palazzo Madama, the Senate, and Turin Cathedral. In 1749 Alfieri began work on the parish church of S. Giorgio at Piovà Massaia, which was not finished until 1774; his project for the belfry of S. Gaudenzio in Novara was completed in 1753. In 1757 he presented the plans for what may be considered his most original work, the parish church of S. Giovanni Battista at Carignano, which was completed in 1764. He was asked to draw up plans for the seminary at Asti in 1762, but his drawings were followed only in part during its erection (1763–75). The parish church of SS. Pietro e Paolo at Monastero Vasco, however, was built in accordance with his plans.

During the last years of his life he built the chapel of S. Evasio in the cathedral at Casale Monferrato. Alfieri undertook a number of assignments to enlarge or decorate residential buildings, and he was also involved in a certain amount of town planning, especially for Turin and Vercelli; he devised a complete plan for the latter in 1761.

ALLIO, DONATO FELICE

Born c. 1690 in Valtellina; died c. 1780 (place of death unknown). Allio established himself in Vienna, where he was a pupil of Johann Bernhard Fischer von Erlach. His only known completed work is the Salesianerinnenkirche in Vienna (1717–30). He made a project to enlarge the convent at Klosterneuburg, but the work, begun in 1730, was broken off in 1750 and never completed.

ALLIPRANDI, GIOVANNI BATTISTA

Born 1665, probably at Laino in Val d'Intelvi; died 1720 at Litomyšl. In Prague he built the Sternberk Palace (1692–1720) in cooperation with Johann Santini Aichel,

and the Kaiserstein, Hrzan, and Lobkowitz (1703) palaces. His garden-palace at Liblice (1699) was a simplified version of Fischer von Erlach's project for a large *Lustgartengebäude*. Alliprandi built the Dreifaltigkeitskìrche at Kusk (after 1707) and began the Piaristenkirche at Litomyšl (1714).

AMARANTE, CARLOS LUIZ FERREIRA DA CRUZ

Born 1748 in Braga; died 1815 in Porto. Amarante's principal works are at Braga: St. Mark's Hospital, erected according to the design for the Johannspital in Salzburg by Fischer von Erlach; the church of Bom Jesus do Monte, with a grand flight of steps; and the Convento do Populo. He also built the church of S. Trinidade e das Almas in Porto. Amarante, an engineer who specialized in bridge construction, built the bridge over the Tâmega in the same town.

AMATO, GIACOMO

Born 1643 in Palermo; died 1732 in Palermo. Apparently Amato turned to architecture only after being in Rome (1671–84), where his first experience was supervising and directing the work on the Maddalena Convent. He then returned to Palermo; in 1686 he started the rebuilding of the church of S. Teresa alla Kalsa there, and in 1687 he was working on the Crossbearers' Novitiate House. Two years later he drew up plans for the church of the Pietà.

Among the secular works he built in Palermo, we should mention the Palazzo Cutò at Porta Maqueda (the plans of which are still in existence), the Palazzo Tarallo, and the Duke of Branciforte's villa; he also directed the modernization of the Palazzo Spaccaforno-Valdina.

ARCHER, THOMAS

Born 1668 at Tanworth-in-Arden; died 1743 in London. Archer was a pupil of Vanbrugh, although his work is nearer to that of Wren and Hawksmoor. His career as an architect lasted only about fifteen years. He studied at Oxford from 1686 to 1689 and then traveled abroad for four years. In 1705 he became Groom Porter, and in 1715 Comptroller of Customs at Newcastle.

His first works were some private buildings: Cascade House in Devonshire (1702), after the plan of Borromini's S. Ivo alla Sapienza; the north façade of Chatsworth House in Derbyshire (1705–7); Heythorp House in Oxfordshire (1705–10); and between 1709 and 1712 two important pavilions in the garden of Wrest (Bedfordshire) for the Duke of Kent. In 1709 he began St. Philip's Church in Birmingham. From this date onward he also made drawings for several houses in London, including Monmouth House in Soho (1709–12), since destroyed, and Roehampton House (1710–12) in Wandsworth, now part of the Queen's Hospital.

Archer was a member of the committee formed for the construction of fifty new churches, for which he designed St. Paul's in Deptford (1712–30) and St. John's at Westminster (1714–18), whose interior was rebuilt after the fire in 1758. (It was again burned down in 1941.)

ASAM, COSMAS DAMIAN and EGID QUIRIN

Cosmas Damian, an architect, sculptor, and painter, was born at Benediktbeuren in 1686 and died at Munich in 1739. His brother Egid Quirin was born at Tegernsee in Bavaria in 1692 and died at Mannheim in 1750. The brothers worked together. They began their training by observing the painting of their father, Hans Georg, who introduced illusionist painting into Bavaria. In 1712–14 the brothers were in Rome, where they came under the influence of Giovanni Battista Gaulli and Andrea Pozzo, and above all of Bernini. The monastery church of Weltenburg, an architectural masterpiece by Cosmas, dates from 1716–18 and contains Egid's altar of 1721; from this same period come their alterations to the church of the old Augustinian monastery at Rohr, which show Bernini's influence.

The delightful church of St. John Nepomuk in Munich dates from 1733; it was magnificently decorated by Egid Quirin and forms a superb artistic unit together with the adjacent house.

Many works were carried out by the Asams between the years of 1736 and 1741: the project for a new high altar and choir for the church of the Holy Sepulchre at Deggendorf; the Ursuline church at Straubing, where the architectural part is by Egid and the frescoes by Cosmas; the remodeling of the south apse in Freising Cathedral (1738); and the altar by Egid for the Maria-Dorfen pilgrimage church.

AUBERT THE YOUNGER, JEAN

Date and place of birth are uncertain; died 1741 in Paris. Aubert worked a great deal in the service of the Condé family, who chose him to carry out alterations on their Chantilly residence. Aubert began work there in 1708, but only the large stables remain. He presented the designs in 1719, and the stables were finished about 1740. He collaborated with Lassurance and above all with Jacques V Gabriel on the Palais Bourbon and the Hôtel Biron (today the Rodin Museum), which was completed in 1731; he also finished the Hôtel de Beauvais. In 1736 (or 1739) he restored Châalis Abbey for the Prince of Clermont, who was abbot of the monastery.

AUGUSTONI, JAKOB

Dates and places of birth and death are unknown, but he was working in Bohemia at the end of the seventeenth century. Some houses for the aristocracy at Plzeň and other buildings in the neighborhood (church of St. Blaise, 1702) were erected by him during the early years of the eighteenth century. Among his works are the church of St. Anne at Plzeň (begun in 1715), and the castles of Přichovice (1718–19), Malesice, Tynec (begun before 1723), and Trpisty (from 1729).

BÄHR, GEORG

Born 1666 at Fürstenwald, near Lauenstein; died 1738 in Dresden. Bähr made a considerable contribution to Protestant religious architecture. His first churches were mainly centralized types in the form of a Greek cross: Loschwitz (1705–8), Schmiedeberg (1713–16), Hohnstein near Pirna (1715–26), and Forchheim near Lenge-feld (1719-21). From 1705 Bähr was the municipal master carpenter of Dresden. His main work is the Frauenkirche in Dresden. The first project for it dates from 1722; construction was begun in 1726 and finished about 1743. The church was completely destroyed during World War II. Bähr cooperated with Pöppelmann on the Dreikönigskirche (from 1732). In Dresden he also worked on the Hôtel de Saxe and the British Palace (c. 1720).

BARONCELLI, GIAN FRANCESCO

Dates and places of birth and death are unknown. He was active between 1672 and 1694 and succeeded Guarini as engineer to Prince Carignano. Baroncelli also assisted Amedeo di Castellamonte, whose work he continued in the Ospedale di S. Giovanni in Turin.

In that city he built the Palazzo Granieri (1682–83) and the Palazzo Barolo, where he was responsible for the central part of the façade, the hall, and the main staircase (1692). In 1684 the sanctuary of S. Maria del Pilone at Moretta was begun in accordance with his plans.

BEER, FRANZ

Born 1660 at Au; died 1726 at Bezau. Together with Michael and Christian Thumb he built the pilgrimage church at Schönenberg, near Ellwangen (1682-95), and the church at Obermarchtal (1686–92). He also erected the abbey churches at Rheinau (1704–11) and St. Urban (1711–15). Beer cooperated with Donato Giuseppe Frisoni, Johann Jakob Herkomer, Christian Thumb, and Kaspar Moosbrugger in designing the chapter church at Weingarten (1715–24). From 1717 to 1724 he directed the construction of the convent church at Weissenau. His church at Pielenhofen dates from 1719.

BEER, JOHANN MICHAEL

Born 1696 at Au; died 1780 at Bildstein. From 1761 to 1769 he built the new east front of the convent church at St. Gall.

BEER, MICHAEL

Born c. 1605; died 1666 (locations unknown). With Johannes Serro, he built the chapter church at Kempten (1651–66), which he probably also designed.

BIBIENA, ANTONIO GALLI DA

Born 1700 in Parma; died 1774, perhaps in Milan. Bibiena belonged to a family of theater architects and scenographers who worked in Italy and were known throughout most of Europe.

Among the religious work carried out by him, the following should be mentioned: the enlargement of the chancel and erection of the high altar in the Peterskirche, Vienna (1730–32); the façade of S. Barbara in Mantua (1737); and the decoration of the Holy Trinity Church in Bratislava.

Antonio's main activity was building theaters. He acted as Francesco Bibiena's assistant on the Teatro Alibert in

Rome, erected the Teatro Scientifico for the Accademia Virgiliana in Mantua (1767–69), and rebuilt the Teatro dei Rinnovati in Siena (1751–53). He drew up the project for the Teatro Civico in Bologna (1755), altered the Teatro della Pergola in Florence, and built the Teatro Rossini at Lugo (1758–61) and the Teatro dei Quattro Cavalieri in Pavia (1763).

BLONDEL, JACQUES-FRANÇOIS

Born 1705 in Rouen; died 1774 in Paris. Blondel was chiefly a theorist and constructed little. One of his first works was the Hôtel Petit de Marivat (1736) at Besançon. He was not asked to design large buildings until he was over fifty, probably because of his immense prestige as a professor and theorist. He founded the École des Arts in Paris (1743), and also published his lectures in book form as the Cours d'architecture civile ou traité de la décoration et construction des bâtiments (Paris, 1771–77, 6 volumes). Blondel became a member of the Academy in 1755 and taught there from 1762. His other publications were L'Architecture française (Paris, 1752–56) and De la Distribution des maisons de plaisances (1737–38). He was engaged by Diderot to direct the writing of the architectural section of the Encyclopédie.

Blondel's major constructions are at Metz, where for the DeChoiseul family he built the girls' college of St. Louis (designed in 1761). During the same period he took part in discussions about the project for the Place des Armes, and was officially entrusted with its creation. The square was bounded on the southwest by the cathedral (façade, 1763–66); parallel to this Blondel built the Hôtel de Ville (town hall) (1764–75), and on the north a corps de garde. Blondel made two more squares around the cathedral: the Place de Chambre, and the square bounded by the Parliament on the south and the bishop's palace on the north.

Blondel also worked for the city of Strasbourg, where he planned the reconstruction of the cathedral dome and a barracks, and submitted a plan for the whole city.

BOFFRAND, GERMAIN

Born 1667 in Nantes; died 1754 in Paris. He was the son of an architect and sculptor. When he was fourteen he was sent to Paris, where he studied under François Girardon and Jules Hardouin-Mansart, with whom he worked on the Orangerie at Versailles in 1685 and on the construction of some façades in the Place Vendôme. In 1690 he was appointed King's Architect and thenceforth was entrusted with important assignments such as the decoration of the Hôtel de Soubise (begun 1735). In 1709 Boffrand was accepted by the Academy of Architecture and through Hardouin-Mansart obtained major commissions from the Duke of Lorraine at Lunéville and at Nancy, where he designed one side of the Place de la Carrière (1715).

Apart from these activities, he carried on brilliant work in Paris, devoting himself in particular to the construction of private houses. In Paris he restored the Hôtel Petit Bourbon for the Princesse de Condé (1710) and the hôtels Amelot de Gournay (1710–13), Broglie (1711), D'Argenson (1711; 1726), Gournay et Villars (1712), and Seignelay (1718). Outside Paris he built the Château de

St-Ouen for the Rohan princes; the Château de Lunéville for the Duke of Lorraine (1709–19); the Château de Malgrange near Nancy (begun 1712); the Ducal Palace at Nancy (1717); and the Château d'Haroué in Lorraine (1720).

From 1725 Boffrand was engaged on some important assignments abroad, among them the designs for the Würzburg Residenz, produced in collaboration with Robert de Cotte. His work on the Hôpital des Enfants Trouvés (1747) and his project for the Place Louis XV (1753; today the Place de la Concorde) date from his last years in Paris.

BONAVIA, SANTIAGO

Born in Piacenza (date unknown); died 1759 at Aranjuez. Bonavia went to Spain about 1731. He was mainly active at Aranjuez, but before settling there he worked in Madrid, where he built the Buen Retiro theater, in which he was engaged more as a scenographer than as an architect. In Madrid he worked on the church of SS. Justo y Pastor, now called S. Miguel; he made the designs in 1739 and directed the construction until 1743.

In 1748 a fire destroyed the palace at Aranjuez. Ferdinand VI immediately ordered it to be reconstructed, and entrusted Bonavia with direction of the works. Although it is difficult to distinguish between the work of the collaborators, one can recognize the hand of Bonavia in the large staircase on the west front and in the chapel of S. Antonio (1748–68). The fire of 1748 prompted a campaign for redeveloping the entire city. In 1750 demolition of the old houses began, and plans for the urban reconstruction of Aranjuez were initiated; Bonavia directed these projects.

BROGGIO, OTTAVIANO

Born c. 1688 at Litoměřice; died 1742 at Litoměřice. His main works are to be found in his native town. In addition to a number of dwellings, he erected the church of St. Wenceslaus (1714–16) and rebuilt the Jesuit church. In 1719 the city appointed him to restore and decorate the cathedral. Broggio also worked on the cathedral of another little town, Raudnitz on the Elbe. At Grossmergthal, near Zvikov, he built the parish church. He is also credited with the main façade of the convent at Osek (1715), the Dominican churches at Litoměřice and Ustì, Ploskovice Palace (c. 1720), and the church at Sobenice.

Other works include the church at Cheb (Eger, 1708–14), the monastery church at Břevnov (1709–15), and the façade of St. Mary of Loreto in Prague (from 1721).

BURLINGTON, RICHARD BOYLE, LORD

Born 1694 in London; died 1753 in London. Lord Burlington had official positions at an early age as Privy Councillor and Lord Treasurer of Ireland; these, however, did not stop him from taking a journey to Italy in 1714–15. He returned there again in 1719 to study the work of Palladio. Lord Burlington was one of the most influential promoters of English Neoclassicism. He financed the publication of William Kent's Designs of I. Jones (1727) and R. Castell's Villas of the Ancients (1728); he himself edited the publication of *Fabbriche antiche disegnate da Andrea Palladio Vicentino e date in luce da Ricardo conte di Burlington* (1730).

In London his finest works include the alterations of Burlington House in Piccadilly (c. 1719), the dormitory of Westminster School (1722–30), and the house of General Wade in Great Burlington Street (1723). At Chiswick (West London), he designed a pavilion for the garden (1717), and then began building a mansion (1724) in imitation of Palladio's Villa Rotonda. This mansion and the Assembly Rooms at York (1730–33) are the most important of Burlington's works. Many others have been destroyed, completely rebuilt, or very much altered: Petersham Lodge, Surrey (c. 1721), Coleshill House, Berkshire (c. 1744), Boynton Hall (Yorkshire), and Kirkby Hall, Ouseburn (Yorkshire), the latter in collaboration with Roger Morris.

CAMPBELL, COLIN

Born in Scotland, date unknown; died 1729 in London. We know little of this Scottish architect's early career; he first appears officially as the agent of William Benson, then Surveyor of the Works, who in 1718 nominated him Chief Clerk of the King's Works and Deputy Surveyor. In 1715 he became widely known, not so much for his constructions (for instance, Wanstead House, Essex), as for the publication of the first volume of *Vitruvius Britannicus,* a collection of engravings of classical English buildings, most of them contemporary (the second and third volumes were issued in 1717 and 1725).

In 1717–18 Campbell built Rolls House in Chancery Lane, London. He then came under the protection of Lord Burlington, for whom he carried out the renovations of Burlington House in Piccadilly (1718–19). Campbell constructed many country mansions, mainly near London, among them Houghton Hall (Norfolk), designed in 1721 for Robert Walpole and built, with modifications, after 1722. Between 1722 and 1725 he built Mereworth Castle in Kent and the Great Room in the Hall Barn at Beaconsfield (Buckinghamshire).

CHIAVERI, GAETANO

Born 1689 in Rome; died 1770 at Foligno. Trained in the environment of late seventeenth-century Rome, he worked mainly in Russia, Poland, and Germany. He went to Russia in 1717 and was in Peter the Great's service until 1727, participating in the rebuilding of St. Petersburg (in 1720 he was appointed a member of the Imperial Chancellory). By order of the Tsarina, he designed the church of the Trinity at Korostino, near Novgorod (1721–23). He worked with Domenico Trezzini on various projects and built a number of public and private buildings. In 1724 Chiaveri succeeded Mattornovij in building the Natural History Museum and the Library of the Academy of Sciences; also in St. Petersburg, he designed the Menšikov Palace and completed St. Isaac's Cathedral.

He then moved to Dresden, where he was appointed court architect. He drew up plans for the Katholische Hofkirche and supervised its erection from 1739 to 1753 (the church was completed by Johann Christoph Knöffel). In Warsaw, about 1740, he designed the façade of the Royal Palace overlooking the Vistula.

Before returning to Rome (1749), Chiaveri built Prince Maximilian's palace in Dresden (its façade was changed in 1783). In Rome, where he was appointed a member of the Accademia di S. Luca, he drew up a plan for the alteration of the dome of St. Peter's, but his works in this city were few and unimportant.

CHURRIGUERA, ALBERTO DE

Born 1676 in Madrid; died 1750 at Orgaz. Alberto was the youngest of the Churriguera brothers. This was the family that gave its name to the so-called "Churrigueresque" style. Alberto did not have an easy career, as he was overshadowed by his brothers José Benito and Joaquín. When Joaquín died in 1725, Alberto was appointed architect of the new cathedral at Salamanca and worked on the choir, the tabernacle of the high altar, and the sacristy (he resigned in 1738, owing to disagreement with the chapter). In 1728 he was entrusted with the construction of the Plaza Mayor in the same city. Its first stone was laid in 1729, and in 1733 the Royal Pavilion was completed; the surrounding palaces were finished in 1755, when Andrés García de Quiñones built the façade of the Ayuntamiento.

Alberto also built the upper part of the façade of Valladolid Cathedral (1729) and the church of S. Sebastián (1731) at Salamanca. He began the Orgaz parish church in 1738, but it was still not completed in 1750, the year of his death. One of his best works is the church of the Assumption at Rueda (1738–47). The large chapel of S. Tecla in Burgos Cathedral (1736) is almost certainly his.

CHURRIGUERA, JOSÉ BENITO DE

Born 1665 in Madrid; died 1725 in Madrid. José Benito is the principal member of this family. His art consisted of ornamental work with cabinet-makers, gilders, and manufacturers of *retablos*. In 1689 he came to official notice as the winner of the competition for the monument to Queen Marie Louise of Orléans, wife of Charles II. In 1690 he worked on the church at Monserrat, which has been destroyed, and was appointed assistant palace designer at the Madrid court. In 1693 he created the *retablo* in the church of S. Esteban in Salamanca, one of his most important works.

He worked as an architect in Madrid mainly between 1700 and 1725, creating the *retablo* in S. Basilio (c. 1717), the façade of S. Cayetano (c. 1722), and the church of S. Tomás (c. 1724; destroyed). But his outstanding achievement is the group of buildings (1722) at Nuevo Batzán, a central block composed of church and palace opening onto three squares. The purchaser was the banker Juan de Goyeneche, for whom he had built a palace at Madrid (now the Academia de S. Fernando, rebuilt by Diego Villanueva in 1774).

CINO, GIUSEPPE

Born 1644 in Lecce; died 1722 in Lecce. Cino worked in his native town on S. Chiara (1687–91), the seminary (1694–1709), S. Maria della Provvidenza (1708), and the rebuilding of the Madonna del Carmine (1711). He was also responsible for the interior decoration of the church of S. Irene and for the façade of SS. Niccolò e Cataldo, both also in Lecce.

COTTE, ROBERT DE

Born 1656 in Paris; died 1737 in Paris. Robert de Cotte was a pupil of and collaborator with Jules Hardouin-Mansart. He was already almost thirty years old when he began to be entrusted with important architectural commissions, but his close collaboration with Hardouin-Mansart prevents one from clearly distinguishing his personal contribution to these projects.

While he was engaged upon the interior of the Château de Maintenon (1686), he was asked to design a *place royale* at Lyon and to adapt and carry out Hardouin-Mansart's design for the Hôtel de Ville in the same city (c. 1700). De Cotte also collaborated with Hardouin-Mansart in the construction of the Invalides, the choir in Notre-Dame at Paris, and the chapel at Versailles.

Upon the death of Hardouin-Mansart (1708), De Cotte inherited the direction of works in the various building yards and the position of King's Architect, which he held until 1734, the year when he fell ill. In the meantime he had become a member of the Royal Academy of Architecture (1687), had undertaken a journey for study purposes in Italy (1689–90), and had attained a high reputation not only in Paris, but in the provinces and at foreign courts. In 1686 he was given the job of reconstructing the bishop's palace at Rheims.

His first entirely independent work was the Hôtel de Ludes (1710). This was soon followed by a series of private mansions, including the Hôtel d'Estrées (1713), the Hôtel de Grenouillière (1716), and the reconstruction of the Hôtel de la Vrillière for the Count of Toulouse (1713–19). De Cotte also worked on public and royal buildings: the reconstruction of the Samaritaine on the Pont-Neuf (1711–15), the fountain at the Château d'Eau in front of the Palais Royal (1719; destroyed in 1848), the design for the façade of St-Roch (1734–35; later carried out by his son), and the installation of the royal library in the Louvre.

In the provinces De Cotte constructed bishops' palaces at Verdun (from 1725) and Châlons-sur-Marne; châteaux at Thouars (1707), Chanteloup, and Issy; and churches (Ste-Croix at Orléans) and town-planning schemes (layout of the Place de la Bourse at Bordeaux, begun in 1730). Perhaps his most interesting work is the Palais de Rohan at Strasbourg (1728–42).

De Cotte was well known and had great influence abroad, and his advice was often sought about important works, as—for example—the castle at Brühl, the Würzburg Residenz, and the Thurn und Taxis Palace in Frankfurt (1727; destroyed in 1944).

COURTONNE, JEAN

Born 1671 in Paris; died 1739 in Paris. Courtonne was a famous architect in his time but very little of his work remains: the Hôtel de Noirmoutier (1720); the Hôtel de Matignon, which the princes of Tingry commissioned in 1721 and sold in 1723, before its completion, to Jacques de Matignon; and the designs for the Cabinet d'Histoire

Naturelle de Bonnier de la Mosson. In 1730 Courtonne was appointed professor at the Academy of Architecture, where he taught until his death.

Among his theoretical works we may mention the *Traité de la perspective avec des remarques sur l'architecture suivi de quelques édifices considérables mis en perspective et de l'invention de l'auteur* (1725) and *Architecture moderne* (1728).

CUVILLIÉS, FRANÇOIS DE

Born 1695 at Soignies; died 1768 in Munich. He entered the service of Elector Maximilian Emanuel of Bavaria, then resident in The Netherlands, at a very early age. In 1715 he followed the Elector to Munich, where he was employed as designer and studied military engineering; in 1720–24 he was in Paris studying architecture. On his return to Munich he was appointed court architect together with Joseph Effner. In 1726 he began construction of the Piosasque de Non Palace in Munich, completed in 1732. In 1728–30 he carried out important work at the castle in Brühl, cooperating with Dominique Girard in decorating and furnishing it and also designing the Falkenlust hunting lodge (1728–29) in its garden.

Cuvilliés did the interior decoration of the green gallery and the Reiche Zimmer in the Munich Residenz (1729–37) in collaboration with Joachim Dietrich, Wenzeslaus Mirofsky, Adam Pichler, and Johann Baptist Zimmermann. He also worked on the Holnstein Palace (1733–37); the Amalienburg hunting lodge (1734–40) in the garden of Nymphenburg Palace for Electress Maria Amalia; the choir of the monastery church at Schäftlarn (1740); and the design for the Wilhelmstal Villa at Kassel.

The best known of Cuvilliés' later works, the Residenztheater in Munich, was built between 1750 and 1753 with his son François. Among his last assignments were the façade of the former Fugger mansion in Munich (1759), the project for enlarging the Munich Residenz (1764–67), and the completion of the façade of the Theatine church of St. Cajetan in Munich (1765–68).

DELAMAIR, PIERRE-ALEXIS

Born 1675 (location unknown); died 1745 at Châtenay. Delamair began his career employed by De Cotte as a master-builder, but was never in agreement with him. Similarly, his collaboration with Boffrand was not very happy either. He suffered from a severe persecution complex, aggravated on his own part by his accusations against his masters.

Elector Maximilian Emanuel of Bavaria had invited him to his estates, but Delamair instead had the good fortune to come under the benevolent protection of the Bishop of Strasbourg, who commissioned him to reconstruct his family's old mansion, the Hôtel de Soubise (1704–9; continued by Boffrand, who worked on it until 1745). Delamair also built the Hôtel de Rohan (1705–8) in Paris for his patron. Both these mansions were later altered. To Delamair is also attributed the Hôtel de Duras (probably only an alteration) and the Hôtel Chanac-Pompadour (built before 1738).

Toward the end of his life Delamair gave up work as

a practicing architect and wrote a book of theory, the manuscript of which was lost after his death.

DE SANCTIS, FRANCESCO

Born 1693 in Rome; died 1740 in Rome. De Sanctis worked mainly in Rome, where his name is linked with the Spanish Stairs, for which he may have prepared designs as early as 1717. From the numerous projects for it submitted by various Roman architects of the period, Pope Innocent XIII selected the design by De Sanctis; work on the great outdoor staircase began in 1723 and ended in 1726. In 1723 De Sanctis was engaged on the façade of SS. Trinità dei Pellegrini in Rome. In Naples he probably designed S. Maria delle Grazie.

DIENTZENHOFER (DIENZENHOFER, DINTZENHOFER), CHRISTOPH

Born 1655 near Aibling; died 1726 in Prague. He worked in Bohemia, especially Prague, where there is evidence of his presence from 1686, although it is probable that he worked there earlier, summoned by Abraham Leuthner.

In 1689 Dientzenhofer was put in charge of work for the pilgrimage church at Kappel and the Teplà convent. In 1690 he was in Marseilles and from 1699 to about 1712 at Obořiště, where he built the convent church, the design of which is very reminiscent of Guarini's Immacolata in Turin. The chapel of the castle at Smiřice and St. Mary Magdalen in Prague date from around the years 1700 to 1713. During this period he also produced projects for the church of St. Nicholas on the Kleinseite in Prague (1703–11), completed by his son Kilian Ignaz between 1737 and 1753. Christoph built St. Clare in Cheb (1707) and the church of St. Margaret (1709–15) at Břevnov, near Prague. It is certain that he also worked on the church of Our Lady of Loreto on the Hradčany, since it is known that he built its façade in 1717–23.

DIENTZENHOFER (DIENZENHOFER, DINTZENHOFER), GEORG

Born 1643 at Aibling; died 1689 at Waldsassen. In 1682 he was working with Abraham Leuthner on the Cistercian abbey church at Waldsassen in Franconia. In 1683 he became a citizen of Amberg, where he took part in building the Jesuit College the following year. From 1684 to 1689 he built the Trinity Chapel (Kappel) near Waldsassen, in the Oberpfalz Forest, the plan and exterior of which symbolize the Trinity, to which it is dedicated. In 1685 he was at Bamberg, working with other artists on the erection of the Jesuit church and the monastery of St. Martin.

DIENTZENHOFER (DIENZENHOFER, DINTZENHOFER), JOHANN

Born 1673 at Aibling; died 1726 at Bamberg. He underwent his apprenticeship in Prague (perhaps with Abraham Leuthner and Jean-Baptiste Mathey) and Italy, visiting Rome in 1699. He then worked mostly at Fulda (1700–11), Bamberg (1711–22), and Würzburg. In 1700 he was made court architect at Fulda, responsible for con-

struction of the great cathedral (1704–12). From 1710 to 1713 he worked on the church of the Benedictine abbey at Banz (consecrated in 1719). Prince-Bishop Lothar Franz von Schönborn commissioned him to build Schloss Pommersfelden, which was to be his main work and on which he was engaged from 1711 to 1718; Hildebrandt and Maximilian von Welsch also contributed to the design. Johann conceived the general lines of the façade for the Neumünster in Würzburg (1712–16) and drew up two projects for the abbey church and cloister at Holzkirchen (c. 1724). At Bamberg he worked on a number of houses for the nobility, among which the Concord (1716–22) must be mentioned.

DIENTZENHOFER (DIENZENHOFER, DINTZENHOFER), JOHANN LEONHARD

Born 1660 (location unknown); died 1707 at Bamberg. As court architect at Bamberg he received commissions of considerable importance. He designed and began to build the Cistercian monastery at Ebrach (1686–88), completed by Balthasar Neumann. At Bamberg, between 1696 and 1702, he was engaged on the partial rebuilding of the Benedictine abbey of St. Michael on the Michaelsberg. At around the same time (1695–1704) he built the Neue Residenz, his main work, for Prince-Bishop Lothar Franz von Schönborn. At Banz he was engaged on altering the abbey (1698–1705), and at Bayreuth he completed the castle begun by Charles-Philippe Dieussart. In 1700 Dientzenhofer began work on a group of buildings which kept him occupied until his death—the Cistercian abbey of Schöntal in Württemberg; he probably also designed the church there, which was built after his death.

DIENTZENHOFER (DIENZENHOFER, DINTZENHOFER), KILIAN IGNAZ

Born 1689 in Prague; died 1751 in Prague. Kilian Ignaz was Christoph's son and worked with his father on the church of Our Lady of Loreto on the Hradčany in Prague. From 1707 to 1717 and again in 1725 it seems that he was staying in Vienna, where he may have studied with Johann Lucas von Hildebrandt.

He worked mainly in Prague, probably from 1717 onward. In the period 1717 to 1720 he built the Villa Amerika in Prague (Count Michna's summer residence), which shows evidence of Hildebrandt's style. He also built the Villa Portheim (1725–28) in Prague for his own family. His work as an architect was, however, mainly carried out for religious orders, for which he designed a series of impressive buildings: the church of St. John Nepomuk on the Hradčany in Prague (1720–29); the pilgrimage church in Nicov (1720–28); the church of the monastery of St. Edwige (1723–31) at Wahlstatt in Silesia; the church of St. Adalbert at Počaply (1724–26); the church of St. Thomas in Prague (1724–31); St. Bartholomew's in Prague for the Jesuits (1725–31); and the monastery at Broumov (project 1726; construction 1728–38).

Dientzenhofer's buildings of the 1730s are particularly important: the invalids' hospice in Prague (1730–37), with its interesting functional solutions; St. John on the Rock in Prague (project 1729; construction 1730–39), one of the finest Bohemian Baroque works; the church of

St. Francis Xavier for the Jesuits (1732–35) at Opařany; St. Nicholas in the Altstadt in Prague (1732–37); and the chapel of St. Peter in Chains (1733–34) at Velenka. Also dating from the same years are St. Clement's at Odolená Voda (construction 1733–43); the Ursuline convent church at Kutná Hora (projects 1734–35; construction 1735–43), left unfinished; St. Mary Magdalen in Karlovy Vary (project 1732; construction 1733–36), considered to be his most outstanding work; and St. Mary of the Seven Sorrows at Dobrá Voda (1733–39).

During his last years Dientzenhofer built the Cathedral of St. Veit in Prague (1737–53); the church of St. Peter and St. Paul at Březno (1739–42); the Sylva-Tarouca Palace in Prague (1743–51); St. Florian's at Kladno (1746–48); St. John the Baptist's at Paštiky (1747–51); and St. Martin's at Chvalenice (1747–53), completed after his death.

DOTTI, CARLO FRANCESCO

Born 1670 in Bologna; died 1759 in Bologna. Most of his work was carried out in this city between 1709 and 1757. Some designs for the Crucifix Chapel in S. Francesco date from 1713. The first drawing for the Arco del Meloncello, which was built in 1732, dates from 1718. The little church of S. Sigismondo, built between 1725 and 1729, may also be placed among his first works. In 1728 Dotti began the modernization of S. Domenico. He also built the Madonna di S. Luca: its first stone was laid in 1723, the new Lady Chapel was begun in 1749, and it was completed only in 1763.

Between 1725 and 1730 Dotti drew up the project for the staircase in the Palazzo Davia-Bargellini, renovated the Carbonesi church (later destroyed), laid out the cloister of the Chiesa dei Celestini, and modernized the church of S. Maria della Morte. In 1732 he won a competition for the parish church of S. Giovanni at Minerbio, which was consecrated in 1737.

As for secular architecture, he was engaged on the Palazzo Monti (later Salina) in Via Barberia (1736–38?), generally attributed to Torreggiani; the Palazzo Agucchi (later Bosdari) in Via Santo Stefano, whose façade dates from 1747–48; and the reading room in the university library.

Dotti's last works include the restoration of the Tempio Malatestiano, as well as a design for the Colonna dell' Immacolata in Piazza Malpighi. In 1752 the chapel of S. Ivo in S. Petronio was built to his design.

EFFNER, JOSEPH

Born 1687 at Dachau; died 1745 in Munich. An architect and decorator, he was the son of the Bavarian Elector Maximilian Emanuel's court gardener and was sent to Paris by the Elector in 1706 to study architecture under Germain Boffrand, with whom he worked on the palace of St-Cloud in 1713.

In 1715 he was again in Munich among the Elector's entourage. The following year he made a trip to Italy, which greatly influenced his artistic evolution. Back in Munich again, he was appointed court architect on Enrico Zuccalli's death in 1724 and director of gardens in 1738. At the Munich court Effner was entrusted with the most

important assignments: the modernization of the old castle of Dachau, for which he devised a new layout for the gardens; and the construction and decoration of the central pavilion at Nymphenburg, and the layout of its adjacent buildings. In collaboration with Girard he planned a new layout for the Nymphenburg grounds, with the waterfall (1716–18), two small castles, the Pagodenburg (1716–19) and Badenburg (1718–28), and a hermitage (Magdalenenklause) (1725-26), in the French style.

In 1719 he added a new story to Schleissheim Castle, the construction of which (begun by Zuccalli in 1701–4) had been suspended. After Maximilian Emanuel's death in 1726 the work was stopped and Effner's plan was not carried out until the nineteenth century. From 1723 to 1728 he built the Preysing Palace in Munich, but after 1730 he was somewhat overshadowed by Cuvilliés, whom the new Elector, Karl Albert, preferred.

EIGTVED, NIELS

Born 1701 at Eigtved; died 1754 in Copenhagen. He studied in Vienna, Paris, and Rome, and worked in Dresden and Warsaw, where he was a master-builder in Pöppelmann's service. Eigtved's name is linked with the renovation of Copenhagen and in particular with the Frederiksstaden quarter there, which was commissioned by Frederik V in 1749.

On his return to Denmark (1735) Eigtved became court architect and director of the Academy of Arts in Copenhagen (1751–54). In the Frederiksstaden quarter, he designed the Amalienborg Square with its surrounding palaces (1750–54), the large Frederiks Kirke (designed 1752), the central block of the hospital founded by Frederik V, and numerous private residences such as the Berkentin Palace, the Prinsens Palais, and the Royal Theater (destroyed).

In the Christianshavn quarter he also designed the Christians Kirke (erected 1755–56), and worked on the interior of Christiansborg Palace (destroyed by fire in 1798). In 1750, together with De Thurah, he erected the Ledreborg Residens near Roskilde.

EOSANDER, JOHANN FRIEDRICH VON

Born c. 1670, perhaps in Riga; died 1729 in Dresden. He worked on fortification projects in Riga, the city to which his family (of Swedish origin) had moved. He entered the Prince of Brandenburg's service in 1696 and was in Berlin in 1699, where he was appointed court architect; his major works are in that city.

Eosander succeeded Andreas Schlüter in taking over the direction of Charlottenburg Castle in 1704, begun by Schlüter and Johann Arnold Nering. He enlarged its main wing and erected the two side wings, the chapel, the Porcelain Room, and the Orangerie (1709–12). At the request of Count Wartenberg, he built the central section of Monbijou Palace in Berlin (1703); he also directed work on the Royal Palace (from 1707), enlarging Schlüter's previous projects. In 1713 Eosander was in the service of Charles XII of Sweden. In 1722 he moved to Dresden and built the Übigau Palace on the Elbe (1724-26) nearby.

FISCHER, JOHANN GEORG

Born 1673 at Füssen am Lech; died in 1747 (location unknown). Fischer was active mainly in Bavarian Swabia during the first half of the eighteenth century. He was commissioned for the first time in 1717 for the construction of the parish church of St. Jakob at Innsbruck; we do not know how much he collaborated with Johann Jakob Herkomer on this. He also worked on the hunting lodge at Markt Oberdorf (1722–25) for the Prince-Archbishop Alexander Sigismund.

He devoted himself almost exclusively to the construction of religious buildings: the parish church at Bertoldshofen (1728), the church at Lindau (1730) on Lake Constance, the interior of Wolfegg Castle (1733), St. Katherine's at Wolfegg (1733–36), the rebuilding of Kisslegg parish church (1734–38), and the Franciscan monastery at Dillingen (1736–40). He may also have been responsible for the chapel (1726) and pilgrimage church (1746) at Steinbach.

FISCHER, JOHANN MICHAEL

Born 1691 at Burglengenfeld; died 1766 in Munich. There is little information about his life and artistic training. After learning the mason's trade from his father, he began a wandering apprenticeship in 1713. His first documented works include rebuilding the monastery church choir at Niederaltaich (1723–24); conversion of St. George's parish church at Schärding (1724–25) in collaboration with Johann Baptist Gunetzhainer and Hans Mayr; and the belfry of the cemetery church at Deggendorf (1724–27). His first fully independent works date from 1726–27: the Baroque reconstruction of the abbey church at Osterhofen, built in 1726–29 and consecrated in 1740; the church of St. Anna-am-Lehel in Munich (1727–33); and the reconstruction of the Benedictine church at Rinchnach (begun 1727). In 1730–32 he built the small parish church of Unering and from 1731 to 1739 the Kollegienkirche at Diessen. In 1735 he designed three important churches: the Franciscan church at Ingolstadt (project 1735; building 1737–39), St. Michael's in Berg am Laim (1735–44), and the pilgrimage church at Aufhausen (project 1735; building 1736–51). Between 1741 and 1752 he carried out the Baroque reconstruction of the Benedictine abbey church of Zwiefalten.

The Benedictine abbey church of Ottobeuren (1748–66), begun in 1737 by Simpert Kraemer, is generally considered Fischer's most important work. To the last years of his life can be dated the chapel of St. Anastasia at Benediktbeuern (1750–58), the church at Bichl (1752), and the rebuilding of the Benedictine monastery church of St. Marinus and St. Arianus at Rott am Inn (1759–66), perhaps his masterpiece. His last project was to rebuild the Benedictine monastery church of the Brigittines in Altomünster, which was begun in 1763 and completed in 1773 after his death.

FISCHER VON ERLACH, JOHANN BERNHARD

Born 1656 in Graz; died 1723 in Vienna. A sculptor's son, he early followed in his father's footsteps, as his first works show. In 1670 he was in Rome, where he worked as a sculptor and painter under Philipp Schorr, through whom he came into contact with some of the most important people of the time: Bellori, Queen Christina of Sweden, Athanasius Kircher, Bernini, and Carlo Fontana.

In 1683 we find him in Naples accompanying Schorr, with whom he carried out some important assignments for the Marquis of Carpi, the viceroy of the city. In 1686 he was back in Austria, where he entered the service of the Althans and Liechtensteins as an architect. The high altar for the sanctuary at Strassengel dates from 1687–92, and the design for the Prince of Liechtenstein's stables at Eisgrub in Moravia from 1688–98.

Fischer's first significant work was the Ahnensaal at the Althan Palace in Frain, which was begun in 1688 but not completed until 1695. In 1689 he was appointed to give daily lessons in architecture to the eleven-year-old crown prince, Joseph I. For Joseph's entry into Vienna, on being crowned King of the Romans in 1690, he built two triumphal arches. In 1693 he designed Schönbrunn Palace for him. The first project, drawn up shortly after Joseph's accession as Emperor, was not implemented, however, and in 1696 Schönbrunn was built in accordance with a reduced and modified plan.

Fischer was appointed court architect and was given important assignments: in 1688 the *Lustgartengebäude* for Count Althan in the Rossau outside Vienna; in 1692 the Strattmann Palace for the court chancellor Strattmann; and in the same years the façade of the court stables at Salzburg for Prince-Bishop Johann Ernst Count Thun-Hohenstein and Engelhartstetten Castle in Niederweiden (c. 1694), which no longer stands. The Dreifaltigkeitskirche in Salzburg was built between 1694 and 1702. The sanctuary in the Kirchental, near Lofer, and the Kollegienkirche in Salzburg (1696–1707), in which he also carried out the decoration, are from the same period. In 1696 he was appointed to build a city-palace for Prince Eugene in Vienna, enlarged in 1723 by Johann Lucas von Hildebrandt. (It is today the Finanzministerium.)

Fischer carried out a number of important works in the early 1700s: the Johannspital and church in Salzburg, the Ursuline church in Salzburg, and the remodeling and enlargement of the Batthyány Palace in Vienna (1699–1706). He was also responsible for the garden-pavilion in the park of Klesheim Castle (1700–9); the portal for the Dietrichstein Palace (1709–11); the Böhmische Hofkanzlei (1708–14); and the Trautson Palace in Vienna (project 1709; construction begun 1710), as well as for the plan to alter the Clam-Gallas Palace in Prague (1713).

In the period from 1715 to 1721 Fischer began a series of projects which were not to be completed until after his death, by his son Joseph Emanuel: the Karlskirche in Vienna (1715–37); the Elector's Chapel in Breslau Cathedral (1716–22); and the Hofbibliothek in Vienna (project 1716; construction 1722–37). In 1721 he published an important work, *Entwurff einer historischen Architektur in Abbildung unterschiedener berühmter Gebäude des Altertums und fremder Völker.*

FISCHER VON ERLACH, JOSEPH EMANUEL

Born 1693 in Vienna; died 1742 in Vienna. He was a pupil of his father, Johann Bernhard, and after 1713 made a series of trips to Rome (1714), Paris (1717–19), and England. Returning to Vienna in 1722, he became court architect. Among his Viennese works are the Hofbibliothek (1723–26), the Hofreitschule (1728–35), the Althan Palace (1729–32), the façade of the Reichskanzleitrakt (1730–31), and the Stiftskirche (1739). He built Seelowitz Castle (1726–28) in Moravia, the Ritterakademie (1726–35) at Liegnitz, the home for the infirm (1727–35) in Budapest, and the parish church at Grossweikersdorf.

Joseph Emanuel also worked on a number of existing buildings in Vienna: the completion of the Karlskirche (1722–23) and the Nepomukspital (1735), Schwarzenberg Palace (1723–25), and La Favorita (1730–37). He also restored a number of mansions in Vienna (1730–37), Austerlitz (Slavkov) Castle in Moravia (1731–32), and Riegersburg Castle (1735). Fischer designed the invalids' hospice in Prague, subsequently built by Kilian Ignaz Dientzenhofer between 1730 and 1737.

FRIGIMELICA, GIROLAMO

Born 1653 in Padua; died 1732 in Modena. In 1696 the rebuilding of Rovigo Cathedral was begun in accordance with his plans. About 1720 his main work, the Villa Pisani at Stra, was started (on his death, Francesco Maria Preti was put in charge of the work). Until 1721–22 he lived in Padua, where he drew up a number of projects, including those for the university library (1718) and the façade of the cathedral (1721–26), neither of which was carried out; and those for the chapel of the Holy Sacrament in the Chiesa del Santo and for S. Maria del Pianto (finished in 1726). In about 1722 Girolamo established himself in Modena, where he built the church of S. Giovanni Battista. In Venice, in 1728, he added the second floor to the Palazzo Pisani.

FRISONI, DONATO GIUSEPPE

Born 1683 at Laino in Val d'Intelvi; died 1735 at Ludwigsburg. He first worked as a stuccoist in Prague, whence he was summoned in 1709 to Ludwigsburg by the Duke of Württemberg. While working as a decorator in the service of Johann Friedrich Nette, he was commissioned by the duke to build the Prinzenbau and the *Lusthaus* (1711) in Stuttgart. Nette died late in 1714, and Frisoni took his place directing works at the Residenz in Ludwigsburg; in addition to the Schlosskirche (1716–19) and the Ordenskapelle (1719–21), he erected numerous pavilions, modifying the general designs of Nette. In the meantime he had been appointed director of constructions in Württemberg and had prepared a town plan for Ludwigsburg. Between 1726 and 1730 he built the parish church there, later altered by his nephews, Paolo and Leopoldo Retti. In 1717 the Benedictine abbot Sebastian Hillerche asked him to come to Weingarten to reconstruct the abbey church; in that year Frisoni designed the bell-towers and the façade, and the year after built the dome and worked on the decoration of the nave. Frisoni was also occupied in rebuilding the castles of Waldenbruck and Karlsruhe, as well as some buildings in the small town of Offingen.

FUGA, FERDINANDO

Born 1699 in Florence; died 1781 in Rome. After an ap-

prenticeship under Giovanni Battista Foggini he moved to Rome in 1717, where he stayed for nine years. His first known work is the design for the façade of S. Giovanni in Laterano (1722); he probably also contributed to the work on the interior of S. Cecilia (c. 1725). Fuga returned to Rome several times and in 1730 he was commissioned to complete the stables and later the Manica Lunga at the Quirinale. Between 1725 and 1730 he was in Naples, where he carried out his first complete work, the Cellamare Chapel (1726–27). In Palermo, he may have built the Milcia Bridge.

Among Fuga's projects in Rome, the following should be mentioned: the Palazzo della Consulta (begun in 1732); the renovation and enlargement of the Palazzo Riario alla Lungara (1736); the café in the Quirinale garden (1741); the façade of the Palazzo Cenci-Bolognetti (1745); the reconstruction of S. Maria dell'Orazione e Morte (1735–37); the façade and portico of S. Maria Maggiore (1735–43); and the designs for the reconstruction of the church of S. Apollinare (1742–48) and the adjacent German-Hungarian College.

In Naples, apart from the Cellamare Chapel, Fuga erected the Albergo dei Poveri (after 1750), the Palazzo Aquino, the Palazzo Rufo (later Giordano), and the Palazzo Caramanico (1780). He also carried out alterations in the king's and queen's apartments in the Palazzo Reale (1775–78), and raised the façade of the church of the Gerolamini (1780).

GABRIEL, ANGE-JACQUES

Born 1698 in Paris; died 1782 in Paris. We know nothing of his childhood and youth. Probably he began by collaborating with his father, Jacques V Gabriel. He studied at the Paris Academy of Architecture and in 1728 was appointed *Contrôleur général des Bâtiments du Roi;* in 1735 he was named *Contrôleur* of Versailles. From 1735, he worked with his father at Dijon, Rennes, the cathedrals at Orléans and La Rochelle, and above all at Bordeaux, where he continued his father's work on the Place Royale (and where he later also built the Exchange, c. 1742–47). In 1737, the Galerie d'Ulysse at Fontainebleau, which contained Primaticcio's frescoes, was demolished; the king wanted to replace it with a series of fifty small rooms; Ange-Jacques, who was still working under his father's guidance, was entrusted with the work.

At Versailles he worked first of all with his father, mainly on decoration of the interior. In 1742, after his father's death, he inherited the position of king's first architect and became president of the Academy. Gabriel's principal works at Versailles are the Pavillon Français at the Grand Trianon (1748–50), the Pavillon du Butard (1750–51), work on the Salle de l'Opéra (begun in 1753, inaugurated in 1770), the Pavillon des Fausses Reposes (1755), and the Petit Trianon (designed in 1761–62). His *grand projet,* which provided for the complete remodeling and enlargement of the entire building complex of Versailles, was prepared in three successive phases, 1742–47, 1759, and 1770–71. For it, Ange-Jacques constructed the Gabriel wing (1739–40), the queen's library, the Ermitage of Madame de Pompadour (1749), and the Gros Pavillon (1750–51). He also began on the decoration and layout of numerous interiors—the Cabinet de Conseil, the Chambre du Roi, and the Dauphin's apartments. However, on the death of the king in 1744, work was interrupted and the whole project was set aside.

Louis XV had also entrusted Gabriel with the modernization and enlargement of numerous small castles: Choisy (1748–63); Compiègne, the final designs for which were drawn up in 1751 and on which he worked until 1775, the year in which he resigned from all his official positions; St-Hubert (1755–63; destroyed in 1855); and the Château de la Muette at St-Germain (1764–68).

Gabriel also had many commissions in Paris. In 1750 he submitted designs for the Ecole Militaire, whose construction he supervised even after he had resigned from the position of court architect. In 1753 he submitted the winning designs for the Place Louis XV (the present-day Place de la Concorde). Between 1755 and 1761 he completed the courtyard of the Louvre and in 1762, in collaboration with Soufflot, the Salle de l'Opéra.

GAGLIARDI, ROSARIO

Born probably c. 1700 in Syracuse; died c. 1770 in Rome. His name is associated with the reconstruction of Noto after the earthquake of 1693. There he built the church of S. Domenico some time after 1727, and in 1743 the Chiesa del Carmine; he supervised the building of the Salvatore monastery and in 1758 designed the church of the Assunta adjoining the convent of S. Chiara.

The following churches are attributed to Gagliardi: the basilica of S. Giorgio at Ragusa Ibla (1746–66), S. Chiara (1749) and S. Giuseppe (1751) at Caltagirone, the Madonna del Bosco and the Madonna Addolorata at Niscemi, S. Giuseppe at Ragusa, and possibly S. Giorgio at Modica.

GALILEI, ALESSANDRO

Born 1691 in Florence; died 1736 in Rome. After his first visit to Rome in order to study its ancient and modern monuments, he was invited to London by John Molesworth in 1714. He met with so much trouble there that he was forced finally to return to Florence, after stopping in Paris, Turin, Milan, and the Venice region.

In Florence, after his first engineering assignments, which consisted of restoring the Acquedotto Montereggi and the tower of the Porta S. Gallo, he became chief architect and superintendent of buildings to Grand Duke Cosimo II.

Summoned to Rome in 1730 by Pope Clement XII, he did work on the Corsini Chapel (1732–35) and on the façades of S. Giovanni in Laterano (1733–36) and S. Giovanni dei Fiorentini (1734).

GALLO, FRANCESCO

Born 1672 in Mondovì; died 1750 in Mondovì. He studied under Antonio Bertola in Turin, and also worked in collaboration with him. He was appointed crown architect and did much work as a military architect, hydraulic engineer, and topographer in Turin and throughout Piedmont.

Gallo was especially active around Cuneo and Mondovì. At Carrù he supervised the building of the parish church of the Assunta (1702–25). In 1703 he began the parish church of S. Ambrogio at Cuneo, where building was sus-

pended, resumed in 1710, and completed in 1743. At Mondovì he built the church of S. Giuseppe for the Discalced Carmelites (1708–17); in 1712 he began work on the church of S. Chiara, and the following year on the Jesuit college, now the Law Courts.

The dome of the Santuario di Vicoforte at Mondovì is regarded as his most important work. The building of this pilgrimage church, begun by Vittozzi, was suspended for many years; Gallo interested himself in it as early as 1702, but he did not work continuously on it until the beginning of 1728, when he began on the dome, which was completed in 1733.

Of Gallo's copious output, special mention should be made of the hospital and church of the SS. Trinità at Fossano (1723–28), the parish church of S. Giovanni Battista at Racconigi (1719–30), the designs for the remodeling of the apse and the sacristy of the church of the Santo Nome di Gesù at Cuneo (c. 1725), and the churches of S. Croce and S. Bernardino at Cavallermaggiore (1737–43).

GAROVE, MICHELANGELO

Born 1650 at Bissone; died 1713 in Turin. Garove collaborated on various undertakings with Guarini, whose work he continued in the church of S. Filippo Neri. In Turin he was responsible for the Palazzo Asinari (begun 1686) and the designs for the courtyard of the University, which was erected after his death (1713–20). After the fire at the Venaria Reale near Turin in 1693, Garove was commissioned to present new designs for the hunting lodge.

The following are also attributed to him: the chapel of Beato Amedeo in Vercelli Cathedral, the sanctuary of the Madonna di S. Giovanni at Sommariva Bosco (designed in 1685), and the parish church of S. Martino at La Morra (1685–95).

GERL, MATHIAS

Born 1712; died 1765 (locations unknown). Gerl worked mainly for the court and archbishopric of Vienna, where his principal works are found: the reconstructions of the Klosterneuburger Hof (1746) and the Simmering parish church (1746–47); works in the Wiener Schottenstift (1754), in St. Thecla's, and in the Piarist convent (1754–56). Outside Vienna he constructed the parish churches at Ober-Laa (1744) and Neulerchenfeld (1765), and the Minorite church (1758–63) at Cheb (Eger).

GERLACH, PHILIPP

Born 1679 at Spandau; died 1748 in Berlin. He succeeded Martin Grünberg in the position of court architect to Friedrich Wilhelm, and in 1720 became general director of royal palaces. He worked mainly on the urban reconstruction of the city of Berlin, being responsible for the Pariserplatz and the Wilhelmstrasse, Charlottenburg Castle (1711), and the Friedrichspital and its adjoining church, whose bell-tower (1726–27) he also erected. Gerlach carried out the enlargement and reconstruction of the crown prince's palace (1732), and built the Law Courts (1734–35) and the house of the State Minister, Von Marschall (later Vosz'sche Palais). At Potsdam he built the garrison church (1730–35), his most important work.

GIBBS, JAMES

Born 1682 at Footdeesmire (Aberdeen); died 1754 in London. He traveled widely in Flanders, France, Switzerland, Germany, and Italy, and was in Rome between 1707 and 1709. He returned to England in 1709, became a member of the committee for the construction of fifty new churches in London, but soon relinquished this post because of hostility on the part of the Whigs.

He had numerous private commissions for mansions, churches, and country residences. His first public work of note was the church of St. Mary-le-Strand in London (1714–17); soon after (1719) he built the steeple of St. Clement Danes and St. Peter's in Vere Street (1721–24), commonly known as Marylebone Chapel. In the same period he constructed his most important church, St. Martin-in-the-Fields, commissioned by a Whig committee. Another of his important churches is All Saints in Derby (1723–25).

Gibbs was just as active in the construction of private houses: he began with Cannons House, Middlesex (1713–19), for the Duke of Chandos, and reached maturity with Ditchley Park, Oxfordshire (1720–22), and Dawley House at Harlington (after 1724). In Cambridge Gibbs built the Senate House and the Fellows' Building at King's College (1724–49).

His finest work was the Radcliffe Camera at Oxford (1737–49), described by him in *Bibliotheca Radcliviana; or Description of the Radcliffe Library at Oxford* (1747).

Gibbs also did sculpture—numerous monuments for tombs—and wrote books of architectural theory, including *A Book of Architecture* (1728), which greatly influenced English architecture of the time, and *Rules for Drawing the Several Parts of Architecture* (1732).

GREGORINI, DOMENICO

Born 1700 in Rome; died 1777 in Rome. He was a pupil of Juvarra and a member of the Accademia di S. Luca. His most significant work is perhaps the restoration of the façade of S. Croce in Gerusalemme, on which he worked in close collaboration with Passalacqua in 1743.

In 1730 he built the oratory of the SS. Sacramento of S. Maria in Via. In the same year he built the *confessio* in the church of S. Lorenzo in Damaso, which was later destroyed by fire and is known to us only through a painting (probably by Pannini).

The following are attributed to Gregorini: the façade of the oratory of Corpus Domini, the Piazza Poli (1731), the rebuilding of the Villa Ludovisi (1748), and the tomb of Prince Ludovisi Boncompagni at Isola del Liri.

GREISING, JOSEPH

Born 1664 at Hohenweiler; died 1721 in Würzburg. Greising worked mainly in Würzburg; he was chief architect to the Prince-Bishop and his greatest works were in the field of religious architecture. His talent is particularly evident in the Baroque reconstruction of the Neumünsterkirche (begun 1711) and the Peterskirche (1717–20) at Würzburg. He built the Herlheim parish church (1717–21) and reconstructed the Grosskomburg capitular church (1706–15). Between 1716 and 1721 he collaborated with Balthasar Neumann in the enlargement and restoration of Ebrach Convent.

Of his civil and private architectural works, the most prominent are those at Würzburg—for instance, the Rückermainhof (1714–21) and the Rosenbach mansion in the Schlossplatz. After the fire of 1699 he worked with Antonio Petrini on the Juliusspital; he also participated (1715–19) in building the north wing of the ecclesiastical seminary (St. Michael's College). The churches at Hauser and Ober-Theres are attributed to Greising.

GRIMM, MAURIZ

Born 1669 in Landshut; died 1757 in Brno. His known works are all at Brno: the Loreto chapel (1716–19), the Minorite church (1729), the Palace of the Diet (1733–36), the church of the monastery of St. Thomas (1734–42), the Jesuit church (1735), and the chapel of St. Maurice in the church of St. Jacob (1736; destroyed).

GUMPP, GEORG ANTON

Born 1682 in Innsbruck; died 1754 in Innsbruck. The works of Pietro da Cortona, Rainaldi, and Borromini, which Gumpp had been able to study on one of his visits to Rome, played a large part in forming his artistic style. In 1722 he succeeded his father, Johann Martin, as court architect. At Innsbruck he reconstructed the grammar school (1722–24), erected the Palace of the Provincial Diet (Landhaus; 1725–31), and worked on the public library (1745). In the same town, the façade of the present Volkskunst Museum (1719), the church of St. Johann am Inn (1729–35), and the Pfeiffenburg and Stockerhaus mansions are also attributed to him. In 1729 Gumpp initiated the rebuilding of the Cistercian monastery and abbey at Stams.

HAWKSMOOR, NICHOLAS

Born 1661 at Ragnall, Nottinghamshire; died 1736 in London. He began his working career in unimportant positions such as secretary to a judge in Yorkshire and copyist to Christopher Wren, who chose him to be his collaborator. Wren made him deputy surveyor at Chelsea Hospital (1682) and Winchester Palace (1683–85), director of works at Kensington Palace, and then his own assistant in St. Paul's Cathedral. In 1698 Hawksmoor became director of works at Greenwich Hospital and the following year he joined Vanbrugh, who made him his first assistant in the construction of country houses (Castle Howard, Yorkshire; Blenheim Palace, Oxfordshire).

About 1702 Hawksmoor began to work on his own. In 1711 he was one of the most active members of the committee formed for the erection of fifty new churches in London; at the same time he worked in Cambridge and Oxford. From 1709 he had been engaged at Queen's College, Oxford, but his activity in this city was particularly intense from 1712 onward: his first design for the Radcliffe Camera (carried out by James Gibbs) is from 1712–13 and that for the Clarendon Building from 1712–15; between 1716 and 1735 he was working at All Souls' College. In 1720 he began the enlargement of King's College in Cambridge (this work also was to be carried out by Gibbs).

Hawksmoor did a great deal of work outside the universities. In 1713 he drew up projects for the enlargement of Wotton House, Surrey. In 1715 he was nominated director of works at Whitehall, at Westminster Abbey (he designed the towers, 1734–45), and at St. James's Palace. He supervised the restoration of Beverly Minster (from 1716) and St. Albans' Abbey (after 1721).

Hawksmoor's activity in the field of religious buildings was extensive. The first church he built was St. Alphege's at Greenwich (1712–14); it was followed by St. George-in-the-East (1714–29), St. Anne's, Limehouse (1714–30), Christ Church, Spitalfields (1714–29), St. Mary Woolnoth (1717–27), and St. George's, Bloomsbury (1720–30). Among his last works were Hockham House in Surrey (1724–29) and the mausoleum at Castle Howard, Yorkshire (1729–40).

HÉRÉ DE CORNY, EMMANUEL

Born 1705 at Nancy; died 1763 at Lunéville. He was court architect to Stanislas Leczinski, Duke of Lorraine and father-in-law of Louis XV. At Nancy Stanislas commissioned Héré to reconstruct the sanctuary of Notre-Dame du Bon-Secours (1738–41), to erect the Hôtel des Missions Royales for the Jesuits (1741–43), and to demolish and rebuild the old Château de Malgrange, which the Duke took over for his own home.

Héré's greatest fame derives from his plan for the urban center of Nancy, consisting of the Place Stanislas (1752–55), the Place de la Carrière, and the Hemicycle or Place du Gouvernement. At Lunéville, Stanislas had the Leopold Castle renovated by Héré, who carried out the interior decoration and finished the chapel and the music room. In the garden he built the Turkish kiosk, le trèfle, the bâtiment de la cascade (1743), and other small pavilions called chartreuses. Héré also worked for Stanislas on the castles of Chanteheux and Einville, at Jolivet, and at Commercy.

With Boffrand Héré worked on the reconstruction of the abbey of St-Jacques at Lunéville (1730–47). Little really remains of his other work: in fact, on the death of Stanislas, Louis XV had Malgrange, Chanteheux, and the chartreuses at Lunéville pulled down, and converted the castle itself into a barracks. Engravings showing Héré's work can be seen in the Recueil des plans, élévations et coupes...des Châteaux, jardins et dépendances que le roi de Pologne occupe en Lorraine, y compris les bâtiments qu'il a fait élever...(Paris, 1750), and in Plans et élévations de la place royale de Nancy et d'autres édifices qui l'environnent bâtis par les ordres du roi de Pologne ... (1753).

HERKOMER (HERKOMMER), JOHANN JAKOB

Born 1648 at Sammeister; died 1717 in Füssen. Herkomer studied in Italy and on his return from Venice built a chapel in his native village (1685–86). In 1701, at Füssen, he began the construction of St. Magnus' Convent and the adjoining church (completed in 1711 and 1717, respectively). At Seeg, near Füssen, he erected the parish church (1710–11). In 1712 he designed the parish church of St. Jakob at Innsbruck, which was not begun until the year of his death. Herkomer supplied other de-

signs for the church of St. Joseph at Büchelbach and the convent church at Fultenbach, begun in 1716. He supervised the alterations of the Heiligkreuzkirche at Augsburg (begun 1716). In the last years of his life he took part in the construction of the church at Weingarten, but we do not know the extent of his contribution.

HILDEBRANDT, JOHANN LUCAS VON

Born 1668 in Genoa; died 1745 in Vienna. Hildebrandt was the son of a German captain who served first the Genoese Republic and later the Imperial army. Around 1690 he went to Rome as a pupil of Carlo Fontana. In 1695–96, as an engineer in the Imperial army, he took part in the Piedmont campaigns in the service of Prince Eugene of Savoy.

In 1696 Hildebrandt settled permanently in Vienna, where in 1700 he was elected court architect. He was commissioned by the court and the nobility to do much important work: the palace for Count Mansfeld-Fondi in Vienna, now called the Schwarzenberg Palace (1697); the Piaristenkirche in Vienna (1698); the church of St. Lawrence at Gabel in Bohemia (1699), mainly derived from Guarini's church of S. Lorenzo in Turin; the Starhemberg-Schönburg Palace in Vienna (1700–6); designs for the Peterskirche in Vienna (1702); Göllersdorf Castle (1710–17); and the Daun-Kinsky Palace in Vienna (1713–16). Hildebrandt also built the Lower Belvedere in Vienna (1714–16) for Prince Eugene of Savoy, the church of the seminary at Linz (1717), the Imperial Chancellery in Vienna (1719), and also designed the extension of the Göttweig monastery on the banks of the Danube (1719). He reconstructed Mirabell Castle at Salzburg in 1721.

The Upper Belvedere—his major work—was built between 1721 and 1722. The designs for the reconstruction of the Hofburg in Vienna date from 1724 and 1725. On the death of Fischer von Erlach in 1723, Hildebrandt was appointed Superintendent of Imperial Constructions, but because of serious differences between him and Fischer's son, the latter succeeded in having him dismissed from court. Although he had fallen into disfavor, Hildebrandt managed nonetheless to secure important work: the design for Marchfeld Castle (1725–32); the building of the Harrach Palace in Vienna (1728–29); designs for the construction of the Residenz at Würzburg, for which he was commissioned by Prince-Bishop Friedrich Karl to work in collaboration with Balthasar Neumann; and the parish church at Göllersdorf (1740–41).

HURTADO IZQUIERDO, FRANCISCO

Born 1669 at Lucena, near Córdoba; died 1725 at Priego, near Córdoba. Hurtado obtained his first official commissions between 1690 and 1700. He may have served his apprenticeship at a school of sculpture where he learned about altars; in fact, his first documented work is a retablo made for the church of S. Lorenzo in Córdoba (1696). It seems that some years before (1693), he may have begun the chapel of Nuestra Señora de la Victoria above the mausoleum of the counts of Buenavista at Málaga. One of his most important works, preserved at Granada, is the monumental Sagrario (Chapel of the Blessed Sacrament) of the Carthusian monastery. The project had already been started, but Hurtado took up work on it in 1702. Another major work is the sanctuary of Granada Cathedral (begun in 1704 and consisting of a small independent church). In 1718 Hurtado designed his last work, the Chapel of the Tabernacle, for the Carthusian monastery at Paular, near Segovia; it was finished by his pupils.

ITTAR, STEFANO

Born in Rome (date unknown); died 1790 in Malta. In Rome Ittar studied the works of such masters as Bernini and Borromini, and had some training at the school of Carlo Fontana. He went to Catania in 1765, where he married into the family of the architect Francesco Battaglia. He worked in conjunction with him on various commissions: designs for the Piazza di S. Filippo (later Mazzini) in 1768–69; the Porta Ferdinandea, or Porta del Fortino (1768); and the façade of the Trinità church.

In 1768 Ittar succeeded Vaccarini in various appointments, including that of Superintendent of Catania University. Ittar built the churches of S. Placido and S. Martino dei Banchi in Catania. Between 1768 and 1780 he produced his major work, the dome of the church of S. Nicola. After it had been finished (about 1783), he left Sicily for Malta, in whose capital (Valletta) he built the library.

JADOT, JEAN-NICOLAS

Born 1710 at Lunéville; died 1761 at Ville-Issey (Belgium). He followed his protector, François of Lorraine, to Vienna when the latter became Emperor of Austria (1745). In 1749, in collaboration with Franz Anton Hildebrandt, he restored Buda Castle. Jadot also erected the mansion at Holič, and in 1753–55 he constructed the old University of Vienna, now the Academy of Sciences. He drew up the designs for the park of Schönbrunn Palace, though they were altered later (c. 1705–6). When François of Lorraine exchanged his dukedom for that of Tuscany, he took Jadot with him; it seems that the architect constructed the Porta S. Gallo in Florence (1738–45).

JENNESSON, JEAN-NICOLAS

Born 1686 in Nancy; died 1755 in Nancy. His principal works are at Nancy, where Jennesson was appointed municipal architect in 1723. He collaborated with other architects in the construction of the cathedral (1709), and erected the barracks in the Rue St-Nicolas (1717), the church of St-Sébastien (1720–31), the sacristy of St-Laurent (c. 1732), and the chapels of St-Pierre and the Missions Royales (1750). He was also engaged in town-planning, altering and designing whole stretches of road, bridges, and private houses. Of his work outside Nancy, mention must be made of the abbatial palace at Remiremont (1750).

JUVARRA (JUARRA, JUVARA, IVARA), FILIPPO

Born 1678 in Messina; died 1736 in Madrid. At the beginning of his career he followed the family profession of goldsmith and carver, preparing himself at the same time for the priesthood.

When still young he went to Rome (1703), where he studied architecture with Carlo Fontana, and in 1706 won a prize offered by Pope Clement XI at Naples for a contest at the Accademia di S. Luca, of which he was appointed a member during the same year. The only work definitely attributed to Juvarra during his Roman period is the Antamori Chapel in the church of S. Girolamo della Carità (1708). In 1714 he went with Vittorio Amedeo II to Messina, where he prepared a design for the Palazzo Reale.

The same year Juvarra went to Piedmont, where he was appointed architect to the king and assigned important works in Turin. For example, he carried out the third city extension toward the west (begun in 1706). His first major efforts date from 1715, with the construction of the church of La Superga and the façade of S. Cristina (1715–18). Between 1716 and 1719 he also built the Palazzo Birago di Borgaro (now Della Valle) and the Palazzo Martini di Cigala. During the years 1716–28 he built the Quartieri Militari at Porta Susa. In 1718 he began the construction of the façade and of the new staircase at the Palazzo Madama and submitted designs for the church of S. Croce, both in Turin, and the castle at Rivoli.

In 1719 Juvarra went to Lisbon, where he prepared a design for the Royal Palace. During his stay in Portugal he also executed designs for the construction of the presbytery and possibly also for the palace-convent at Mafra.

The following year he left Lisbon and returned to Turin. He designed the church of S. Filippo, reconstructed after the collapse of Guarini's dome (1722). In 1725 he went to Rome, where he succeeded Carlo Fontana as architect of St. Peter's. Back in Piedmont, he completed a series of important works in Turin: the Palazzo d'Ormea (1730), the façade of the Palazzo Guarene, the Stupinigi hunting lodge (1729–31), and the Chiesa del Carmine (1732–36). He also submitted designs for a number of towns in the kingdom of Savoy and in Lombardy.

In 1735 Juvarra was summoned to Spain by Philip V and began building the new Royal Palace in Madrid. At the same time he submitted designs for La Granja Palace at S. Ildefonso and for the castle at Aranjuez. These designs were executed after his death by his pupil, Giovanni Battista Sacchetti.

KANKA, FRANZ MAXIMILIAN

Born 1674 in Prague; died 1766 in Prague. After probable training in Italy, he was active mainly in Prague during the first half of the eighteenth century. He worked on the rebuilding of St. Clement's at Clementinum (1711–15) and on the building of the tower of the church of Our Savior (1714).

Stylistically he was very close to the Dientzenhofers, and collaborated with Kilian Ignaz on the convent adjoining St. Nicholas in the Altstadt (1717–30) and the rebuilding of St. Catherine's (1737–41). In the period 1719–26 he was engaged on the Piarist monastery at Litomyšl. He also carried out some work on the Czernin Palace in Prague (1725), and built Vinor Castle (1720–25) in the neighborhood of the city. Kanka planned the rebuilding of the convent church of St. John Nepomuk at Kutná Hora and the church at Donaueschingen (1724). Following

plans by Kilian Ignaz Dientzenhofer, it was he who probably built the church of the Assumption at Zlonice between 1727 and 1735.

KENT, WILLIAM

Born 1685 at Bridlington, Yorkshire; died 1748 in London. Kent served his apprenticeship as a decorator, and the first part of his life was devoted exclusively to painting. He was in Rome for about ten years, where he met Lord Burlington, who invited him to decorate Burlington House. Under his guidance, Kent turned to architecture, and an inseparable collaboration between the two artists began.

Thanks to Lord Burlington, Kent occupied positions of importance as Master Carpenter in the Works in 1725, Master Mason in 1735, and two years later, Deputy Surveyor. On the advice of his protector, he edited a collection of the drawings of Inigo Jones in 1727.

The most fruitful period of Kent's career was between 1730 and 1739. In 1732 he built the Clock Court at Hampton Court Palace. In 1732 and in 1735 he drew up designs for Parliament in Westminster. These designs, like those for the Horse Guards at Whitehall, were carried out after his death. His best work was Holkham Hall, Norfolk (1734). Between 1730 and 1740 Kent also designed the gardens of Chiswick, Stowe, and Rousham, in which he initiated the tradition of the English landscape garden, abandoning the symbolic geometry of Le Nôtre and the Baroque garden.

KNOBELSDORFF, GEORG WENZESLAUS VON

Born 1699 at Kuckädel; died 1754 in Berlin. His studies took him to Italy in 1736 and to Paris in 1740. In the latter year he assumed the post of Superintendent of Castles and Gardens for Frederick of Prussia. On his return from Italy he completed Rheinsberg Castle and laid out the grounds (1737–39). In Berlin he enlarged Monbijou Palace (1740–42), supervised the new east wing of Charlottenburg Castle (1740–43; destroyed during World War II), and created his masterpiece, the Opera House on Unter den Linden (1741–43).

Von Knobelsdorff worked in Potsdam during the last years of his life, from 1744 onward, devoting himself to military works and private houses; his major projects were designs for conversion of the Stadtschloss (1744–51) and for Frederick the Great's pleasure palace, Sanssouci (1745–47). He also drew up a plan for the renovation of Dessau Castle (1747), which was only partially carried out.

KROHNE, GOTTFRIED HEINRICH

Born 1703 in Dresden; died 1756 (location unknown). He worked at the court of the dukes of Weimar—at first in cooperation with Johann Adolf Richter—on hunting lodges at Troistedt, Brembach, and Stützerbach; on the ducal residences at Hardisleben, Ilmenau, Apolda, and Dornburg (1732–44); and at Langheim Monastery, near Bamberg.

After a visit to Vienna, Krohne built the new castle at Eisenach (1741). In 1743 he was appointed supervisor of the construction of the pilgrimage church of Vierzehnheiligen, designed by Balthasar Neumann. Because he did not follow Neumann's project, he was replaced by Johann Jakob Michael Küchel in 1744, whereupon he returned to the court at Weimar and built a number of summer residences and hunting lodges (Klemme, Wilhelmstal, Hohe Sonne). He then worked at the court of the dukes of Gotha (1747) and at Ilmenau, reconstructing that town after the fire of 1751.

KÜCHEL, JOHANN JAKOB MICHAEL

Born 1703 in Bamberg; died 1769 in Bamberg. He worked in Franconia, where he built churches and monasteries. In 1735 he returned to Bamberg and in 1749 took up the post of court engineer. Küchel's main works are there; from 1744 to 1756 he restored the city hall and the tower on the upper bridge. He also built houses for noblemen (Ebracherhof, 1750), the archbishop's palace, and the residence for the parish priest of St. Stephen's.

Küchel collaborated with Johann Dientzenhofer and Balthasar Neumann in building the cloister of the monastery at Banz (completed in 1755). In addition, he was entrusted with carrying out one of Neumann's major projects, the pilgrimage church of Vierzehnheiligen, for which he also designed the high altar (1744–63).

LA GUEPIÈRE, PHILIPPE DE

Born c. 1715 (location unknown); died 1773 in Paris. He probably studied at the Paris Academy and was one of J.-F. Blondel's pupils. In 1752 he was called to Württemberg by Duke Karl Eugen to complete the ducal palace. He built the ducal residences of Mon Repos (from 1760) in Ludwigsburg Park and La Solitude (1763–67) near Stuttgart, taking part also in the work on Karlsruhe Castle and the conversion of Villa Schiekhardt (Stuttgart) into an opera house. La Guepière is credited with the town hall at Montbéliard and the plan for the Bibliothèque Ste-Geneviève in Paris. He published *Recueil d'esquisses d'architecture* in 1759.

LASSURANCE (CAILLETEAU DE L'ASSURANCE), PIERRE

Born 1655; died 1724 (locations unknown). Lassurance began his career in 1678 as a stone-mason at Clagny and as one of Jules Hardouin-Mansart's collaborators. In 1711 he became an academician.

Working independently between 1700 and 1724, Lassurance built numerous private houses. About 1700 he erected the Hôtel Rothelin d'Argenson. In 1704 the king's secretary, Thomas Rivié, commissioned him to build a mansion (later the Hôtel Desmarets). It was followed in 1708 by the Hôtel d'Auvergne, the Hôtel de Maison, and the Hôtel de Neufchâtel; in 1711 by the Hôtel Passort in Rue St-Honoré for Adrien-Maurice, the Duc de Noailles; and in 1719 by the Hôtel de Rohan-Montbazon. He also built the Château d'Evry-Petit-Bourg.

Lassurance collaborated with Giardini in the construction of the Palais de Bourbon (1720–22) and the Hôtel de Lassay (1722), succeeding him later in the direction of those works. His last work seems to have been the Hôtel

de Roquelaure, begun in 1722 and finished by Jean-Baptiste Leroux in 1736.

LE BLOND, ALEXANDRE-JEAN-BAPTISTE

Born 1679 in Paris; died 1719 in St. Petersburg. Le Blond was the son of a painter; in his youth he was engaged on interior decoration and garden architecture. The first buildings erected by him in Paris were the Palais Vendôme (1705–6; enlarged in 1714–16), the Palais Clermont (1708–14; destroyed), and the Palais Dunoyer (1708). Among his early works mention must also be made of the archbishop's palace at Auch, which was completely reconstructed about the middle of the eighteenth century. Le Blond worked in Narbonne, Canet, and Châtillon-sous-Bagneux, mostly on the layouts for gardens and parks.

In 1716, at the invitation of Le Fort, Le Blond moved to St. Petersburg, to the court of Tsar Peter the Great, where he replaced Andreas Schlüter as chief architect. His design for a general urban renewal scheme was opposed by Menšikov, the Tsar's favorite. Le Blond supplied designs for the two royal palaces of Strel'na and Mon Plaisir at Peterhof, work which was continued later by Rastrelli and Michetti.

From 1710 on, Le Blond edited the posthumous edition of Charles-Augustin Daviler's *Cours d'Architecture;* probably participated in drawing up the *Théorie et pratique du jardinage,* published anonymously in Paris in 1709; and wrote a treatise on interior and exterior decoration, the manuscript of which has been lost.

LEUTHNER (VON GRUNDT), ABRAHAM

Born at Wildenstein (date unknown); died 1700 in Prague. He worked in Prague from 1665 until his death. He became Chief Master-Builder in Bohemia and teacher of the Dientzenhofers. Leuthner took part in the erection of Czernin Palace (1669–76), in cooperation with Francesco Caratti; built the town hall at Elbogen (1682–85); and started work on the Cistercian church and monastery at Waldsassen (1682–85), which was completed by Christoph and Georg Dientzenhofer.

LISBOA, ANTÓNIO FRANCISCO (ALEIJADINHO)

Born 1738 at Villa Rica, Brazil; died 1814 at Villa Rica. Son of a Portuguese architect who had settled in Brazil, Lisboa worked chiefly in the Minas Gerais region. He served his apprenticeship as a decorator. As a result of an illness when he was thirty-nine, he became deformed, which made work difficult for him and earned him the nickname of Aleijadinho ("the lame one").

Lisboa's first known work is the church of S. Francisco at Ouro Preto (1766–94). Later he designed the church of S. Pedro at Mariana, with an elliptical plan; it was actually built by Sousa Calheiros in 1771–73. At Ouro Preto he also designed the *retablo* for the high altar of S. José (1772). From 1773 he worked on the façade and the pulpits of the church of Nostra Señora do Carmo at Sabará, also leaving many sculptural works there.

Lisboa's best sculptures (a series of statues of the twelve prophets) are to be found in his church of Bom Jesus de Matozinhos at Congonhas do Campo (1796–1805). In

1774 Lisboa prepared the designs for the church of S. Francisco at São João del Rei.

LUDOVICE, JOÃO FEDERICO (LUDWIG, JOHANN FRIEDRICH)

Born 1670 in Regensburg; died 1752 in Lisbon. Of German origin, he developed his artistic style in Italy, where he worked for Andrea Pozzo on the altar of S. Ignazio in Il Gesù. From about 1700 he was in Portugal, where King João V had commissioned him to build the palace-convent at Mafra. The final monumental solution (1717–30) includes a convent, a palace, a church, and a barracks. Ludovice also designed the library at Coimbra University (1716–23) and the Mór Chapel in Évora Cathedral (1718–46).

LURAGO, ANSELMO

Born 1702 in Como; died 1765 in Prague. He worked most of his life in the latter city, collaborating for a long time with Kilian Ignaz Dientzenhofer on the church of St. Nicholas on the Kleinseite in Prague (Lurago did the top floor and spire of the belfry) and in building and enlarging the Sylva-Tarouca (Piccolomini) Palace, which Lurago completed in 1751. He rebuilt Liběšice Palace (1738–54) and Kladno Palace. He also worked on the large convent at Dolní Rocov (1746–65), Czernin Palace (1747–50), and the church of Our Lady of the Assumption at Přestice (1748–75). He built the Golz-Kinsky Palace in Prague (1755–65) and at Maria Theresa's request worked on altering the imperial castle (1758 onward).

MAROT, DANIEL

Born 1663 in Paris; died 1752 at The Hague. Marot settled in The Hague at the time of the repeal of the Edict of Nantes (1685). He soon became William of Orange's architect. He was in London between 1695 and 1696. At Gorssel he built Voorst-en-Gueldre Castle (1697–1700), which William III had asked Daniel Gittard to design in 1684. At The Hague Marot worked on the audience room of the Seat of the States General (1696-98) and on the town hall (1733–39). After 1700 he mainly constructed private houses at Amsterdam. His best works in this city are the Royal Library (1734–37) and the enlargement of the Huis ten Bosch (1734–37).

MASSARI, GIORGIO

Born 1687 in Venice; died 1766 in Venice. The first definite information we have on his work as an architect concerns the villa at Istrana, which we know he completed in 1715. The works attributed to him as a young man include the Palazzo Civran on the Grand Canal in Venice and the church of S. Maria della Pace in Brescia, which was begun in 1720 and consecrated in 1746. From 1726 to 1736 Massari worked on the Chiesa dei Gesuati in Venice, and in 1751 he began working on the adjoining convent, which was only partially completed.

While working on the Gesuati Massari also replanned the Ospizio dei Catecumeni and the Scuola di S. Giovanni Evangelista (1727); he reconstructed the home and church of the Penitenti (1738–43). He won a contest held in 1735 for the reconstruction of the church and the home of S. Maria della Pietà, and began work on it in 1744. After completing the church of S. Maria della Consolazione (1750–53), the architect worked on the mansions of the Grassi family (after 1748) and the Rezzonico family (1750–66). In 1755 he agreed to rebuild the façade for the Scuola della Carità.

Massari's work outside Venice includes the apse in the church of S. Filippo Neri and the Palazzo Vecchia-Romanelli (1748–49) at Vicenza; the church of S. Maria delle Grazie (Cappella dell'Immagine Miracolosa, c. 1730) and the façade of S. Antonio (1733) at Udine; the Villa Cardellina (1735–60) at Montecchio; and the Villa Giovannelli (completed in 1739) at Noventa Padovana.

MEISSONIER, JUSTE-AURÈLE

Born 1695 in Turin; died 1750 in Paris. In his native city he made the acquaintance of Guarini and studied architecture with him. He began his career in France as a goldsmith, being awarded the title of *Orfèvre du Roi* in 1724. On the death of Jean Berain the Younger, he became *Dessinateur de la Chambre du Roi*. Meissonier was also engaged as superintendent of funeral ceremonies, *fêtes galantes*, firework displays, and theatrical costumes and decorations.

He designed altars and tombs in various churches—for example, the altars for St-Leu in Paris and St-Aignon in Orléans. He also devoted much of his energies to more specifically architectural work: in 1726 he submitted the plans for the façade of St-Sulpice to the prior of the church, followed by those for the chapel of the Virgin and the high altar in 1727.

The Maison Brethous in Bayonne (1733) is Meissonier's only work still in existence. Owing to his exceptionally fluid and dynamic decorativism, Meissonier is considered to be the major figure of the French Rococo. All the documentation for his works may be found in the collection of 118 plates entitled *Oeuvre de Juste-Aurèle Meissonier* (1742–50).

MICHELA, COSTANZO

Born c. 1690 at Agliè; died 1754 at Agliè. He was active in the Canavese district (c. 1731–49) and was possibly an assistant to Juvarra at Stupinigi. The first information we have about Michela refers to work done in the sanctuary of the Madonna delle Grazie at Cintano Canavese (1731). He built the parish church of S. Giacomo at Rivarolo Canavese (after 1734). Between 1739 and 1749 he reconstructed the church of the Confraternità della SS. Trinità at Valperga. In 1740 Michela began the church of S. Marta at Agliè, and in 1749 he submitted the drawings for the parish church of Borgomasino, which was later built according to designs by Vittone.

MICHETTI, NICOLA

Born 1675 (location unknown); died 1759 in Rome. Michetti was Carlo Fontana's assistant on the construction of the Ospizio di S. Michele a Ripa, in Rome. His own career really commenced about 1710. Nominated architect of the Rospigliosi family, he built the church of S. Pietro at Zagarolo (1717–30) and the chapel of S. Francesco a Ripa (1710–21). These two buildings had not been completed when Nicola left for Russia in 1718.

At the court of Peter the Great he took part in the construction of the Tsar's palace (Mon Plaisir) at Peterhof, the Summer Palace at St. Petersburg, the Kadriorg Palace at Tallinn (begun in 1718), and Strel'na Palace (begun in 1720).

Michetti returned to Rome in 1723. Two years later he became a member of the Accademia di S. Luca and took part in the competition for a palace announced in 1725. His most important work after his return to Rome was the restoration of the Palazzo Colonna, undertaken in 1730 and completed by Paolo Posi.

MIČURIN, IVAN FËDOROVIČ

Born c. 1700; died 1763 (locations unknown). Mičurin was a pupil of Michetti and went to Holland (1723–28) to complete his studies. In Moscow he erected the church of the Trinity and the church in the monastery of Zlatouskovskij; he continued the general layout of the city (1734), already begun by Mordvinov, and supervised the new construction of the synod's printing office. Keeping to Rastrelli's designs, he erected the church of St. Andrew in Kiev (1747–53). Numerous works in other cities—Brjansk, Kolna, Tver (Kalinin)—are also attributed to Mičurin, since it is presumed he drew up the designs.

MOOSBRUGGER, KASPAR

Born 1656 at Au in the Bregenzerwald; died 1723 at Einsiedeln. He was one of the main representatives of the Vorarlberg builders. From 1670 to 1673 he served his apprenticeship as a stone-carver in Au. At the age of twenty-five he entered the Benedictine monastery at Einsiedeln as a novice and worked there until his death, making frequent visits to other Benedictine monasteries in order to give architectural advice. At Einsiedeln he built the monastery itself (1684–87) and the Meinrad Chapel (1698); in 1703 he began the designs for the monastery church. In the same year it was decided to rebuild the monastery: Moosbrugger erected the east, south, and north sides between 1704 and 1711, and in 1713 he made changes in the design of the west side. In 1719 he drew up the final plan for the monastery church and began the work; it was consecrated in 1735.

Moosbrugger also directed a number of minor projects and dispensed advice. In 1684 the abbot of Weingarten consulted him on the renovation of his church (which was begun only in 1715 according to final plans by Moosbrugger). In 1684 he also visited the abbeys at Fischingen and Münsterlingen. He supplied advice and perhaps complete plans for the monastery at Muri (from 1685). Moosbrugger worked on the convents at Sarnen (1687), Katherinenthal (1689), Seedorf (1695–99), and Kalchrain (1697 and 1702), the Holy Cross Sanctuary at Grafenort (1689), and the chapels of St. Ulrich at St. Urban (1690), St. Anne at Schindellegi (1697; destroyed), and St. Serena at Zug (1705–10). He supplied designs for the Carthusian monastery at Ittingen (1697), the monastery church at Pfäfers (1697), and the churches at Rheinau (1702), Lachen (1703), Engelberg (1704), and Netstal (1704).

MUNGGENAST, JOSEPH

Born 1680 at Schnann; died 1741 at St. Pölten. He belonged to a family of Tyrolean architects and worked almost entirely in abbey churches and monasteries. He was one of Prandtauer's pupils and followers. According to his master's designs, Munggenast built the church for the Augustinian monastery at Herzogenberg (1714–40). At Melk, in 1728, he rebuilt the two bell-towers of the church of St. Peter and St. Paul and completed the adjacent Benedictine abbey, begun by Prandtauer in 1702; at Sonntagsberg he continued Prandtauer's work of building the Holy Trinity Sanctuary and St. Michael's (1718–32). Munggenast worked on the abbeys at Dürnstein (1721–33) and Zwettl (1722–35), and rebuilt the old chapter house at St. Pölten (c. 1722–39). He directed the erection of the monastery at Geras (1731–40) and of the abbey church and library at Altenburg (1730–33).

NAPOLI, TOMMASO MARIA

Born 1655 in Palermo; died 1725 in Palermo. A member of the Dominican order, he was a student of mathematics and wrote theoretical works: *Utriusque Architecturae compendium in duos libros* ("Compendium of Both Architectures in Two Volumes") in 1708, and *Breve ristretto dell'architettura militare e fortificazione offensiva e difensiva* ("Brief Summary of Military Architecture and Offensive and Defensive Fortification") in 1723. Napoli's name is associated with the Villa Palagonia (1715, in collaboration with Agatino Daidone) at Bagheria and with the Villa Valguarnera (1721). At Palermo, he built the Colonna dell'Immacolata in Piazza S. Domenico, and then began work on the layout of the whole piazza—a project that was completed in 1726 by Giovanni Biagio Amico.

NETTE, JOHANN FRIEDRICH

Born 1672 (location unknown); died 1714 in Nancy. Nette, together with Donato Giuseppe Frisoni, played a decisive part in building the Residenz in Ludwigsburg, where he erected the upper floors of the central section, the south wing, and the pavilion on the west corner (1704–14). He assembled the plans for the Residenz in a volume of prints called *Vues et parties principales de Louisburg* (1712). At roughly the same time he worked on the façade and enlargement of the Prinzenbau at Stuttgart.

NEUMANN, BALTHASAR

Born 1687 in Cheb (Bohemia); died 1753 at Würzburg. After completing his apprenticeship at a casting-house in Cheb, he moved in 1711 to Würzburg, where he worked as a modeler and decorator in the workshop of Ignaz Kopp. Here his work came to the notice of Andreas Müller, who taught him the first elements of architecture and military engineering. In 1714 he became the pupil of Joseph Greising, chief architect to the Prince-Bishop. After taking part in 1717 in the conquest of the fortress of Belgrade, Neumann went to Vienna in the service of the Imperial Governor, on whose behalf the following year he went to Milan and Turin, where he became acquainted with Italian architecture, in particular the works of Guarini and Juvarra.

In 1719 Count Johann Philipp Franz von Schönborn, who had been appointed Prince-Bishop of Würzburg, transferred his court from Marienberg to Würzburg and commissioned Neumann to build the Residenz and to prepare designs for the improvement of this city. In 1721 Neumann started building the Schönborn Chapel in the same town and a year later, as head of the building commission, he had working with him a skilled team of collaborators: Johann Dientzenhofer, Maximilian von Welsch, and Johann Lucas von Hildebrandt.

In 1723 Neumann went to Paris, where he established contact with Germain Boffrand and Robert de Cotte. During his stay there he elaborated the designs for the Würzburg Residenz, which he had begun to work on as early as 1719, while keeping up an active correspondence with the people who had commissioned the work and with his collaborators. The Residenz (which was completed only in 1744) is Neumann's major work, and is one of the most noteworthy examples of German Baroque.

Between 1727 and 1732 he built the parish church of Wiesentheid, his first large religious building; the Benedictine church at Münsterschwarzach (since demolished); and the church at Holzkirchen, which was begun by Johann Dientzenhofer. In 1728 Neumann was commissioned by the Bishop of Speyer to complete the castle at Bruchsal, which had already been begun by Anselm Franz Freiherr von Ritter zu Grünstein. The castle, for which he provided the huge central staircase, was finished in 1731. He was appointed to teach civil and military architecture at the University of Würzburg.

In 1729 Friedrich Karl von Schönborn succeeded Johann Philipp Franz as Prince-Bishop of Würzburg, and he commissioned Neumann to do some important works: to complete the Würzburg Residenz, to supervise military work, to control all the building projects of the region, and to devise a town plan for Würzburg.

In 1733 Neumann began building the castle of Werneck, and during the same year he was commissioned by Elector Clemens August von Wittelsbach to continue work at the castle in Brühl, previously attended to by Von Schlaun and Cuvilliés.

Neumann's interest in problems of space is also revealed in the architecture of his numerous churches between 1729 and 1745: the pilgrimage church of Gössweinstein (1729–39), the Hofkirche in the Würzburg Residenz (1731–32), and the churches at Heusenstamm (1739–56), Gaibach (1740–45), and Etwashausen (1740–45). In 1742 he also produced the designs for the church of the Jesuits at Mainz (consecrated in 1746; demolished in 1805) and for the pilgrimage church of Vierzehnheiligen (consecrated 1772).

On the death of Friedrich Karl von Schönborn in 1746, Neumann was relieved of his appointment as court architect. He left Würzburg and went to Vienna, where he augmented Joseph Emanuel Fischer von Erlach's and Hildebrandt's earlier designs for the new imperial residence, the Hofburg (1746–47). At the same time he prepared designs for the Residenz in Stuttgart (1747–49) and for the palace at Karlsruhe (1750); the latter was rejected because it was considered to be too grandiose in style. To this period also belong the church of St. Mary on the Nikolausberg above Würzburg, known as the Käppele (foundation-stone 1748), and the completion of the Benedictine church at Neresheim (from 1747), in which Neumann successfully combines the basilical plan with a structure based on a central plan. In 1749 the new bishop of Würzburg, Karl Philipp von Greiffenklau, assigned to him again the duties taken from him.

OPPENORD, GILLES-MARIE

Born 1672 in Paris; died 1742 in Paris. Son of a cabinet-maker, he joined Jules Hardouin-Mansart's circle and, thanks to him, obtained a grant to study at the French Academy in Rome. During his stay in Italy, which lasted seven years, he devoted himself to the study of Roman monuments and contemporary architecture, and traveled in northern Italy, staying mainly in Venice and Lombardy; before leaving Rome he designed the tomb of the Bouillon family (today at the Hôtel-Dieu in Cluny), which was executed by Legros.

On his return to Paris (1699), Oppenord supplied designs for the tomb of the Countess of Relingue in the church of the Dominican Novitiates, the high altar in St-Germain-des-Près, and the chapel of St-Jean-du-Voeu in Amiens Cathedral (1709–11). He also planned the decoration for the choir in the church of St-Victoire (1709), though it was never executed. He played an important part in the building of St-Sulpice: the high altar (1704), the completion of the north front, begun by Gittard, and the construction of the south front (1719–26) are all the work of Oppenord.

In 1713 he renovated the interior of the Château de Bercy. About 1717 he entered the service of the Duke of Orléans and also began work on the Palais Royal; in 1719 and 1720 he was working on the large hall and decoration of the Aeneas Gallery. In 1720–21, for the Duke of Orléans, he enlarged and renovated the Hôtel du Grand Prieur du Temple in Paris, which had been constructed in 1667 by Delisle and Hardouin-Mansart, and decorated numerous rooms in the Château de Viller-Cotterêts. He also worked for the younger Crozat, in the Rue de Richelieu, where he built the gallery (which collapsed in 1721); he also built for him an orangerie in his park at Montmorency.

A series of drawings made by Oppenord between 1731 and 1742 for the Hôtel Gaudion are kept in the Musée des Arts Décoratifs in Paris. Oppenord worked abroad too: he supplied the Elector of Cologne with several designs for the palace at Bonn and for the Falkenlust pavilion of the castle at Brühl.

His works were collected and published in two volumes by Huquier: *Le grand Oppenord* and *Le petit Oppenord* (Paris, c. 1715).

PACASSI, NIKOLAUS FRANZ LEONHARD

Born 1716 at Wiener-Neustadt; died 1790 in Vienna. He came from a family of artists originating in Gorizia. Pacassi's name is linked above all with the completion of Schönbrunn Palace (1744–49) in Vienna, begun by Johann Bernhard Fischer von Erlach, and with the conversion at Wiener-Neustadt of the old castle into a military academy (1751).

From 1745 he was in the service of the court in Vienna, where he did work on the Kreuzkirche (1755–63), the archers' barracks (1761–63), the Belvedere, the restoration of the Hofbibliothek (1763–69), the Mint, Prince Karl von Lothringen's palace, plans for the interior of the Hungarian Guards' quarters (1766), and renovation of the Hofburg (c. 1764).

In Prague Pacassi was engaged on the convent of the Virgin Mary (1754) and the adjacent church (1769). He worked on the castles at Bratislava, Prague, Laxenburg, Troja, and Erlau (Starhemberg Castle, from 1767). At Klagenfurt he built the archbishop's palace (1769–71); in Gorizia he erected the Fountain of Neptune and the Attimis Palace.

PALMA, ANDREA

Born 1664 at Trapani; died 1730 at Palermo. He was a pupil of Giacomo Amato. Between 1728 and 1754 the façade of the cathedral at Syracuse was built to his designs. Palma also decorated the aisles and the transept chapel in the church of S. Caterina in Palermo.

PASSALACQUA, PIETRO

Born in Messina (date unknown); died 1748 in Rome. He worked in Rome on the façade of S. Francesco d'Assisi at Monte Mario (1728–29) and on the rebuilding of S. Croce in Gerusalemme (1743), in collaboration with Domenico Gregorini. In addition, he built the oratories of the Annunziata and of the Arciconfraternità di S. Spirito in Sassia (1745).

PINEAU, NICOLAS

Born 1684 in Paris; died 1754 in Paris. Son of a sculptor, Nicolas probably served his apprenticeship in his father's atelier, and it seems that he came into contact with the greatest Parisian artists of his time—Boffrand the architect, Coysevox the sculptor, and Thomas Germain the decorative artist.

The most important moment in his career was his departure for Russia in Le Blond's suite. Of all Pineau's work at the Tsar's court, only the *Cabinet* of Peter the Great at Peterhof remains. On Le Blond's death, he succeeded him in his architectural functions and supplied designs for an arsenal, an entertainment hall, a church, and several *pavillons d'agrément*. He remained in Russia about twelve years.

On his return to France in 1727, Pineau abandoned architecture and limited himself to supplying drawings for decorators, for all the best architects of the time wanted him to collaborate with them. In Rome he was made a teacher at the Accademia di S. Luca in 1739 and was nominated director in 1747.

PLANTERY, GIAN GIACOMO

Born 1680 in Turin; died 1756 in Turin. He held public appointments in the kingdom of Savoy, and this enabled him to leave a lasting mark on the town-planning and architectural works of his time, especially in Turin. He worked a great deal in Savigliano, where in 1708 he presented designs for the churches of the Confraternita dell'Assunta and S. Croce, also known as S. Maria del Pianto.

In Turin Plantery interested himself in particular in domestic building: between 1715 and 1722 he built the Palazzo Saluzzo-Paesana; around 1729 he built the Palazzo Cavour; after 1753 he began the Palazzo Fontana di Cravanzana. At Fossano in 1724 he presented changes in the designs Gallo had prepared for the hospital, while at Cavallermaggiore he left designs for the Carmelite monastery.

Buildings attributed to Plantery include the Palazzo Cigliano (1707–8) and the Palazzo Capris di Cigliè (1730) in Turin, as well as the sanctuary of S. Ignazio at Lanzo Torinese (1725–29).

PÖPPELMANN, MATHAES DANIEL

Born 1662 at Herford (Westphalia); died 1736 in Dresden. In 1684 he was in Dresden as a pupil of Wolf Caspar von Klengel, who was engaged in rebuilding the district of Alt-Dresden, destroyed by a fire. On his master's death, Pöppelmann continued his work.

In 1691 he was appointed director of building in Dresden and in 1710 *Geheim Cämmeriere* (Privy Councillor). For the Royal Palace in Dresden, destroyed by fire, Pöppelmann drew up a series of projects, of which those of 1705-7 and 1716 are particularly important. In 1709 he began to draw up the plans for his main work, the Zwinger in Dresden. After erection of the palace's northwest wing he designed and built the symmetrical southeast section (from 1718).

In 1713 Pöppelmann was working in Warsaw; his plans for the Royal Palace and later for the Saxon Palace were never carried into effect, owing to a lack of funds. Between 1713 and 1729 he designed Joachimstein Castle near Zittau. From 1720 he was building the castle at Pillnitz on the Elbe and, from 1723, the Bergkirche; by request of Augustus the Strong he transformed the hunting castle at Moritzburg (1723–33). After enlarging Graditz Castle (1722–23) at Torgau and designing the Niedertorbrücke and the Frauentorbrücke in Zwickau, he concentrated his work in Dresden again: the Augustusbrücke (1727–31), the conversion of the Dutch Palace to the Japanese Palace (from 1727), and—with Georg Bähr—the Dreikönigskirche (from 1732). The church of St. Matthew (1728–30) and the façade of the Chancellory Palace (1733) are attributed to him.

PRANDTAUER, JACOB

Born 1662 at Stanz (Tyrol); died 1726 at St. Pölten. Nothing is known about his activity up to 1689, the year in which he was working as a sculptor at St. Pölten. Especially at first, his work as an architect was connected with the reconstruction of places destroyed by the Turkish invasion. His first large projects were at Count Gurland's castle in Thalheim (c. 1690) and at some monasteries in Lower Austria. In 1692 Prandtauer was at Dürnstein, where he probably left plans for the parish church of Our Lady of the Assumption. In 1700 he was made a citizen of St. Pölten and given the title of Master-Builder. In the same year he was appointed by Abbot Dietmayr to carry out his main work, the rebuilding and enlargement of the Benedictine abbey at Melk (he was engaged on it from 1702 to 1718, although the abbey was not finished until 1727).

Between 1701 and 1704 Prandtauer made the acquaintance of Fischer von Erlach and Hildebrandt in Vienna. His plans for the reconstruction of the Augustinian monastery at Klosterneuburg (1706) were never carried into effect. The work he undertook for the sanctuary of the Holy Trinity (1706) and St. Michael's at the Sonntagsberg was continued in 1718 by Munggenast, who also completed the renovation and enlargement of the Augustinian monastery at Herzogenburg, on which Prandtauer was engaged from 1714 to 1725.

Prandtauer finished a number of works undertaken by the Italian Carlo Antonio Carlone: in 1708 the parish church at Cristkindl (begun in 1703) and the Benedictine monastery at Garsten (begun after 1695); and in 1714 the Augustinian monastery at St. Florian, for which Carlone had drawn up a first project in 1686. Between 1713 and 1717 Prandtauer built the Benedictine abbey at Kremsmünster. He planned the alteration of Neupernstein Castle (1715–17) and erected the parish church at Maria Ponsee (1716–26) and a little later (1719) the bishop's residence at Linz. He worked on the Baroque conversion of St. Pölten Cathedral (1721–22) and the erection of the church of Our Lady of the Assumption at Ravelsbach (1721–25). During the last years of his life Prandtauer designed the little hunting castle (built by Jacob Steinhuber) at Hehenbrunn near St. Florian and remodeled the church of St. George at Wullersdorf.

PRUNNER, JOHANN MICHAEL

Born 1669 at Linz; died 1739 at Linz. Prunner may have studied in Rome and Florence. He had his early working experience in Prague and Vienna. Returning to his native town in 1705, he quickly became the leading architect in Upper Austria. There are numerous private buildings and churches in Linz on which Prunner was engaged, particularly on the façades: the Carmelite church (1710); Count Thürheim's house (1710); plans for the Minorite church (1713; not carried out) and monastery (1716); houses for the barons Weissenwolff (begun in 1715), Zeppenfeld (c. 1715), and Mannstorff (1716–18); the Seminary church, where he directed the work from 1717 to 1725 according to Hildebrandt's plans; and Wels Palace (1739).

About 1712 Prunner was involved in drawing up the plans for rebuilding Kammer Castle at Attersee. He also completed the library in Schlierbach Monastery (begun by Carlo Antonio Carlone), built the Kalvarienbergkirche at Schenkenfelden, and altered the church of St. Nicholas at Passau. Prunner's most important buildings include the Trinitätskirche at Paura near Lambach (1714–24), built to a triangular design with three towers; the collegiate church of Our Lady of the Assumption at Spital am Pyhrn (1714–36); and the wool mill on the banks of the Danube (1722–23). In 1725 he enlarged and renovated Gstatt Castle at Öblarn; from 1727 to 1731 he rebuilt Lamber Castle at Steyr.

QUIÑONES, ANDRÉS GARCÍA DE

Active about the middle of the eighteenth century; precise birth and death dates unknown. Quiñones is probably the architect of the towers and courtyard of the Clerecía and the Ayuntamiento at Salamanca (1750–55); his designs for the towers built in the Clerecía were originally intended for the Ayuntamiento.

RAGUZZINI, FILIPPO

Born 1680 in Naples; died 1771 in Rome. His first works were commissioned at the time of the reconstruction of Benevento after the earthquake of 1702. There he became acquainted with Cardinal Orsini, later Pope Benedict XIII, an association which led to commissions after his arrival in Rome in 1724.

Of his works in Benevento, the following are worthy of mention: the chapel of S. Gennaro in the church of the Annunziata, the designs for the churches of S. Filippo and S. Bartolomeo, and the Palazzetto De Simone.

In Rome Raguzzini held important appointments only until the death of Benedict XIII (1730). Nevertheless, in 1733 he was successful in obtaining the appointment of Architect of the Roman People, and in entering both the Congregazione dei Virtuosi del Pantheon and the Accademia di S. Luca.

His first major work in Rome was the church and hospital of S. Gallicano (1724–26). In 1725 the chapel of S. Domenico in S. Maria sopra Minerva was inaugurated, and in the same year Raguzzini supervised restoration work in S. Sisto Vecchio, which was followed by similar work in the Sistine Chapel of S. Maria Maggiore and in the Cappella del Crocefisso of S. Maria sopra Minerva. During the same period he built the façade of the church of the Madonna delle Fornaci and the chapel of the Presepio in S. Maria in Trastevere (c. 1726).

Between 1727 and 1731 Raguzzini supervised work on the church of the Madonna della Quercia, the planning of Piazza S. Ignazio (1727–28), and the Chiesetta del Divino Amore at Campo Marzio (1729). In 1731 he took part in the contest for the façade of S. Giovanni in Laterano; in the same year he submitted a design for the restoration of the Spanish Stairs.

RASTRELLI, BARTOLOMEO

Born 1700, probably in Paris; died 1771 in St. Petersburg. At fifteen he went with his father to Russia, and while still very young did a great deal of work with him. Except for brief visits to France and Italy, Rastrelli was to do the greater part of his work as an architect in Russia.

He began work there when the Tsarina Anna Ivanova came to the throne (1730), and produced buildings in which he successfully harmonized the national Russian style with the European Baroque. Between 1730 and 1736 he built a series of mansions in wood at Annenhof near Moscow, the Kantemir Palace at St. Petersburg, and his masterpiece, the Winter Palace at St. Petersburg (1732–36), which was destroyed and rebuilt by Rastrelli himself between 1753 and 1762. In 1736 he was appointed court architect, and with the accession of Elizabeth in 1741 he became the chief interpreter of the reconstruction and layout plans desired by the Tsarina.

Rastrelli's output between 1736 and 1757 was especially intense: the Biron Palace (1736–40); the Aničkov Palace (1744–50); the Summer Palace at St. Petersburg (1740–44), which was altered more than once; the design for the church of St. Andrew (1747–48) at Kiev, which was later built by Mičurin; the restoration and extension of the great palace of Mon Plaisir at Peterhof (1747–52); the design for the group of buildings for

Smolny Convent (1744–57) at St. Petersburg; the Voronzov Palace (1746–55) and the Stroganov Palace at St. Petersburg (1750–54); and the reconstruction of the great palace of Tsarskoe Selo with new interior decorations (1752–56).

RETTI, LEOPOLDO

Born 1705 at Laino (or Vienna?); died 1751 in Vienna. He studied in Vienna, then moved to Ludwigsburg, where he became court architect in 1727, probably working on the Residenz and drawing up the plans for the whole city. As first court architect he built the Orangerie (1735) and the Caroline Gymnasium (1736), renovated the Gumpertuskirche (1736-38), and erected the synagogue (1743) and various private houses.

After winning a competitive examination for the Stuttgart Residenz, Retti personally directed work on the building (probably begun in 1744), which was continued after his death by Philippe de la Guepière. As chief architect in Württemberg he built various castles—including Kirchberg and Eschenau (1745)—and the churches at Weidenbach and Schwenningen.

RODRÍGUEZ, VENTURA

Born 1717 in Madrid; died 1785 in Madrid. During his early years he came into contact with Étienne Marchand, Filippo Juvarra, and Giovanni Battista Sacchetti. He worked as an apprentice at the Royal Palace in Madrid; by 1741 he was one of the first assistants and in 1757 took over the direction of the "outside works, squares, galleries, and gardens of the Palace."

After the death of his protector, Ferdinand VI, he lost his position and had to look for new patrons. In the meantime, however, Rodríguez had undertaken numerous other works: the church of S. Marcos in Madrid (1749–53), the renovation and completion of the basilica of S. María del Pilar at Saragossa (commissioned in 1750), designs for the *Transparente* of Cuenca Cathedral and for the destroyed church of S. Norberto in Madrid (1754), and the reconstruction of the interior of the church of the Incarnation, also in Madrid (designed in 1755).

His designs for the Augustinian monastery at Valladolid (1760) and for the adjoining church were followed by a group of works in which Rodríguez attempted the combination of a central plan with an imposing choir: the chapel of the Colegio Mayor de S. Ildefonso in Alcalá de Henares (1760), the Covadonga Basilica (1779), and the Vittoria church at Córdoba (1772–78).

In 1761 Rodríguez designed the Royal College of Surgery in Barcelona—not his only work of this kind, since he had earlier designed Madrid's General Hospital (1755) and was later to design the chapel in the Hospicio at Oviedo (1768), the Trillo Sanatorium (1775), and the S. Lázaro Hospital at Málaga (1783). His last important work was the façade of Pamplona Cathedral (1783 or 1784).

ROSSI, DOMENICO EGIDIO

Born 1678 at Fano, in The Marches; died 1742 in Venice. Rossi was both an architect and a painter. He was in Bologna for some time, before 1704. After working in Vienna and Prague, he was appointed in 1698 to build Count Czernin's hunting castle at Rastatt (completed in 1702). In 1698 Rossi submitted the plans for Scheibenhard Castle at Karlsruhe, which he built between 1699 and 1701.

RUDOLF, KONRAD

Born between 1650 and 1675 in Germany; died 1732 in Vienna. He served his apprenticeship in Paris and Rome. Between 1701 and 1707 he was at Valencia, where he commenced the main portal of the cathedral in 1703 and later extended his work to the entire façade. In 1707, however, when he left the city, only the lower part of the façade had been erected, and work was continued on it until 1740 by Francisco Stolf and Francisco Vergara. About 1713 Rudolf moved to Vienna, where he assumed the position of *Hof- und Kammer-Statuarius* in 1714.

SALVI, NICOLA

Born 1697 in Rome; died 1751 in Rome. After studying painting under Nicolò Ricciolini and Antonio Canevari, he was appointed member of the Accademia di S. Luca in 1733, and in 1745 entered the Congregazione dei Virtuosi del Pantheon. His first works include the baptistery of S. Paolo fuori le Mura (1727), later destroyed; the designs for the façade of S. Giovanni in Laterano, made on the occasion of a competition in which Alessandro Algardi, Alessandro Galilei, and Luigi Vanvitelli also participated; and the designs for the Trevi Fountain (1732), his principal work, which was completed by Giuseppe Pannini in 1762.

In 1735 Salvi executed work for the Ruffo Chapel in S. Lorenzo in Damaso, Rome, and three years later he reconstructed the church of S. Maria de' Gradi at Viterbo. He collaborated with Vanvitelli on the chapel of S. João in the church of S. Roch in Lisbon (1742) and on the rebuilding of the Odescalchi Palace (1745) in Rome. The following year he presented designs for the new façade of the SS. Apostoli, which were not executed.

SANFELICE, FERDINANDO

Born 1675 in Naples; died 1748 in Naples. Sanfelice was extremely prolific as a scenographer as well as an architect. Of his numerous decors and arrangements for state occasions, the following must be mentioned: the decorations for the funeral of Carlo II (1701, the year of his debut as an architect), those for the visit of Philip V (1702), the entry into Naples of Don Carlos of Bourbon (1734), the king's marriage (1738), and the birth of the queen's first child (1740).

One of the first churches built by Sanfelice was S. Maria delle Periclitanti at Pontecorvaro (1701). In 1701 he also did restoration work on the church of the Cappuccini at Pozzuoli. Rebuilding and restoration work in fact occupied him for the rest of his life: in Naples, in the churches of the Redenzione dei Cattivi (1706), S. Gaudioso (1733), and the church and monastery of Donnaregina; outside Naples, in the cathedrals at Nardò (1715) and Salerno (1723–30).

The churches of Villanova at Posillipo, of the Nunziatella (possibly built in 1736), and of S. Maria succurre miseris in Naples are of unknown date. In 1724 he built the church of S. Maria della Purità at Nardò, the church of S. Chiara at Nola, and the façade of S. Lorenzo in Naples (1743).

Sanfelice's civil architecture is of greater importance. He worked on numerous palazzi: Pignatelli (1718), Filomarino, Maggiocco, Palmarici, and Casamassima. He built the Palazzo Sanfelice for his own family at Vergini (1725–28), the Palazzo Serra-Cassano (1725), and the Palazzo Di Majo.

The solution Sanfelice adopted for steps is especially worthy of note: see, for example, the flight of steps *(scalinata)* at the church of S. Giovanni a Carbonara (1708) and the staircases of the Palazzo Di Majo, the Palazzo Serra-Cassano, and the Palazzo Capuano.

SANTINI AICHEL, JOHANN (SANTINI, GIOVANNI)

Born 1677 in Prague; died 1723 in Prague. Aichel, who was of Italian extraction, may be considered the most original representative of the Bohemian Baroque. He probably visited Italy, Holland, and England, which had an influence on him. Among his Neo-Gothic works we should mention the Cistercian abbey church at Sedlec near Kutná Hora (1703), and the abbey at Kladruby (1712–26), both based on pre-existing medieval buildings. His shrine of St. John Nepomuk on the Green Mountain near Žďár (Saar) in Moravia (1719–22) is star-shaped.

Among his more Baroque works, the first which can be attributed to him with certainty is the chapel at Panenské Břežany (Jungfernbřežan) to the north of Prague (1705-7). The chapel at Lomec, in southern Bohemia (completed in 1702), is almost certainly by him.

Among Santini Aichel's other interesting works are the sanctuaries of Mariánské Týnice (1711-18) and Křtiny (1713–35) in Moravia; Zbraslav Monastery (from 1716) at Königsaal, near Prague, probably his best-known work; the Thun-Hohenstein Palace (1710–20; sculptural work after 1720) and the Morzin Palace (1713–14), both in Prague; Karlová Koruna (Karlskrone) Castle (1720–21) near Chlumec on the Cidlina; and the design for Plasy Monastery. Santini Aichel's last work was the convent church at Rajhrad near Brno (1722).

SARDI, GIUSEPPE

Born c. 1680 at S. Angelo in Vado; died 1753 in Rome. He was self-taught and developed outside the world of Roman culture. When the church of S. Maria del Rosario in Marino (1710–13) was attributed to Sardi, it became possible to reconstruct the career of this architect who was active in Rome during the first half of the eighteenth century. He probably worked on the restoration of S. Maria in Monticelli (c. 1715), an occasion which would have brought him into contact with Fontana's school.

In 1721 he completed the front elevation of S. Paolino alla Regola and built the baptismal chapel of S. Lorenzo in Lucina. We have no further information about Sardi until 1732, when he worked under Manoel Rodrigues dos Santos on the church of the Trinità on Rome's Via Condotti. It is probable that during the period 1734–35 he supervised work on the façade of S. Maria Maddalena. The façade of S. Maria ad Nives is generally attributed to Sardi. His last known works are the convent and church of the SS. Quaranta in Trastevere (1735–47).

SCHÄDEL, GOTTFRIED

Born c. 1680 at Wandsbeck, near Hamburg; died 1752 at Kiev. In 1713 he accompanied Andreas Schlüter to St. Petersburg, where he began constructing the Menšikov Palace and Oranienbaum Castle (1713–25) near the city, probably working in collaboration with Giovanni Maria Fontana.

At Kiev he restored and altered the ancient Academy (from 1735), erected the bell-tower of the Lavra Kievo-Pečërskaja (1736–45), constructed the west door and the bell-tower of the church of St. Sophia (1746), and collaborated on St. Andrew's Cathedral (1747–52).

SCHLAUN, JOHANN CONRAD VON

Born 1695 at Nörde (Warburg); died 1773 at Münster. He worked in Westphalia, especially in Münster, where in 1720 he was given the post of engineer to the archbishopric. A pupil for some time in Balthasar Neumann's school, he was able to obtain direct knowledge of the Roman Baroque, since he was in Rome in 1722, of the French Rococo, and of the architecture of southern Germany, where he traveled in 1742.

Schlaun designed and constructed many buildings in Münster: the cathedral's courtyard (1720) and walk (1722); the Capuchin church (1724–29); the Customs Office (1731); the fortifications and penitentiary (1732); Velen House (1752); and the church of St. Maurice (1758). Particular importance attaches to the Schloss, the bishop's residence, for which a first project dates from 1733, though it was built only between 1767 and 1773, and to St. Clement's (1745–48) and the Erbdrostenhof (1755–57), which were seriously damaged during World War II.

From 1724 to 1728 Schlaun directed the construction of the castle for Elector Clemens August von Wittelsbach at Brühl; he was succeeded by François de Cuvilliés (1728) and Balthasar Neumann (1733). Near Münster, at Soegel, he built the Clemenswerth hunting lodge for Clemens August (1736–50). He worked in a number of Westphalian towns in the service of princes, bishops, and religious orders: for the Jesuits he built a college at Büren (1716–20) and a school at Cologne (1728–29); for the Capuchins the churches at Brakel (1715–18) and Witten (with the adjacent monastery, 1730); he also erected the archbishop's palace at Paderborn. Other works by Schlaun include Arnsburg Castle (1725–30), Rösberg Castle at Bonn (1730), Totenhausen Castle (c. 1737), the Rüschhaus (1745–48) near Münster, and the castles at Rheder (1720), Hovestadt, and Ahaus (1767–73).

SINATRA, VINCENZO

Dates and places of birth and death unknown. Sinatra is one of the Sicilian architects who collaborated on the rebuilding of the towns hit by the famous earthquake of 1693. At Noto he built the Palazzo Ducerio (1764); a little earlier he had built the church of Montevergine. The church of S. Paolo at Palazzolo Acreide (c. 1750) has been attributed to Sinatra after analysis of its style. As for S. Giorgio at Modica, there is still much doubt as to whether it is in fact Sinatra's work or that of Rosario Gagliardi.

SPECCHI, ALESSANDRO

Born 1668 in Rome; died 1729 in Rome. Most of Specchi's buildings are in his native city, where his principal work is the port of the Ripetta (1703–5). In 1706 he built the S. Fabiano Chapel in the church of S. Sebastiano fuori le Mura; in 1710 he worked on the reconstruction of the Palazzo Pichini (later called the Palazzo Roccagiovane) in the Piazza Farnese, and also on the restoration of the Palazzo Albani del Drago, in which he was responsible for the courtyard, the entrance in Via del Quirinale, and the interior decoration. In 1714 he began work on the Palazzo De Carolis al Corso, which was finished in 1724. Between 1717 and 1720 he prepared a series of designs for the Spanish Stairs.

A member of the Accademia di S. Luca, Specchi was forced to resign his membership in 1719. He was nonetheless successful in obtaining assignments: he was appointed architect of the Camera Capitolina, and from 1721 onward was Architect and Measurer of the Fabric of St. Peter's. In 1725 Specchi ceased to work as an architect after the collapse of the colonnade of S. Paolo, the work which he was supervising. It is doubtful whether he had any part in building the coach-houses of the Quirinale or in the restoration of S. Maria della Neve at Frosinone.

SPECHT, JOHANN JAKOB

Born 1720 at Lindenberg; died 1803 at Lindenberg. He belonged to Peter Thumb's school. Between 1772 and 1781 Specht built the large convent church at Wiblingen, based on a design by Johann Michael Fischer. He also erected the parish church at Wiggenbach and the chapel of St. Leonard at Rimpach.

STARCEV, OSIP DMITRIEVIČ

Born in Moscow; life dates and place of death unknown. Active in the second half of the seventeenth century, this Russian architect worked mainly in Moscow, where he built the refectory of Simonovskij Monastery (1680–83), Krutickij Teremok Palace (c. 1694), and decorated Krutickoe Podvor'e. Starcev also worked in the Ukraine. At Kiev, he erected the churches of the Bratskij and Nikol'skij monasteries after 1690.

STEINL, MATTHIAS

Born 1644 in Vienna; died 1727 in Vienna. He was responsible for the renovation of the parish church of Our Lady of the Assumption at Dürnstein, which belonged to the old Augustinian convent. Steinl drew up the designs with Prandtauer and directed the actual construction between 1721 and 1725 with Munggenast, who finished it by 1733. He also designed the tower-façade of the abbey church at Zwettl (1722). Steinl executed some works which are not purely architectural: the pulpit and high altar in the Cistercian church at Vorau (1700–4) and the monstrance for the church of Our Lady at Klosterneuburg (1714). His façade for St. Dorothy's in Vienna (1698–1702) has been destroyed.

THUMB, CHRISTIAN

Born c. 1640 at Bregenz; died 1726 at Au. He belonged to a family of architects and painters from the Bregenzerwald. In 1682, with Franz Beer and his brother Michael Thumb, he began to erect the pilgrimage church at Schönenberg, near Ellwangen, one of the first examples of the so-called *Vorarlberger Münsterschema*. On his brother's death in 1690, he continued to work on the church at Obermarchthal, with Beer's cooperation. Christian may also have worked with Beer on the chapter church at Weingarten between 1715 and 1721. During the same period, about 1720, he designed the monastery at Ottobeuren, which was not carried out. Christian Thumb was one of the main exponents of the Vorarlberg school.

THUMB, PETER

Born 1681 at Bezau; died 1766 at Constance. Michael Thumb's son, he belonged to the Vorarlberg school. In 1704 he began to work with Franz Beer, first on the abbey church at Rheinau (Switzerland). Between 1709 and 1715 he worked on the church and monastery at Ebersmünster, which he rebuilt himself in 1719–25. Thumb worked almost entirely on abbeys: St. Trudpert, Ettenheimmünster (1718–29), Schuttern (church tower, 1722), Schwarzach (1724), Friedenweiler (1725–26), Baden-Lichtental (1728), Günstertal (1728–30), and Königsbrück (c. 1729).

Among his major works, mention should be made of the library at the monastery of St. Peter in the Black Forest (1737); the sanctuary at Birnau on Lake Constance, considered to be his main work (1746–49); and the rebuilding of the abbey church of St. Gall (designed 1749, rebuilt 1744–66) and of the library in the abbey's annex (1758–66).

Thumb worked on other religious buildings also: these include the Benedictine church at Villingen in the Black Forest (from 1729), the parish churches at Biengen (1730) and St. Ulrich (1739–40) in Breisgau, and those at Mundelfingen in Baden (1750–51) and Tiengen (1753–57) on the Upper Rhine.

THURAH, LAURIDS DE

Born 1706 at Aarhus; died 1759 in Copenhagen. De Thurah worked mainly in Copenhagen, where he built Hirschholm Castle (1733–44; destroyed); the bell-tower of the church of Our Savior (1750), which was inspired by Borromini's lantern of S. Ivo alla Sapienza in Rome; the Frederiks Hospital (begun in 1752 in collaboration with Niels Eigtved, in the new quarter constructed by Frederik V); a wing of Frederiksborg Castle; and Christiansborg Castle.

Near Copenhagen he built the Eremitage hunting lodge (1734–36) and the royal mansion of Sorgenfrei (1743–45), at Lyngby, begun by Charles-Philippe Dieussart in 1705. At Roskilde De Thurah constructed the Palaiset (1732) and the Ledreborg Residens (c. 1750) nearby. At Sorø he contributed to the erection of the Academy with the two buildings used as teachers' houses (1738–43).

De Thurah's name is associated with a theoretical work of capital importance for the history of eighteenth-century Danish architecture, *Den Danske Vitruvius* (1746–49).

TOMÉ, NARCISO

Born perhaps 1690 in Toro; died 1742 in Toledo. He belonged to a family of sculptors and decorators active in Castile at the beginning of the eighteenth century. His first independent work, which brought him great fame, is the *Transparente* in Toledo Cathedral (1721–32), commissioned by Archbishop Diego de Astorga y Céspedes. About 1736, again for Toledo Cathedral, he designed the alterations to the choir. It seems that he also supplied designs for the pedestal of the tabernacle and worked on the chapel of S. Pedro.

In 1738 Tomé was engaged on a marble *retablo* for the chapel of the Baronesa Convent of the Discalced Carmelites at Madrid. His last known work is the high altar of León Cathedral, preserved in fragments in the Capuchin church at León.

TREZZINI (TRESSINI), DOMENICO

Born c. 1670 in Astano, Switzerland; died 1734 at St. Petersburg. He spent the thirty years of his career as an architect at St. Petersburg, and Peter the Great nominated him director of building works of the city, particularly of the new royal residence (until 1716).

Trezzini's most important works in St. Petersburg are the Twelve Colleges (1722–32), the University (1722–42), and above all the cathedral of St. Peter and St. Paul (1712–33) and the Fortress (1717–18). In 1717 he began the *lavra* (group of monastic cells and church) of Alexander Nevsky, which was continued later according to other designs. He also worked on the Summer Palace (1710–14), a wing of the Winter Palace (1726), and on the hospital in the Vyborg quarter (1715–34). Trezzini carried out much fortification work, especially in the provinces—at Narva, Kronstadt, and Schlüsselburg.

VACCARINI, GIOVANNI BATTISTA

Born 1702 in Palermo; died 1769 at Milazzo. When still very young he went to Rome, where he studied architecture under Carlo Fontana and in the circles of the Accademia di S. Luca.

He resided in Catania from 1730 onward, and led a very active life there for thirty years, during which he rebuilt the center of the city, which had been completely destroyed by an earthquake.

Vaccarini devoted himself almost entirely to designing, building, and decorating churches, private and public edifices, and monuments. They include the front elevation of the cathedral (1734–58); the rebuilding of the façade of the Palazzo Senatorio (1732–50); the courtyard of the University of Catania (after 1730); and the Fontana dell'Elefante.

His best works include two churches which occupied him for a long time: S. Giuliano (1738–60) and S. Agata (1735–67), both built on a central plan. Vaccarini's most noteworthy domestic works are the courtyards of the Palazzo Reburdone and the Collegio Cutelli (1754), the Palazzo Valle, and the Palazzo Serravalle.

VACCARO, DOMENICO ANTONIO

Born c. 1681 in Naples; died 1750 in Naples. He was a pupil of Francesco Solimena and began his career as a painter and sculptor before changing to architecture. He worked almost exclusively in Naples, on the Teatro Nuovo (1724), which was destroyed by fire in 1934; on the church of the Concezione at Montecalvario (c. 1726); and on the church of S. Michele (1730). The Caravita hunting lodge and the Palazzo Spinelli di Tarsia were built to his designs. He also designed a building for the harbor master's office on the Immacolatella Vecchia, commissioned by Don Carlos of Bourbon. The renovation of the church of S. Chiara and the adjoining cloister was executed in 1734 (or 1724?). Outside Naples, Vaccaro worked at Capua, Teano, Nola, and Calvizzano. At Anacapri he built the church of SS. Sofia e Michele (1719).

VALVASSORI, GABRIELE

Born 1683 in Rome; died 1761 in Rome. He was educated at the Accademia di S. Luca, of which he became a member in 1737, and early in his career entered the service of the Doria princes. He was commissioned by them to execute the high altar of S. Agnese in Piazza Navona (1720); the new façade for the Palazzo Doria (1731–33) and the building connecting it with the adjoining church of S. Maria in Via Lata; and the renovation of the Villa Doria-Pamphili (1732). Perhaps his most characteristic work is the interior of the church of S. Maria della Luce in Trastevere (1730).

Valvassori is mentioned in a number of documents relating to the reconstruction of the church of S. Bartolomeo dei Bergamaschi (1732–33). Between 1741 and 1750 he restored the church of SS. Quirico e Giulitta. About 1760 he did much work on the reconstruction of the Via Angelo Brunetti wing of the Palazzo Rondanini.

VANBRUGH, JOHN

Born 1664 in London; died 1726 in London. Vanbrugh's adventurous life was at first divided between a military career and theatrical interests; he was, in fact, a brilliant playwright, and turned to architecture relatively late. His first architectural designs date from 1699, when Charles Howard, Earl of Carlisle, summoned him, together with Hawksmoor, to direct the construction of his country house—Castle Howard in Yorkshire. His final link with the theatrical world was the construction of the Queen's Opera House in London, inaugurated in 1705 (since destroyed).

In the meantime Vanbrugh had begun his close collaboration with Hawksmoor, which was to last for his entire architectural career and would produce the most important works of the English Late Baroque. In 1702 he was nominated Comptroller of Works, involving the administration of royal buildings. In 1705 he received the commission for his greatest work: the construction of Blenheim Palace, near Woodstock, which Queen Anne and Parliament offered to the Duke of Marlborough after his great victory over Louis XIV in 1704. In 1712 work was interrupted following Marlborough's exile; it was begun again in 1716, but Vanbrugh was compelled to resign as a result of his disagreement with the Duchess of Marlborough (Hawksmoor completed Blenheim in 1727). Also in 1716, Vanbrugh replaced Sir Christopher Wren as superin-

dent of the work on Greenwich Hospital: under his direction the Great Hall was completed and the King William Block erected.

Vanbrugh did not neglect private commissions: in addition to a series of houses at Greenwich (c. 1717), he built other larger and more important ones: at Eastbury in Dorsetshire (1718), at Seaton Delaval in Northumberland (1720–21), and at Grimsthorpe in Lincolnshire (1722). For himself he built Claremont House in Surrey (1710), which he later sold. He also drew up a plan for the gardens at Stowe in Buckinghamshire (1719). Although invited to join the commission for the construction of fifty new churches, Vanbrugh never put his hand to works of a religious nature.

VANVITELLI, LUIGI

Born 1700 in Naples; died 1773 in Caserta. He was the son of the painter Gaspar van Wittel (known in Italian as Vanvitelli) and while still very young he moved to Rome, where he began to study under the guidance of Filippo Juvarra. After an early period devoted to painting of no particular importance, he began his architectural career: the restoration of the Palazzo Albani and the churches of S. Francesco and S. Domenico at Urbino (1730–32), possibly in collaboration with Filippo Barigiani, and the church of S. Pietro at Pesaro. With Nicola Salvi he executed the aqueduct at Vermicino near Frascati (1730–31) and extended the façade of the Palazzo Odescalchi in Rome. In 1726 he was appointed Architect of the Fabric of St. Peter's with Antonio Valeri (an appointment he was to hold alone from 1736).

After successfully participating in the competition for the façade of S. Giovanni in Laterano (1732), Vanvitelli was assigned by Pope Clement XII to do some building work in The Marches: at Ancona he built the Lazzaretto (1733), the Arco Clementino (1733), the Cappella delle Reliquie in S. Ciriaco (1738), and the church of Gesù. The work for the church and monastery of the Olivetani at Perugia and for the church of the Misericordia at Macerata; the completion of the bell-tower of the basilica at Loreto; and the remodeling of the church of S. Agostino at Siena (1747) were executed according to his designs.

In 1735 Vanvitelli was appointed architect of the basilica of St. Peter's and returned to Rome, where he worked on the monastery of the Augustinians, the transformation of the *tepidarium* of the Terme di Diocleziano into the church of S. Maria degli Angeli (begun by Michelangelo), and the completion of the dome of St. Peter's. In 1751 he was invited by Don Carlos of Bourbon, King of Naples, to build the new Royal Palace at Caserta (completed in 1774 by his son Carlo). He also built the Acquedotto Carolino (1752–53), the façade of the Palazzo Calabritto (c. 1755), the barracks at the Ponte della Maddalena, the church of the SS. Annunziata at Caserta, and Prince Campolieto's villa at Resina (c. 1766). He later restored the hunting lodge at Persano and the church of S. Maria della Rotonda, also preparing the designs for the Palazzo d'Angri in Naples.

In about 1769 Vanvitelli was invited to Milan to make alterations to the Palazzo Reale, later executed by Piermarini, and to construct the new façade of the cathedral, for which he drew up a design. During his later years he was responsible for the interior of the great hall of the Palazzo Vecchio at Brescia, which was never completed.

VISCARDI, GIOVANNI ANTONIO

Born 1645 at San Vittore (Grisons); died 1713 in Munich. He went to Bavaria in 1670, where he succeeded Enrico Zuccalli in 1678 as court master-mason, and in 1686 was appointed chief architect. His masterpieces are the monastery and church at Fürstenfeld, near Munich; the monastery was built between 1692 and 1704, and the church was built after his death (1718-36).

For Marshal Tilly's family he built Helfenberg Castle and the church of Our Lady of Succour at Freystadt (1700-8). In 1701 he prepared plans for the Dreifaltigkeitskirche in Munich (begun in 1711 and completed by Zuccalli after his death). At Nymphenburg in 1702 Viscardi began to build the two new side wings of the castle. For the Jesuits he built the Bürgersaal in Munich (1709-10). He also planned the church at Neustift-Freising (1712), near Munich, and restored and decorated the church of St. Salvatore in Augsburg. The barracks at Straubing, Vohburg, and Kösching, as well as the fortifications at Ingolstadt are his work.

VITTONE, BERNARDO ANTONIO

Born 1705 in Turin; died 1770 in Turin. He went to Rome and took part in the competition held by Pope Clement XII for S. Giovanni in Laterano; he also won first prize in a competition held by the Accademia di S. Luca. He returned to Turin in 1733 and began a vast series of minor architectural works, hardly ever concerning himself with official appointments. His first major work was the pilgrimage chapel of the Visitation at Vallinotto, near Carignano (1738-39), whose ideas were repeated in the cemetery church of S. Luigi Gonzaga in Corteranzo (c. 1740). Between 1740 and 1744 he supervised the completion of the church of S. Bernardino at Chieri. In 1742 he built the church of S. Chiara at Brà. In 1744 building was begun on the Albergo di Carità (almshouse) at Carignano, according to his designs, and the following year on the Ospedale di Carità at Casale Monferrato.

Vittone prepared the designs for the church of S. Chiara in Turin (c. 1745) and for the church of S. Gaetano in Nizza (c. 1745); between 1750 and 1756 he supervised the building of the church and convent of S. Chiara at Vercelli. Shortly afterward he built the church of S. Maria di Piazza in Turin (the façade dates from the nineteenth century). In 1755 he built the church of S. Croce in Villanova di Mondovì.

He was responsible for numerous parish churches in Piedmont and left many designs: S. Maria della Neve at Pecetto Torinese (begun in 1730), S. Maria Maddalena at Foglizzo (1741-46), the Assunta at Grignasco (begun in 1750), S. Michele at Rivarolo Canavese (begun in 1758) and at Borgo d'Ale (1770-78), and a design for S. Salvatore at Borgomasino (1755).

Among Vittone's domestic buildings we should point out the Palazzo Giriodi at Castigliole Saluzzo, the almshouse at Pinerolo (1740), the Collegio delle Province in Turin (c. 1750), and the town hall at Brà (attributed to him).

Vittone left numerous designs and plans, and his interest in the theory of architecture is noteworthy. He was responsible for the posthumous publication of Guarini's *Architettura civile* (published in 1737). He himself wrote *Istruzioni elementari per indirizzo dei giovani allo studio dell'Architettura civile* ("Elementary Instructions for the Guidance of the Young in the Study of Domestic Architecture") (Lugano, 1760) and *Istruzioni diverse concernenti l'officio dell'Architettura civile* ("Miscellaneous Instructions Concerning the Practice of Domestic Architecture") (Lugano, 1766).

WELSCH, JOHANN MAXIMILIAN VON

Born 1671 at Kronach; died 1745 in Mainz. During the architect's formative period he took a number of trips abroad, especially to Vienna, where he met Fischer von Erlach. He worked mainly under the protection of the Prince-Bishop of Mainz (who was also Elector of the Holy Roman Empire) and the Archbishop of Bamberg.

His first works were a series of castles: a project for Idstein Castle for the dukes of Nassau (1709), work on Biebrich Castle (from 1710), the castle of La Favorita at Mainz (1710-18), and, again for the dukes of Nassau, the grounds of the Residenz at Usingen (1714). At Erfurt, between 1710 and 1720, he built the Governor's Palace, and in Bamberg he drew up a series of projects for the Böttingerhaus (1713). He was engaged as a military architect on the fortifications at Erfurt and Mainz from 1714.

At Pommersfelden, in the palace for Elector Lothar Franz von Schönborn, Von Welsch worked with Johann Dientzenhofer and Hildebrandt; the great stables there (1717-18) are by Von Welsch. From 1720, at the request of the Schönborn family, he drew up projects for Bruchsal Castle for the Bishop Damian Hugo, and took part in drafting plans for the new Residenz at Würzburg. In 1721 he designed the Schönborn Chapel in Würzburg Cathedral, which was subsequently built in accordance with a modified plan by Balthasar Neumann. He took part unsuccessfully in the competitive examination for the pilgrimage church of Vierzehnheiligen in 1742. The same year he prepared designs for the rebuilding of the Benedictine abbey at Amorbach; of his work there, only the two west towers remain.

WOOD THE ELDER, JOHN

Born 1704 in Bath; died 1754 in Bath. He was the creator of the urban expansion of Bath. In London, where he lived between 1725 and 1727 in the service of the Duke of Chandos, he succeeded in getting his designs for Bath accepted by the landowner R. Gay.

Wood settled in Bath in 1727 and began the construction of numerous landmarks: Gay Street, St. John's Hospital (1727-30), and Queen Square (1728-34). In 1740 he built a series of houses in South Parade; in 1754 he began construction of the King's Circus, which was later continued by his son. He rebuilt Prior Park near Bath (1735-48) and erected the loggia of Titan Barrow (1748). Wood left numerous writings, mostly of historical value, such as his book on the Bristol Exchange (1745).

WOOD THE YOUNGER, JOHN

Born 1728 in Bath; died 1781 in Bath. He was the son of John Wood the Elder, upon whose death (1754) he continued work as architect of the city of Bath, including the completion of the King's Circus in 1758. In 1766 he bought some land near the Circus to begin the construction of the Royal Crescent (1767-74), his masterpiece.

Among Wood's principal works at Bath are Brock Street (1765), St. Margaret's Chapel (1773; destroyed during World War II), the New Assembly Rooms (1769-72), Rivers Street (c. 1770), and Catherine Place (c. 1780).

ZIMMERMANN, DOMINIKUS

Born 1685 at Wessobrunn; died 1766 at Wies. He worked as an architect and painter and was the leading stuccoist of his time. He first learned the rudiments of stucco work from Christoph Schäffler and Johann Schmutzer, and on the death of the latter in 1701 he formed an association with Johann Jakob Herkomer. His first important work (1710-12), greatly influenced by Herkomer, was the rebuilding of the church and library of the monastery at Buxheim, on which he worked with his brother Johann Baptist. During this period he was also in contact with the Vorarlberg builders. In 1716 Zimmermann moved to Landsberg am Lech, where he was granted citizenship rights and where, with his brother, he worked on the decoration of the town hall and the Altar of the Rosary in the parish church; in 1725 he built the Ursuline convent there. From 1716 to 1729 he lived at Maria Mödingen, where he worked on the convent of the Dominican nuns and on the reconstruction of the church.

The church of St. Mark, which forms part of the Dominican convent at Siessen, and the pilgrimage church of Steinhausen (1727-33)—which is the first example in Germany of the *Hallenkirche* on an elliptical plan—were inspired by the Vorarlberg school. In 1732 Zimmermann prepared the two designs, which were not executed, for the church of the abbey at Ottobeuren, and in 1735 it seems (though it has not been confirmed) that he did some work on the monastery of St. Blasien.

Between 1736 and 1741 he built the parish church of Our Lady at Günzburg, on the Danube. During this period he also built the Little Castle and the chapel at Pöring, the church of St. John at Landsberg am Lech, and the church of Ingenried near Schongau. In 1752 Zimmermann retired to the house he had built for himself at Wies, where he built the sanctuary (project 1744; construction 1745-54). Of his later works we should recall the parish church of Tapfheim (1747), the design for the rebuilding of the church and monastery of the Premonstratensians at Schussenried (1747-48), and the rebuilding of the parish church at Eresing (1756-57).

SELECTED BIBLIOGRAPHY

SOURCES

BLONDEL, J.-F., *Cours d'architecture civile*, Paris, 1771–77.

———, *De la distribution des maisons de plaisance*, Paris, 1737–38.

———, *L'Architecture française*, Paris, 1752–56.

BOFFRAND, G., *Livre d'Architecture*, Paris, 1745.

CAMPBELL, C., *Vitruvius Britannicus*, London, 1715–25.

DAVILER, A.C., *Cours d'Architecture*, Paris, 1720.

DECKER, P., *Fürstlicher Baumeister*, Augsburg, 1711–13.

FISCHER VON ERLACH, J.B., *Entwurff einer historischen Architektur*. . . .Vienna, 1721.

KLEINER, S., *Wunderwürdiges Kriegs- und Siegslager*, Vienna, 1731–40.

MARIETTE, J., *L'Architecture française*, Paris, 1727.

PATTE, P., *Monuments érigés à la gloire de Louis XV*, Paris, 1765.

STURM, C.L., *Vollständige Anweisung aller Art Kirchen recht anzugeben*, Augsburg, 1718.

VITTONE, B. A., *Istruzioni diverse concernenti l'officio dell'Architettura civile*, Lugano, 1766.

———, *Istruzioni elementari per indirizzo dei giovani allo studio dell'Architettura civile*, Lugano, 1760.

MODERN WORKS

ANDEREGG-TILLE, M., *Die Schule Guarinis*, Winterthur, 1962.

ANDERSEN, L., *Studien zu Profanbauformen Balthasar Neumanns*, Munich, 1966.

BACHMANN, E., "Architektur," *Barock in Böhmen*, ed. K.M. Swoboda, Munich, 1964.

———, "Balthasar Neumann und das Mittelalter," *Stifter-Jahrbuch*, III, 1953.

———, *Residenz Würzburg*, Munich, 1970.

BAUER, H., *Rocaille*, Berlin, 1962.

BLUNT, A., *Sicilian Baroque*, London, 1968.

BOSCARINO, S., *Studi e rilievi di architettura siciliana*, Messina, 1961.

BOURKE, J., *Baroque Churches of Central Europe*, London, 1958.

BRAUNFELS, W., *François de Cuvilliés*, Würzburg, 1938.

BRINCKMANN, A.E., *Baukunst des 17. und 18. Jahrhunderts in den romanischen Ländern*, Berlin, 1919.

———, *Stadtbaukunst*, Wildpark-Potsdam, 1925.

———, *Theatrum Novum Pedemontii*, Düsseldorf, 1931.

———, *Von Guarino Guarini bis Balthasar Neumann*, Berlin, 1932.

BUSCH, H., and LOHSE, B., *Baroque Europe*, New York, 1962.

CARBONERI, N., *L'architetto Francesco Gallo*, Turin, 1954.

CAVALLARI-MURAT, A., *Forma urbana ed architettura nella Torino barocca*, Turin, 1968.

CONNOLLY, C., and ZERBE, J., *Les Pavillons: French Pavillons of the 18th Century*, London-New York, 1962.

DE SIMONE, M., *Ville Palermitane*, Genoa, 1968.

DÖRING, B.A., *Matthes Daniel Pöppelmann*, Dresden, 1930.

DOWNES, K., *English Baroque Architecture*, London, 1966.

———, *Hawksmoor*, London, 1959 (new edition, 1969).

FICHERA, F., *G.B. Vaccarini e l'architettura del settecento in Sicilia*, Rome, 1934.

———, *Luigi Vanvitelli*, Rome, 1937.

FRANZ, H.G., *Bauten und Baumeistern der Barockzeit in Böhmen*, Leipzig, 1962.

———, *Die deutsche Barockbaukunst Mährens*, Munich, 1943.

———, *Die Kirchenbauten des Christoph Dientzenhofer*, Brno-Munich-Vienna, 1942.

———, "Die Klosterkirche Banz und die Kirchen Balthasar Neumanns in ihrem Verhältnis zur böhmischen Barockbaukunst," *Zeitschrift für Kunstgeschichte*, Berlin, 1947.

———, "Gotik und Barock im Werk des Johann Santini Aichel," *Wiener Jahrbuch für Kunstgeschichte*, XIV, 1950.

———, *Studien zur Barockarchitektur in Böhmen und Mähren*, Brno-Munich-Vienna, 1943.

FREEDEN, M.H. VON, *Balthasar Neumann*, Munich-Berlin, 1953.

GIEDION, S., *Space, Time and Architecture*, Cambridge, Mass., 1967.

GRABAR, I.E., LASAREW, W.N., and KEMENOW, W.S., *Geschichte der russischen Kunst*, V, Dresden, 1970.

GRIMSCHITZ, B., *Johann Lucas von Hildebrandt*, Vienna-Munich, 1959.

———, *Johann Michael Prunner*, Vienna-Munich, 1960.

———, *Wiener Barockpaläste*, Vienna, 1947.

GRISERI, A., *Le metamorfosi del barocco*, Turin, 1967.

GRUNDMANN, G., *Schlesische Barockkirchen und Klöster*, Lindau, 1958.

HAGEN-DEMPF, F., *Der Zentralbaugedanke bei Johann Michael Fischer*, Munich, 1954.

———, *Die Kollegienkirche in Salzburg*, Vienna, 1949.

HAGER, W., *Architektur des Barock*, Baden-Baden, 1968.

———, *Die Bauten des deutschen Barocks*, Jena, 1942.

HAMILTON, G.H., *The Art and Architecture of Russia*, Harmondsworth, 1954.

HANFSTAENGEL, E., *Die Brüder Asam*, Munich-Berlin, 1955.

HANTSCH, H., *Jakob Prandtauer*, Vienna, 1926.

HAUSER, A., *The Social History of Art*, London, 1962.

HAUTECOEUR, L., *Histoire de l'architecture classique en France*, Paris, 1943–57.

HAUTMANN, M., *Geschichte der kirchlichen Baukunst in Bayern, Schwaben und Franken 1550–1780*, Munich, 1921.

HEGEMANN, H.W., *Die deutsche Barockbaukunst Böhmens*, Munich, 1943.

HEMPEL, E., *Baroque Art and Architecture in Central Europe*, Harmondsworth, 1965.

———, *Der Zwinger zu Dresden*, Berlin, 1961.

———, *Gaetano Chiaveri*, Hanau, 1956.

HITCHCOCK, H.-R., *German Rococo*, London, 1968.

———, *Rococo Architecture in Southern Germany*, London, 1968.

KIMBALL, F., *Le Style Louis XV: Origine et évolution du Rococo*, Paris, 1949.

KÖMSTEDT, R., *Von Bauten und Baumeistern des fränkischen Barocks*, Berlin, 1963.

KREISEL, H., *Das Schloss zu Pommersfelden*, Munich, 1953.

KUBLER, G., and SORIA, M., *Art and Architecture in Spain and Portugal 1500–1800*, Harmondsworth, 1959.

KUNOTH, G., *Die historische Architektur Fischers von Erlach*, Düsseldorf, 1956.

LAMB, C., *Die Wies*, Munich, 1964.

LANDOLT, H., *Schweizer Barockkirchen*, Frauenfeld, 1948.

LAVEDAN, P., *French Architecture*, Harmondsworth, 1956.

———, *Les villes françaises*, Paris, 1960.

LIEB, N., *Barockkirchen zwischen Donau und Alpen*, Munich, 1953.

———, and DIEDL, F., *Die Vorarlberger Barockbaumeister*, Munich-Zurich, 1960.

LÖFFLER, F., *Das alte Dresden*, Dresden, 1958.

MILLON, H., *Baroque and Rococo Architecture*, New York, 1961.

MINISSI, F., *Aspetti dell'architettura religiosa del settecento in Sicilia*, Rome, 1958.

MUNGENAST, E., *Joseph Munggenast*, Vienna, 1963.

NEUMANN, G., *Neresheim*, Munich, 1947.

NEUMANN, J., *Cesky barok*, Prague, 1969.

NORBERG-SCHULZ, C., *Kilian Ignaz Dientzenhofer e il barocco boemo*, Rome, 1968.

———, "Lo spazio nell'architettura post-Guariniana," *Guarino Guarini e l'internazionalità del barocco* (ed. V. Viale), Turin, 1970.

OLIVERO, E., *Le opere di Bernardo Antonio Vittone*, Turin, 1920.

PANE, R., *Architettura dell'età barocca in Napoli*, Naples, 1939.

———, *Ferdinando Fuga*, Naples, 1956.

PEVSNER, N., *An Outline of European Architecture*, Harmondsworth, 1960.

PILLEMENT, G., *Les Hôtels de Paris*, Paris, 1965.

PINDER, W., *Deutscher Barock*, Düsseldorf-Leipzig, 1912.

POMMER, R., *Eighteenth-Century Architecture in Piedmont*, New York, 1967.

PORTOGHESI, P., *Bernardo Vittone*, Rome, 1966.

——— (ed.), *Dizionario Enciclopedico di architettura e urbanistica*, Rome, 1968–69.

———, *Guarino Guarini*, Milan, 1956.

———, *Roma barocca*, Cambridge, Mass., 1971.

POWELL, N., *From Baroque to Rococo: an Introduction to Austrian and German Architecture from 1580 to 1790*, London, 1959.

RENSING, T., *Johann Conrad Schlaun*, Munich-Berlin, 1954.

REUTHER, H., *Die Kirchenbauten Balthasar Neumanns*, Berlin, 1960.

ROTILI, M., *Filippo Raguzzini e il rococò romano*, Rome, 1951.

ROVERE, L., VITALE, V., and BRINCKMANN, A.E., *Filippo Juvarra*, Milan, 1937.

SCHÖNBERGER, A., and SOEHNER, H., *The Rococo Age*, London-New York, 1960.

SEDLMAYR, H., *Epochen und Werke*, II, Vienna-Munich, 1960.

————, *Johann Bernhard Fischer von Erlach*, Vienna-Munich, 1956.

————, *Österreichische Barockarchitektur*, Vienna, 1930.

————, "Rococo," *Enciclopedia Universale dell'Arte*, XI, Venice-Rome, 1963.

SITWELL, S., *Southern Baroque Art*, London, 1924.

STREICHHAN, A., *Knobelsdorff und das friderizianische Rokoko*, Burg bei Magdeburg, 1932.

SUMMERSON, J., *Architecture in Britain 1530–1830*, Harmondsworth, 1953.

TELLUCCHINI, A., *L'arte dell'architetto Filippo Juvarra in Piemonte*, Turin, 1926.

TEUFEL, R., *Vierzehnheiligen*, Lichtenfels, 1957.

TINTELNOT, H., *Barocktheater und barocke Kunst*, Berlin, 1929.

WACKERNAGEL, M., *Baukunst des 17. und 18. Jahrhunderts in den germanischen Ländern*, Berlin, 1915.

WAGNER, V., *Czech Baroque*, Prague, 1940.

WHISTLER, L., *Sir John Vanbrugh, Architect and Dramatist*, London, 1938.

WOLF, F., *François de Cuvilliés*, Munich, 1967.

INDEX

LIST OF PLATES

NOTE: *The abbreviations D.A.U. and E.U.A. stand for Dizionario di Architettura e Urbanistica and Enciclopedia Universale dell'Arte, respectively.*